TEXAS COWBOYS

TEXAS COWBOYS

Memories of the Early Days

Edited by Jim Lanning
and Judy Lanning

Texas A&M University Press   COLLEGE STATION

Manufactured in the United States of America
Fourth printing, 2004

Library of Congress Cataloging-in-Publication Data
Main entry under title:

Texas cowboys.

Bibliography: p.
1. Cowboys—Texas—History—Addresses, essays, lectures.
2. Cowboys—Texas—Biography—Addresses, essays, lectures
3. Ranch life—Texas—History—Addresses, essays, lectures.
4. Texas—Social life and customs—Addresses, essays, lectures.
5. Texas—Biography—Addresses, essays, lectures.
I. Lanning, Jim, 1942–   II. Lanning, Judy, 1943–
F391.T3813   1984   976.4   83-40494
ISBN 0-89096-658-3 (pbk.)

Contents

Acknowledgments

THIS project could not have been accomplished without the assistance of Joseph D. Sullivan, Manuscript Librarian, Manuscript Division, Library of Congress. His expertise on both the Federal Writers' Project and its product, the first-person narratives of Texas cowboys, was provided to us in the true spirit and tradition of a public-domain depository.

From the National Archives, Dorothy Provine and Richard C. Crawford, Archivists, Scientific, Economic and Natural Resources Branch, greatly assisted in providing the necessary documents of record on the FWP efforts in Texas.

Others consulted in gathering material were Gregory Malak, Curator of the Will Rogers Memorial Museum; Charles Endress, Head of the History Department at San Angelo State University; and many staff members of the *San Angelo Standard-Times*.

Contributors who either read or assisted in the editing are Eunice Lanning Andrus, Lee and Linda Lanning, Fred Henshaw, Stanley Edwards, Steve and Genell Edwards, Virginia Madeiros, Carolyn Griffith, Chuck Nelson, and Clara Scanlan.

The kind words of encouragement and permission from Mrs. L. M. Pettis, Bonham, Texas, sister of Erwin E. Smith, to use selected prints from the Erwin E. Smith Collection of the Library of Congress Prints Section are also greatly appreciated.

Special tribute must be given to Everett McAulay for his willingness to interview and record the experiences of his mother, Mrs. Annie McAulay, who served as a field interviewer in Texas. Without her memories this book would not have been complete.

A delightful afternoon spent at the home of the daughters of Mollie and "Booger Red" Privett lent insight on this notable couple and their contribution to early-day Wild West shows. We appreciate the use of the photograph of their parents which they willingly entrusted to us.

Finally, but not least, we want to acknowledge the efforts of our typist and friend, Sally Mendoza Robertson, whose cheerful and professional attitude never faltered, even when faced with required deadlines.

Introduction

TOWARD the end of the Great Depression an unheralded federal project left its mark on Texas history. Nationally known as the Work Projects Administration[1]–Federal Writers' Project (WPA-FWP), this short-lived relief program authorized and produced the largest collection of narratives of personal life history ever assembled in the United States.

The Federal Writers' Project was organized as a means of providing relief to white-collar workers (authors, writers, editors, researchers, journalists, and so on), whose task was to compile for publication a comprehensive information book, on the entire United States, to be named *The American Guide*. As the collection of information grew to an enormous size, the project was quickly redefined, with each state assigned the task of compiling its own guidebook using the same basic outline as envisioned for the national guide. The FWP of Texas published *Texas: A Guide to the Lone Star State* in 1940; because of its popularity it remains in print today.

Meanwhile, in 1938, with the state guide series well underway, the FWP formally expanded its scope and authorized the collection of folklore materials, setting the stage for Texas writers to locate, interview, and record subjects of state and local interest. Their efforts resulted in the collection of stories of old cowboys and former slaves. No effort was made to compile the stories of any other distinctive Texas group.

On October 21, 1940, instructions were issued by the national WPA office in Washington, D.C., requiring that duplicate records in nearly all categories, including state folklore, be forwarded to Washington.[2] When the sheer bulk of the files be-

---

[1]Originally Works Progress Administration.

[2]Katherine H. Davidson, comp., *Preliminary Inventory of the Records of the Federal Writers' Project, Works Projects Administration, 1935–44 (Record Group 69)*, National Archives Publication No. 54-2 (Washington, D.C.: National Archives, 1953), p. 6.

came apparent, these instructions were quickly amended, but the Texas office has already shipped many of their records. (A review of *The University of Texas Archives: A Guide to the Historical Manuscript Collections in the University of Texas Library* reveals extensive WPA-FWP holdings about the grazing and cattle industry of Texas. As the policy normally was to send only copies to Washington, it is plausible that duplicates of these narratives survive in the WPA-FWP collection in Austin.) These files sat untouched for the next forty years.

Ann Banks, research associate at Boston College's American Studies Center, was the first person to read the more than ten thousand life story narratives at the Library of Congress. After first reviewing and cataloging them, she published *First Person America* in 1980. Both that book and an article by her, "*Getting By In Hard Times,*" in the October 12, 1980, Sunday magazine of the *Washington Post* inspired our research. In early 1982, we obtained access to the narrative manuscripts at the Library of Congress. Joseph D. Sullivan of the manuscript division explained that the WPA-FWP folklore collection containing first-person narratives had been transferred to his charge from the Archive of Folk Culture and was being formally cataloged. Assisting our pursuit of Texas-related subjects, Mr. Sullivan suggested that we begin with six library file boxes of the Texas Rangelore Collection. We went no further.

From the approximately four hundred narratives reviewed, we have selected thirty-two. To our knowledge, this is the first publication of any of these narratives. It was a pleasant discovery to find interviews conducted with women, blacks, and Mexican Americans, although their presence on the range is historical fact. George W. Saunders, of the Texas Trail Drivers Association, estimated that of the approximately 35,000 men who participated in trail drives during their heyday, 1866–1895, about one-third were minority members (blacks and Mexicans). Of these, it is estimated that blacks outnumbered Mexicans by more than two to one.[3] It can be deduced, therefore, that the

---

[3] J. Marvin Hunter, ed., *The Trail Drivers of Texas*, p. 453; Kenneth Wiggins Porter, *The Negro on the American Frontier*, p. 495.

larger group from which these trail drivers were drawn was approximately the same general demographic mix.

The singular reason for this book is to present first-person narratives of old-time Texas cowboys recounting their perceptions of range life. These were the men and women who helped ranchers as renowned as King, Kenedy, Slaughter, Swenson, Waggoner, and Burnett shape the open rangeland into economic empires. Using their narratives as a bridge, we can experience the fun of initiating a new "greener," the hours of tedious riding, the bite of dust clouds on the cattle trail, the monotonous routine of bland chuck washed down with Arbuckle coffee, and the terror of facing a stampede—and all for minimal wages. It is small wonder that old cowboys were hard to find.

When we grew up in West Texas it was still possible to go into town on a Saturday afternoon and gaze at the cowhands climbing out of old pickups or loitering in front of the Red & White or Piggly Wiggly killing time. None of these men resembled John Wayne or Gary Cooper, and all seemed to be over sixty. Yet they retained an air of gallantry in the old-fashioned tip of their hats and a bit of swagger in the way they leaned against the store front, their boots resting against the brick wall. They could have told us the stories we found at the Library of Congress, but we were too impatient to listen. Larry McMurtry's novels *The Last Picture Show* and *Horseman, Pass By* describe masterfully why we struggled to leave as soon as possible. When we finally were far enough away from home—both in distance and time—to appreciate our heritage, most of the old-time cowboys had left for the Best of Pastures.

The task of selecting these narratives for publication was influenced by our memories of these men. As we read the stories of their contemporaries recorded and saved by the Federal Writers' Project, we felt a reaffirmation to their way of life.

First Person America is not the only other book based on FWP interviews. Three other works whose central theses were recording oral history from the viewpoint of the individual himself have been published. Unlike Ann Banks's work, all are regionally based. The first, *These Are Our Lives*, compiled by William T. Couch in 1939, is drawn from informants in North

Carolina, Tennessee, and Georgia. The second, *Such As Us: Southern Voices of the Thirties*, edited in 1978 by Tom E. Terrill and Jerrold Hirsch, was basically a sequel to *These Are Our Lives* and consisted of life narratives from the Southeast. It includes an excellent bibliographical essay for those who desire to learn more about the work of the FWP and life histories. The third, *Hispano Folklife of New Mexico: The Lorin W. Brown Federal Writers' Project Manuscripts*, edited in 1978 by Lorin W. Brown, Charles L. Briggs, and Marta Weigle, focused on the FWP efforts in New Mexico.

The narratives of slaves recorded by FWP workers in Texas have also been published as George P. Rawick's *The American Slave: A Composite Autobiography*, Volumes 4–5, *Texas Narratives*, a reprint of slave narratives held in the Rare Book Room Collection of the Library of Congress, and as *The American Slave; A Composite Autobiography*, Volumes 2–10, Texas Narratives, *Supplement*, Series 2, for narratives not included in the Library of Congress Rare Book Room. A second reprint of the Library of Congress typewritten records of slave narratives was published under the title *The Federal Writers' Project, Slave Narratives: A Folk History of Slavery in the United States from Interviews with Former Slaves*, Volumes 3–4, *Texas Narratives*.

For additional study of the FWP, a new publication of the Library of Congress, *Pickaxe and Pencil: Reference for the Study of the WPA*, published in 1982, is excellent. The sections "Literature in the Depression: The Federal Writers' Project" and "Where Is It Now? Collectors and Collections" contain bibliographies that answer the recent interest in the FWP, what it did, and what became of it.

The Federal Writers' Projects operated in each state under the control of the Office of the federal director, Henry G. Alsberg, located in Washington, D.C. J. Frank Davis, author of the acclaimed work *The Road to San Jacinto* and a prolific writer, served as the Texas state supervisor. With headquarters located in San Antonio, Texas was organized into twenty districts because of its size. From the beginning Texas had difficulty in filling its authorized quota of employees because of the lack of qualified workers on relief and other general organizational problems. As a result, the national office downgraded the state quota from an authorized high of 258 to 158 employees on January 15, 1936.[4] By November 1, 1938, the time period critical to the collection of cowboy narratives, the total authorized staff had increased to 170 employees.[5]

Excluding secretarial and clerical workers, the state had eighty-one workers on the roll as of April 5, 1938. Before joining the Federal Writers' Project, ten had held important editorial posts, fourteen had a year's experience with a newspaper, and eleven had sold articles to magazines or newspapers.[6] This group had the task of writing the entire list of the Writers' Program publications and many unpublished works, including the cowboy narratives.

From a review of federal correspondence with the Texas office it appears that a significant discriminator for prospective writers was their financial need, although it was not an absolute prerequisite that one had to be on relief to be hired. Personnel with previous reportorial or editorial newspaper experience were best prepared for the job. Because of the general subject matter of the Writers' Program topics, minimal technical knowledge was required of the writers and supervisors.

For a six-month period in Texas, from July 1 to December 31, 1938, the FWP was authorized a sum of $68,207.00 for the employment of 150 workers. Additionally, the nonlabor costs (telephone, office supplies, and so on) could not exceed 7.1 percent ($4,852.70) of the project cost. The balance resulted in an average monthly wage of $70.39 per worker.[7]

[4]Letter, Henry G. Alsberg to J. Frank Davis, January 15, 1936, Records of the Federal Writers' Project, WPA, Administrative Correspondence, 1935–39, Texas File, Record Group 69, National Archives (hereafter cited as RG 69, NA).
[5]Letter, Ellen S. Woodward to H. P. Drought, October 28, 1938, Records of the Federal Writers' Project, WPA, Administrative Correspondence, 1935–39, Texas File 657.317, RG 69, NA.
[6]Letter and memorandum, J. Frank Davis to Henry G. Alsberg, May 16, 1938, Records of the Federal Writers' Project, WPA, Administrative Correspondence, 1935–39, Texas File, RG 69, NA.
[7]Letter, Ellen S. Woodward to H. P. Drought, September 8, 1938, Records of the Federal Writers' Project, WPA, Administrative Correspondence, 1935–39, Texas File 657.317, RG 69, NA.

After an intensive search for a living FWP worker in Texas, we were fortunate to locate Mrs. Annie McAulay, a field interviewer and daughter-in-law of the W. L. McAulay whose narrative is recorded in the section "Waddies." With the assistance of her son, Everett McAulay of Beeville, Texas, we obtained the following information based on her experience with the FWP:

> While a summer school student at Texas Tech College in Lubbock, Texas, I was selected for employment. I had read their job announcement, took a test, and submitted a story for review. I received no formal training other than topical guidelines on what was desired about cowboys. Basically, I devised my own questions and in a three–four month time period conducted 25–30 interviews. Cowboys were selected by talking to old-timers and from a review of court house records. Interviews were in the subjects' homes and usually lasted one day; although a few took longer. All narratives were typed from notes taken with pencil and paper. I found the cowboys were all glad to be interviewed and enjoyed talking about their experiences. One man, Mr. Padgett, wanted me to write a book. I was paid $60.00 per month for three or four months. Most everything I wrote about was the truth as far as I could determine. I felt they were telling the truth, not "spinning tales." They were telling it "like it was." To my knowledge, none of these stories were ever published. My supervisor never critiqued my work and everything was sent to the University of Texas at Austin, Texas.[8]

How authentic are these narratives? Are they true? These questions may be approached on two accounts. First, were the informants telling the truth without changing the stories to reflect the way they wished things might have been? The passing of years has been known to dull memories and lead to occasional faulty recollections. Second, how proficient and reliable were the recorders working for the FWP? What was the "trade-off" between quantity of work and quality of composition? The topic of authenticity of FWP narratives has been examined in the periodical *The Oral History Review* by interested parties presenting both sides of the issue. In an article, "Replies to Leonard

[8]Questionnaire completed by Everett McAulay and Mrs. Annie McAulay for J. W. Lanning, May 10, 1983.

Rapport's 'How Valid Are the Federal Writers' Project Life Stories: An Iconoclast among the True Believers,'" Tom E. Terrill and Jerrold Hirsch warn that it is simplistic to argue that the only authentic life histories are verbatim accounts, especially since the FWP effort was before the days of the tape recorder. Further, they point out that viewing the question of perceived authenticity in either/or terms creates a false dichotomy which can only lead to a simplistic use of the materials. Researchers should remember that the narratives are a result of collaboration of a conversational dialogue (narrative) between an interviewer and an interviewee and, like other historical sources, are most valuable when used in conjunction with as many other sources as possible. They close by acknowledging the challenge of using FWP materials; however, it would be unfortunate if we lost the opportunity for study because we shied away from the challenge.[9]

Marguerite D. Bloxom, in *Pickaxe and Pencil*, also warns: "All these first person documents can provide valuable source material for scholars if appropriate precautions are taken. Those who intend to use published narratives as primary material will want to inform themselves about the amount and type of editing the material received before publication."[10] Since the people involved in the gathering of narratives are virtually all unavailable for verification, you must in the final judgment draw your own conclusions. It is our feeling, however, that these cowboy stories are basically substantive.

A careful review of nearly every interview provides information on which its validity can be based. For example, Mrs. C. C. West stated that her husband established the first post office in Eldorado and was the first justice of the peace in Schleicher County. This information is corroborated by the publication *Schleicher County; or, Eighty Years of Development in Southwest Texas.* As another example, Mr. J. K. Millwee's claim of

[9]Tom E. Terrill and Jerrold Hirsch, "Replies to Leonard Rapport's, 'How Valid Are the Federal Writers' Project Life Stories: An Iconoclast among the True Believers,'" *Oral History Review,* 1980, pp. 81–89.

[10]Marguerite D. Bloxom, comp., *Pickaxe and Pencil: References for the Study of WPA* (Washington, D.C.: Library of Congress, 1982), p. 63.

serving as the ranch manager of the IOA Ranch is supported by
the book *Rollie Burns: An Account of the Ranching Industry on
the South Plains,* in which Mr. Burns states, "When he [David
Boaz] had started stocking the range [IOA Ranch] with cattle,
Boaz installed J. K. Millwee as ranch manager."[11]

On the other hand, the claim by H. P. Cook of an association with the young Will Rogers cannot be substantiated. Gregory Malak, curator of the Will Rogers Museum in Claremore,
Oklahoma, writes us:

> There is no way to conclusively prove or disprove Mr. Cook's
> story about Will Rogers. Oral history is a valuable resource in
> studying history but it has a major drawback in that people can be
> very selective in what they remember and sometimes will embel-
> lish stories over the years. Will Rogers was only in Texas for about
> six months in 1898 and if he did everything claimed of him he
> would have been an extremely busy man. Another point that
> needs to be made is that Rogers was and is a common name for
> this area of the country. As an example, our Will Rogers was often
> confused during his early life in the Cooweescoowee District, In-
> dian Territory, with another person by that name.[12]

Several oldtimers savored remembrances of outlaws they
claimed to have known. James Cape told of his experience as a
stock tender for Jesse James. George Bedo claimed that as a child
he lived on the Pat Garrett ranch, and he recalled overhearing
an interesting dialogue between Billy the Kid and Pat Garrett
even though he was only five years old when Garrett killed the
Kid at Maxwell's Ranch (not a Mexican shack, as Bedo says). Several other narratives were excluded from the book because of
too many obvious disparities between the cowboys' stories and
historical fact.

In editing, we took the lead from the explanation in the Introduction of Ann Banks's book: "I restored corruptions of spell-
ing to standard English. In addition, I edited the narratives for

[11] William C. Holden, *Rollie Burns; or, An Account of the Ranching Industry on
the South Plains,* p. 149.
[12] Letter, Gregory Malak, Curator, Will Rogers Memorial, Claremore, Oklahoma,
to J. W. Lanning, November 17, 1982.

the sake of continuity and readability, while trying not to distort the tone or content of the original version."[13] The reader should be aware that we changed so-called black dialect used by the federal writers to contemporary English and in a few stories substituted an acceptable term in place of derogatory racial terms. This decision was not made to imply that equality existed for all people on the frontier. Certainly discrimination existed, but among trail crews the superior-subordinate relationship was blurred because of the commonality of labor and singularness of purpose.

We chose to use the informants' real names rather than to substitute fictitious ones. It is our understanding that the instructions to federal writers included a release statement so that the names of informants could be used when their stories were published. We feel that this written record made some forty-five years ago will be well received and appreciated by readers who recognize in it the names of their loved ones.

Photographs, unless otherwise identified, are from the Erwin E. Smith Collection, Library of Congress. Mr. Smith, who was based in Bonham, Texas, made extensive photographs throughout West Texas during the period 1905–1915. The pictures we selected represent a typical event or situation described in the text. Captions for the photographs are Smith's and are not intended to represent any location or personality in this book.

[13] Ann Banks, ed., *First Person America*, p. xxiv.

WADDIES

Three charter members of the Texas and Southwestern Cattle Raisers' Association at the golden anniversary convention, Fort Worth, 1926. (*L to r*) Hillary G. Bedford, Midland, Texas; D. B. Gardner, founder of the Pitchfork Ranch (Dickens County); and Joe H. Graham, Lovington, New Mexico.

W. E. Oglesby

I was born in Lincoln County, Tennessee, on December 11, 1863. My father, John H. Oglesby, lived on a farm, and there I was born and reared until I was nine years old, when my parents moved to Texas. I have lived in Texas since the first day I put a foot on its soil.

It was in 1872 that the Oglesby family joined with seventeen other families which constituted an immigrant train of eighteen covered wagons which left for Texas. Most of the families were Tennessee citizens. There were a couple of the families from Alabama. Two families of Johnsons were from Alabama. The Tennessee folks were Jack Abner's, ——— Gray's, Hugo Garrison's, Dr. Miller's, Hall's, and others' whose names I can't recall.

All the people had sold more or less property and had a little money, not much, because in those days real estate did not sell for much. They all loaded their personal effects into covered wagons and started for Texas with high hopes to do better.

During those days immigrant trains were compelled to meet the menace of white bandits and Indian raiders. The white bandits were interested in getting the money the immigrants had, and the Indians were after anything they could get, and in some cases the scalps of the white people. Therefore, each adult, men and women, carried firearms and a store of ammunition.

The immigrant party organized for the trip. Some were designated to be trail leaders, some acted as scouts, and some were on guard duty. There was no trouble anticipated until the Red River.

The Red River was high and the ferry could take only one wagon at a time to do the job safely. It took the ferry all day to put wagons, stock, and humans on Texas soil.

Until we arrived in the Indian Territory (now Oklahoma) we did not see any sinister-looking parties, but thereafter parties of

Indians were seen frequently and then everyone became alert. The Indians never gave us any trouble, except to beg for trinkets, food, a horse, and anything they trusted we might part with.

Each night, during the entire trip, the wagons were placed in a circle when we camped, and armed guards rode in the vicinity of the circle at all hours. After we began to see Indians we doubled the night guard and everyone kept their guns at their side.

Most of the women were fair shots. My mother was an excellent shot. She and father went hunting game regularly back in Tennessee. Therefore, the women were ready to shoot in defense of the train at any time. But there was no occasion for using the guns on the entire trip.

Everything went well after we crossed the Red River until we arrived on black land south of Paris, Texas. There had been a three-day rain, and that mud was so sticky we could not travel because it balled up on the wheels and on the animals' feet till movement was impossible. We were compelled to camp in that mud for five days before it dried so travel was possible.

While camping in that sticky mud, our worries about bandits and Indian raids were dispelled. There was a way one could travel and that was on a horse, but a horse could travel no faster than a walk. We knew that no raider was going to travel through that muck.

The last day we were camping, waiting for the mud to dry, cooking became a problem. Each wagon carried wood for emergency purposes, but the supply gave out and we were where fuel could not be found.

We finally arrived at Dallas, and from there we traveled to Waxahachie and then back to Fort Worth. It was five months and twelve days after we had left Lincoln County, Tennessee, when we arrived.

My father and Jack Abner settled in Fort Worth. The rest of the party continued on and settled in various places.

After we arrived in Fort Worth there has been one family or more of us living in the city and more or less of the men engaged in the carpenter trade.

Father could not find a vacant house of any kind into which

he could move his family when we arrived. The winter
on us, and it looked as though we would have to li\
wagon or a tent. Captain Fields owned a building in \
stored feed. It was located at what is now the corner oı Lamar
and Belknap streets. The floor of the building was covered with
corn, but Fields told father that if he could find room enough,
after moving the corn to one part of the room, he could live
there temporarily. Father accepted the offer of Fields, and we
moved the corn to one side, then moved in using the vacant
space for living purposes until spring.

It was in 1878 when I went on a ranch. I secured a job with
the Hop Lowe ranch located in Jack County, and the cattle grazed
in the Keechi Valley section of that country. Dave Mayhorn was
ranch foreman. "Top screw" was what the cowhands called a
foreman, and "big auger," "bull moose," and similar terms were
used when referring to the owner. Negro Sam was our cooky and
a good one. Among the steady hands were Henry and Ward
Lowe, sons of the owner. In addition there were Jeff Hart,
Bill McGonegal, Joe Jephart, and "Highpocket." The ranch employed on an average fifteen hands. We had a well-constructed
bunkhouse for sleeping quarters and a cook shack for our eating
place. The chuck was plain but well cooked. Of course, beef was
the main item on the menu, beans came next, then sourdough
and cornbread and canned vegetables trailed behind. Black coffee was always made and ready for all who wanted some at
any time.

We did night riding on the HL Ranch. HL was what the
ranch was called and it was the brand. The night riding was done
in four shifts, with four men to the crew. Four was enough to
keep watch during the night, because the cattle always bedded
down about dusk. During the day while the cattle were grazing
it required around ten men to keep together the herd, which
numbered around five thousand.

The only time we would have trouble was before or during
a severe storm and in the event something scared some of the
cattle. All that was necessary to start a stomp from a scare was for
just one or two of the animals to be scared, and fear would be
transmitted to the entire herd, then a stampede would start. Be-

fore a hard storm arrived, the animals would become fretful and had a tendency to drift. During those times we were compelled to ride hard and steady in order to keep the herd from drifting off. We always were compelled to work the hardest during the worst weather.

However, during the time I worked on the HL Ranch our worst trouble was with sheepherders and sheepmen who came in on the cattle range with their sheep. Wherever sheep graze, the territory is spoiled for cattle. Cattle will not graze after sheep. The range was open and free, and the sheepmen had a legal right to it equal with the cowmen, but when the sheepmen came in, the ranchmen instructed the waddies to shoot the sheep. Their idea was to scare the sheepmen off and prevent the range from being spoiled for cattle by sheep.

The cowboy felt as the ranch owners did, in respect to the grazing of sheep. The dominating idea was that the cowmen came on the range first and thus had prior rights. We wanted the sheepmen to leave with their sheep because we felt it was wrong for them to spoil the range for cattle and not because we wanted to monopolize the range. Also, we knew there was no legal action we could take. Therefore, it was a case of protecting the range for cattle by the law of might in the absence of a right law.

Lowe gave us orders, like the other ranchers gave their waddies, and we began to shoot sheep. When the sheepmen discovered their sheep were being shot, they gave orders to their herders to shoot the cowboys whom they met molesting sheep. Then followed shooting which resulted in several men getting wounded and a few killed. Then us waddies received orders to shoot every sheepman we saw, as we would shoot prairie dogs, and there was a number of sheepmen killed.

The HL waddies got into one of the worst battles in the Keechi Valley section during those days of the sheep war in that section. We were always watching for sheepmen, and of course they were watching for us. One day about ten of us met an equal number of herders, and each side opened fire. It was a battle that last about forty-five minutes, and during that time everybody was doing their best and fastest shooting.

Everyone took to whatever shelter was available, behind horses, sage brush, or just flat on the ground. All men on each side were shooting at the spot where they knew an opponent was lying.

Joe Jephart was the first one of us to get shot. He was hit in the hip but continued to fight. Jack Lowe was the next to get hit, and he received a shoulder wound but stayed in the fight. Then it was I that received a wound. I was hit in the forearm, and the bullet is still inbedded in my right arm. We three wounded men were bleeding profusely. Our guns and part of our clothing were covered with blood, but the excitement and anger that possessed all of us kept us in the fight. The next fellow to get hit was Jack McGonegal, and the hit was fatal. He never did arise to his feet.

While the herders were hitting us, we were hitting them and to such extent that shortly after McGonegal was killed, they that were still alive retreated. We did not follow the herders because we were anxious to have a cessation so that we could repair our injuries. After that battle the cowboys hunted sheepmen earnestly.

It was but a short time after this HL battle when the sheepmen left the Keechi Valley section. They moved their sheep to the rough section of Palo Pinto County. In Palo Pinto County there is considerable rough territory which is unfit for cattle but suitable for sheep, and sheep are still grazing there.

The thing that we waddies lived in fear of every minute was the stampede. A run could be expected at any time of the night or day. However, the worst mess caused by a run that I ever watched was a stampede by three thousand head of cattle which wore the Burk Burnett brand.[1]

The herd was being driven into Fort Worth, and I happened to be gathering firewood off of the banks of Sycamore Creek. I heard the thunder of running feet and the clashing horns, and I looked to see where the noise was coming from and saw the herd

---

[1]Burk Burnett, friend of Comanche Chief Quanah Parker, established the 6666 Ranch in 1870 in Wichita and Baylor counties. See the chapter "Burk Burnett of the Four Sixes," in Claude L. Douglas, *Cattle Kings of Texas.*

coming. I was directly in its path. I started to run, to my right, at my best speed and succeeded in getting out of the herd's path by the width of a hair. If I had failed I would not be sitting here now talking about it.

Those cattle were equaling a ranch horse in speed. It appeared to me that the cattle were jumping twice their length with each leap. The riders were shooting their guns in the faces of the cattle and yelling their loudest, but were not accomplishing a thing. When the herd reached the creek, some crossed, some went up, and others went down the stream. Most of the herd was headed towards town and became scattered in the residential district. When the animals began to run in all directions among the buildings, people ran for the houses to clear the way for the wild steers. The cowboys were one whole day getting the animals out of the district, and until they did, people were afraid to venture outside.

Shooting out the lights of a saloon and using the bar fixtures for a target was a frequent happening in Fort Worth. The cowboys did that to satisfy their devilment emotions and not to be destructive or vindictive. The owner of a place which was shot up could always depend on the boys returning to settle for the damage. The cowboys were greatly amused by seeing the people duck for cover, as a covey of quails would go, when the shooting started, and that amusement was their purpose behind the shooting. Generally no one was hurt during the sprees.

I saw one shooting deal which turned to what appeared would be serious during the cowboys' play. There was a party of about a dozen cowboys making the rounds of the saloons and other places of entertainment. Among the crowd were two of the McClain boys, who ran a ranch near Fort Worth. That crowd was getting a little boisterous but was not hurting anything. A policeman, whose name I forget, walked up to one of the McClain boys and insisted that they start for their camp. That demand was taken as an affront by the boys. McClain told the policeman that he was going home when he was ready and that the policeman could not arrest them.

The officer started, what may have been a bluff, to draw his gun. When the officer's hand moved toward the gun, McClain hit him flush on the jaw. The blow knocked the policeman out, and the boy took the officer's gun. When the officer's senses returned, he announced that he was going to call his associates and the sheriff for assistance and arrest McClain. The crowd of cowboys asserted that they would not allow the officers to take McClain. The cowboys mounted their horses and rode from place to place buying drinks and shooting in the air while traveling. When they came to a place in which they could ride their horses, they rode in and insisted on being served sitting in the saddle. The boys were taunting the officer because they were riled and wanted a fight.

It was not long till a large crowd gathered and were following the cowboys expecting to see a gun battle, which appeared imminent. Sheriff Courtwright was seen coming towards the cowboys after about thirty of the boys started to ride and shoot. The atmosphere was tense, but not for long. The sheriff walked up to McClain and told him he or his friends need not fear arrest as long as they confined themselves to having fun without hurting anyone, but he would appreciate it if they would cut their play time short under the circumstances.

The action of the sheriff saved having trouble and satisfied the cowboys. The boys then headed out of town and showed their appreciation for the sheriff's good sense by shooting out the lights in only one block as they rode away. But they were back the next day and settled for the lights.

Sheldon F. Gauthier

W. L. Newman

I have always called Fort Worth my home, as it's my birth-place and was my business center for many years. We moved to Jack County when I was four years of age; however, this does not keep me from remembering how we dreaded those redskins. My mother would hang quilts and blankets over the windows of our little one-room log cabin to hide our light so that the Indians might not locate our destination when they were out depredating.

Our nearest and dearest neighbors were old Mary and Britt Johnson (Negroes). I have visited and eaten many times with this old couple. Mary was a good cook and Britt a good provider, so we got along just fine.

One day the Indians came and captured old Mary and kept her several months before she was returned. Old Britt made some kind of trade with the Indians and got her back, but no one ever knew what this trade was.

Britt had a very pretty white horse that he kept tied to the corner of his house when he was not riding or driving him. He often remarked that no Indian should ever ride his horse.

Old Negro Britt was a freighter—carried supplies from Fort Worth to Fort Griffin where the ranchers could get their supplies. One time he and six more Negroes were coming from Fort Worth with a four-wagon train and pulled down on Salt Creek in Young County to spend the night. The next morning they got up early, pulled out about sunrise, and heard the Indians coming. They pulled their train in a circle and were completely surrounded by about two hundred wild redskins, shouting, shooting, and giving their war cry. The fight began—five Negroes were killed in the wagons, one Negro boy escaped, and old Britt was on the back axle under his wagon, pouring lead. One hundred and forty-four empty shotgun shells ran out and a hand-to-hand battle was staged. The escaped Negro boy ran and walked into Jacksboro barefooted to get help. My father and a brother of Hez Lowe, the present sheriff of Tom Green County, were in the bunch that went out. They found old Britt's body mutilated; his eyes were punched out, body split open, and the internal organs removed and replaced by meal; his ears were cut off and his scalp taken.

The white horse that Britt was so crazy about was killed with shots from his gun. It was believed that Britt would not take chances on escaping, and he killed his horse to make his statement hold true, that no Indian should ever ride his white horse.

I have gone to Britt's grave with old Mary many times to share her sorrow. Just after his death, the Indians came in again and massacred the Cameron family that lived on a little creek and this has been known as Cameron Creek since that time.

Massacring the seven members of the Cameron family was not enough; that very day the Indians went on down the creek about one mile, where they killed Mr. and Mrs. Pete Lynn and took their scalps. Mr. and Mrs. Lynn had two children, boy, four, and a girl, two, that escaped death as they happened to be playing away from the house in some tall grass. My father and other rangers found this tragedy about two days afterward, and the baby girl was nursing the dead mother's breast. The little boy was looking his parents over, wondering what it was all about.

The rangers carried the two children to their grandfather Lynn's home, where they lived afterward. When the boy was about seventeen years of age I carried him to his parents' grave and related the story of their death as best I could. My father had told me so much about the pitiful sight I would never forget the details. Old Uncle Billie Kutch and Mr. Manning organized a memorial association and erected tombstones for the unfortunate citizens' graves. I have visited them many times and right today could go point them out, then tell how each met his doom.

I worked for the Loving Cattle Company about sixteen years.[2] James Loving was the first and only secretary, until his

[2]Oliver Loving, one of the fathers of Texas trail driving, drove the first herd of longhorns from his Palo Pinto County ranch through the Indian Nations to Illinois in 1858 and, in like manner, pioneered the first trail to Colorado in 1859. It was on another drive to New

death, for the Cattle Raisers' Association. This organization was formed under a big oak tree at Graham, Texas. Colonel C. C. Slaughter, Burk Burnett, and James Loving were among the charter members. The famous old oak tree has always been cherished by the older cattle men because of what the organization has meant to the cowman.

I'm a cowman that has never suffered the hardships of going up the trail; I could have gone many times but stayed on the range by choice. We always carried our cattle to Henrietta up in Clay County. It was the largest cattle shipping point in the United States at that time; we were only ninety miles from there and it was to our advantage to ship by rail. Sometimes we would carry a thousand or more cattle to Henrietta, then have to wait a week or more for our turn to load on the train.

Stampedes were numerous, as the ground was strange. Any little unusual commotion, as a polecat, rabbit, thunder, or such like, would give the cattle a start. Our boss always expected us to stay with our cattle regardless of the number in charge.

This rodeo business they have now—I never go to such tommy-rot. I used to see better ones every morning than these boys stage here annually. We would have fourteen or fifteen horses rearing, pitching, and snorting all at once when we got ready to go out on the range. Believe me we sure would have to pull leather to stay on. We never had to make our horses pitch.

When I worked for the Loving Cattle Company I rode a little horse by the name of Mack. I had trained that little horse from a colt to be a fine cutter. I rode him about four years when a darned old cattle buyer came in and bought a bunch of cattle and had me cutting them out. I thought to myself I was doing a pretty job of it; I always did when I was on Mack. The old cattle buyer rode over to me and asked about the horse. I said, "He ain't for sale." Well that guy went on to Mr. Loving about it and bought him. Was I mad? I had a notion of quitting, but had another that beat that one, so I stayed. The fellow paid three times as much

---

Mexico in 1867 that Loving was fatally wounded by hostile Indians. Upon his death, his son, James C. Loving, took over the business. See the chapter "The Odyssey of Oliver Loving," in Douglas, *Cattle Kings of Texas.*

for him as he would an ordinary horse, but I hated to let him go. That taught me a lesson; I never took much interest in the other fellow's horse.

I began to ride old Long, and that devil pitched every time I got on him for four years. He threw me and I never rode him again. We decided to make a work horse out of him, but he got to pitching one day and fell dead. I guess he must have broke a blood vessel, but I never let that worry me.

We were not rough on the new cowboys, but I really caught everything when I went in. I was just a kid and those other fellows were much older. They kind of slowed down when they put me on a bad horse and I rode him. If they see there's any stuff in you, they like you and all that hazing stops.

We always had our fun when an Englishman or some guy from the East that knew nothing came in for that wild stuff.

Ruby Mosley

W. H. Childers

Yes sir, I was born on the range when it was all open, and my whole family, kinfolks and all, were on it at the time. While the range itself has changed completely, I still have a son in the saddle and making good. His name's Cecil Childers, and he's a polo and rodeo rider. He's in the show at the Fort Worth rodeo right now and stands pretty high. I reckon you've heard about him, though, so I'll tell you about myself. He sort of took after his dad about his hoss topping.

Now to begin with, I was born on my dad's stock farm in Wood County, Texas, September 5, 1866. I don't recollect much about the first place because my dad moved the family to Sivells Bend in Cooke County when I wasn't but two years old. He done that to work with A. Y. and W. W. Gunter, a couple of uncles of mine who ran stock in Cooke County.

I'd already begun to ride ponies when my dad decided to move back to Wood County when I wasn't but four. I still don't recollect much about that, either, but I do know that he put up the first one-hoss gin in Wood County that year. The next year he'd sold out his gin at a good profit and moved back to Sivells Bend, taking four wagonloads of lumber to build a house with.

Now there's a thing about that country that can't be seen anywhere today, and that's the grass they had then. It was so high that when the lumber was unloaded, the men'd have to hunt for it to find it. Actually, it was so high that in later years when I rode man-size hosses, the grass'd turn the rowels on my boots, and I'd be topping a hoss about fourteen hands high. It was from knee- to hip-high on an ordinary man, and when we'd be in there, running the mowing machine and putting up hay for the winter, we'd never see the blade. The only way we knowed where the blade was, was by watching the grass right even to the right of where we had the machine. It'd rise up, then lean to one side. It was so thick that it didn't even fall when it was cut but leaned

JA Ranch, Texas. The chuck wagon for the JA group camped on Cotton-wood Creek, 1907.

on other grass. It only fell when we came along and stacked it for drying. You've seen the big haystacks they have on farms? Well, that's what I mean. Another thing, too, and that's when cattle laid down. You just had to almost stumble over them to find them in the grass.

The location of the place Dad built was just north of where Gainesville is now, and on the old Buffalo Hide Trail. Just after we settled there, my Uncle Harper Gunter moved in with a fair-sized hoss herd, and he hadn't been there two months until the Indians raided his hoss herd and got every head. Now, the way they done it was to shoot the old grey bell mare with arrows to keep her from giving the alarm, then they drove the herd off. Soon's Uncle Harper found it out, he organized a bunch of the neighbors and chased the Indians. They lost a lot of time because they had to trail the Indians every step of the way. Just to show you how the oldtimers could do it, though, they caught up with the Indians in the Territory and would have fought them if they hadn't run. The trailers might have lost the hoss herd if they'd have give chase, so they let the redskins go and took care of the hosses. They got every head back.

I really didn't pay much attention to Dad's place while a kid, but I can tell you about myself. I learned to ride hosses so well that by the time I was six, I could ride a running hoss bare-backed. In fact, I never had a real saddle until I was fourteen years old. On my birthday, Dad made me a present of a saddle that cost exactly fourteen dollars—a good one for those days.

Prior to that time, when I wanted a saddle, I'd get an old tree with the leather all worn off, take a rope and work a short loop around the hoss, and then tie it up short. I didn't even have any stirrups, and must have looked a sight while riding around over the country in that rig.

Not having a good saddle didn't bother my cow work, though, because I just went right ahead, and worked like a regular cowhand with my dad's stock. My dad was the first to have the Turkey Track iron in Cooke County.[3] That was his iron, and

---

[3]This brand should not be confused with that of the more famous Turkey Track Ranch located in Hutchinson and Hansford counties. This name and brand were used by several other ranches at different times and places in Texas and New Mexico.

nobody else ran it until he went in partners with old Colonel Jot Gunter, who had another ranch in Grayson County.

I reckon I was about thirteen years old when Dad and the Colonel done that. They established the Childers-Gunter spread in Cooke County and run around three thousand head in the Turkey Track iron. I don't recall just how many acres there were in the spread, but it was so big it run from Saint Jo on the north to Myra on the east and to Muenster on the southwest. It was about four miles across, and about nine miles long.

The family never went to the Turkey Track but stayed right on the stock farm. In fact, Dad put me and my younger bud, Cyrus, in charge of the place and with orders not to neglect it but to work it like it belonged to us. And, that we done. Cy and me sure run that place, even though he wasn't but nine and I was thirteen when Dad left.

That was the way of the oldtimer days, though. Kids got to be men a heap quicker than they do nowadays, and Cy and me went to the roundups just like we were men. You see, all the neighbors got together and rounded up all the cattle in that part of the country then cut out what belonged to each other.

We had quite a bit of trouble with a man named Bill Mallock, though, because he fenced a forty-acre pasture and so many cattle were ruined on the fence. We never lost any except when we went to driving, and they'd head right for that fence every time, it seemed. You see, it wasn't but a one-strand fence, but the strand, even when it was on the top of the posts, would just barely be hid by the tall grass, and the cattle would run right into it. When they ran sideways into it, the barbs never failed to cut leg muscles, and we'd then have to shoot the poor critter. Sure made a lot of folks mad around there, and they cut it down humpteen times, but old Bill put it right back every time and they finally let it stand. So many head of stock were ruined that it's always been a wonder to me why some of those crusty old pioneers didn't cut Bill down.

The real reason they didn't was because Bill was noted for being a bad shot, but he could fistfight and rough-and-tumble wrestle. In those days men didn't shoot unarmed men, but when two of them had an argument, they'd give each other the same chance and shoot it out. Most of the arguments settled thataway were settled right in town. They'd be across the street from each other, see each other, and start walking to the middle of the street. They'd usually get about thirty paces from each other, then both would draw their pistols at the same time. The truest first shot then won the fight.

But Bill Mallock was a problem. He wouldn't even tote a gun. Instead, he would dare a man to meet him in a man-to-man fistfight or any way he wanted to make it, and the other man always got the worst of it when that happened. All the trouble quieted down when more people moved in and fenced their places. Then, the first thing you knew, the whole range was fenced in.

I was just a happy-go-lucky kid on the stock farm, and that's the reason I can't tell you a whole lot more about the old place before I went to the Turkey Track. I know we had a few stampedes, but not any big ones. And there were drouths, and soon that come to bother the cattlemen, but I can't say much about those things.

When I reached my eighteenth birthday, Dad sent for me to come to the Turkey Track. When I got there, I was hired as a cow punch at twenty dollars a month and chuck.

About the first thing I done in the line of work after I reached the Turkey Track was to go with some other cow puncher over to the T-Anchor, Colonel Jot's other ranch in Elm Flats in Grayson County. This was a bigger spread, covering over twenty-five thousand acres and running around eight thousand head of stock on it. The iron was made like this: $\bot$.[4]

There was quite a difference between the T-Anchor iron and the Turkey Track. To make the Turkey Track, we only had one running iron and made three burns at a time. When it was finished, it looked like this: $\uparrow$. When these cow punchers I spoke of and myself went over to the Turkey Track, we went after fifty

[4]Though the main T-Anchor ranch was in Randall County, the T-Anchor brand was originated in 1881 by Jules Gunter, nephew of Jot Gunter (onetime president of the Texas State Fair and promoter of the Gunter Hotel, San Antonio), on their land in Montague County. C. Boone McClure, "A Review of the T-Anchor Ranch," *Panhandle Plains Historical Review*, 3 (1930).

hosses that had been shipped from the King Ranch and busted on Colonel Jot's hoss ranch he had in connection with his cattle. He run so many hosses, and sold, too, that he had to have a regular hoss ranch and he'd ship them in from South Texas after the wild ones around his ranch played out.

These fifty must have been earmarked for the Turkey Track, because Colonel Jot's T-Anchor hadn't been put on them, but they'd used a running iron instead and put the Turkey Track iron on. We were certainly glad of that, because it's a lot of work to brand wild hosses, or hosses that have been fresh busted. You see, they're still wilder than a jack rabbit and liable to cause a lot of trouble when they're still fresh busted and you go to put some iron on them. While the men Jot hired regular as hoss busters were experts in that matter, they didn't take to that part of the work themselves.

We started that drive, and it's still a nightmare to me how much trouble them ornery critters gave us cow punchers. They would bolt at every opportunity, and when one was bolting one way, some of the others would try to bolt another. We were a whole week making a drive across the country when we should have made it in a day's time.

You see, it wasn't over fifty miles for the whole trip, but if Dad hadn't sent as many as he did to make the drive, we'd have never made it back with all the hosses. The way we worked it was, when a bunch bolted, some of us would take after them while the rest stayed with the herd. When they'd get back, we'd drive on, then another bunch would bolt. That's the way it was the whole trip over.

When I got back to the ranch, Dad sent me out as a check line rider. Our duties as check liners were to keep the cattle back from the fence where there was one. You see, the whole range still wasn't fenced except in valleys. Then we repaired wire where somebody would go through and leave it down, see about water holes and drive the stock across country to other holes, and in general see to the welfare of the stock.

I rode the check line for a whole year before Dad sent for Cy to come over on the Turkey Track. When he came over, Dad went to Houston County to buy cattle. A couple of weeks after he left, we got a wire telling us to go to Houston County. He met us when we got there and took us out to a place where some cattlemen were driving in a bunch of Spanish longhorn steers. There were three trainloads when Dad got them loaded up, and he went back with one, Cy went with one, and I came back to the Turkey Track with the other.

These cattle were put out on a fenced pasture for a year where they fattened. After they fattened enough, Dad had them drove to the railroad and loaded up again for Kansas City. This time, Cy and myself went with the cattle. Out of Oklahoma City, the cattle were put in two trains instead of three, because the trains were able to haul more there. That's the way trains were in the olden days.

You know, when the cattle train come out of Houston County, I'd catch the engine and ride there until about halfway to the next stopping point, then I'd swing off and watch the cars as they passed by me. If I'd see any of the critters down, I'd swing on and prod them up before they were stomped to death, then I'd get off and let the rest of the train pass by until the caboose reached me, then I'd swing on. When the train went out of Oklahoma City, I noticed that I had trouble making my catch, but I done it anyway. Then when we got to Kansas City, the beef price wasn't as much as Dad thought it should have been, so he ordered us by wire to take the cattle on to Chicago. Well, that we done. I caught the engine as usual, and when we got along a way, I swung off at the top of a hill, but I noticed that the hill didn't make so awful much difference to the engine and that it was catching up speed pretty fast, so I swung back on. Then I got to studying things over, and you know, if I hadn't swung back on there at the first, I'd have been left way out there, miles from nowhere. Those big eastern engines were a heap different from the little old hoggers Texas had in them days. Of course it's all the same now, but it wasn't then.

We were met at the train by the commission company Dad had to handle the beef, and they took things over from then on. Cy and me then took the town in, and I expect the town must have took us in, too, because they certainly did stare at us. I can well recall how they stared, but we stared right back because we thought they certainly did dude themselves up funny when they went out anywhere. We took in a number of dance halls and saloons and were invited in on gambling games a number of times. That was one thing Dad had warned us against, though, so we didn't accept any of their kind invitations.

The second day there, Cy and me decided that we wanted to dodge all the attention we were getting, so we stepped into a men's clothes emporium and had them fit us out with the regular duds the ordinary people in Chicago sported. We didn't cause anybody to stare at us then and made the same rounds we made the day before to see if anybody would make any remarks about what we'd done. Very few of them showed they recognized us, and when they did, it was only by a nod of some sort.

Along in the evening of the third day we decided we'd had enough of the big city and were figuring on leaving the next morning when we come out of a dive and saw two men holding up a third. Since this place was downstairs, and the door stood open, these fellows couldn't have known we were coming out right then. I just don't know what to think about it now, but when Cy and me saw what they were doing, we decided to get in on the fun. We walked up behind the fellow that's got the gun on the victim, and Cy says, "Reckon you fellows better high-tail it before we ventilate you."

They looked around and Cy's big old bucker was in his fist, and one of them said, "They're from Texas. Let's beat it." And, sure enough, they ran away as hard as they could go it. The victim thanked us, gave us a card, and told us to see him the next day and he'd show us a good time. We looked at the card, and it had the name of a dive just like the one we'd come out of, so we decided not to look in on him. I still had that old card around in my stuff until a couple of years ago when I throwed it away. Dad said it was some kind of a skin game and we done right.

When we got back to the Turkey Track, we fell into the regular work as cow punchers until I was about twenty-one. At that time, Colonel Jot had already colonized and sold off his T-Anchor property, and Dad and him were setting out to colonize the Turkey Track. As they colonized a section, they'd round up cattle from off another section and sell them. Then they'd sell off that bunch and so on until I helped drive the last head off the Turkey Track when I was twenty-three years old.

Dad made a wad of money off that deal but had to split it all with the Colonel, of course. We all went back to the stock farm and raised fine stock until dad died just after the turn of the century. Not so long after he died, Cy and me split up the inheritance and I moved out to Abilene, Texas, where I still live. Among the children my wife and I've raised was Cecil, and he made a real hossman, as I told you when I first met you. And he's just starting in the game, too. If he can stick and stay until he gets more rodeo experience, he'll make a top notcher yet.

Woody Phipps

Fogg Coffey

AFTER being born in Parker County in 1863, I moved in 1865 with my family, Rich Coffey's, in a wagon drawn by oxen to a settlement consisting of five families. It was called Picketville and located near Elm Creek on the Colorado River in Runnels County. They built their houses by putting posts in the ground as close together as possible, then they put a few poles and brush on top and stretched buffalo hides over all that. My mother said it made a very comfortable shelter.

I think we dreaded the Indians in the early days more than anything. We had to be on the watch constantly or they'd take all we had. A bunch of redskins (Comanches, I think they were) visited our settlement on June 1, 1871. We had just got all the cattle and horses rounded up. There were 1,050 head of cattle and fifty-four saddle horses. The men had left a few boys to guard the herds while they went to take another look for stragglers, and some to eat. Nobody suspected an attack, for they'd seen no Indians or signs or nothing.

Well, before the men could get in their saddles, them low-down Indians had drove off every cow and all the horses except three or four. Two of our men were killed, and my brother John, then just a boy, was wounded.

The very next Christmas them Indians came back and drove off 350 head of cattle. There weren't more than twenty men in the neighborhood, and they were scattered, of course, so before they could get together the Comanches were gone.

My brother Bill and me had a little run-in with the Indians when I wasn't more than eight or nine years old. My father had sent us out to look for some horses near our home. We was afoot and saw the Indians after the horses before they saw us. We managed to catch two of the horses and beat them back to the house. They took after us, and all the time they was shooting at us with old flintlock guns. We was some scared boys, but nobody took a little thing like that too serious them days.

When I was just a small shaver I was sent with my brother John to look for some stock one day. We had gotten hold of a small cap-and-ball pistol. Brother John rode off one way and me another. He let me keep the gun, but told me to be sure and not fire it unless I saw Indians. A gunshot was a signal for help. I didn't go far before I ran onto a polecat and I let loose shooting. It wasn't any time at all before my brother and everybody in hearing distance was there on the spot. They thought, of course, we had spotted some Indians. My father sure gave me a trimming down. It was worth it though, just to get to shoot that gun.

I remember another incident that happened when I was a boy that sure did tickle me. Old Dad Guest had a hog ranch at Fort Chadbourne along in the early seventies. He came by our house one day on his way to Fort Chadbourne, and I teased my father and my mother to let me go with him. They consented, and I rigged me up an old shotgun muzzler and started off feeling proud as a young cock.

When we were in a few miles of the fort we looked around and saw a band of Indians coming not more than a half mile away. They chased us to the fort, shooting and yelling for all they was worth. When we got there some of the folks asked Dad if they'd shot at him. He said, "Yes, we heard the bullets twice, once when they passed us, and again when we passed them." If they had attacked us a little further back, before we got so near the fort, they'd have scalped us for sure.

I never did any long trail driving; I worked on the range always. I guess I was a pretty fair bronc rider, but everybody was in them days. We had to be good riders. It was useless to try to live if you couldn't ride and shoot. I rode, or broke, lots of wild horses when I was a young fellow.

I remember some Rangers came to our house from Coleman as late as 1875 or '76. They had camped the night before in Curley Hatchet Bend about one-half mile from our house. The Indians had stolen their horses and left them afoot. My father thought that was a good joke on the Rangers.

The biggest roundup I ever helped with was along about 1887. We rounded fifty thousand head of cattle and brought them together over on Fuzzy Creek. The cattle had drifted into

Concho, Coleman, and other counties. Jim Johnson was big boss of the roundup. Other bosses were Irie Fitzgerald, Bill McAuley, and John Davison. It took several days to gather the cattle. They was worked in three bunches. After we'd worked (cut and branded) them they was turned loose again.

There was a man by the name of McMahon killed in that outfit. He was shot and killed by a boy who worked for him, whom he had whipped. The boy drew his gun and told him to apologize to him, and pay him. But McMahon laughed instead, and the boy killed him on the spot.

My father built a two-story rock building on the line of Concho and Runnels counties and near the Colorado River in 1881. The house is still standing. Practically all my life, with the exception of a few years, has been spent in that part of the country.

I live at Leaday now. I have been in the sheep business for many years. I was the first man in West Texas to run sheep on open range.

The sheep and cowmen didn't mix in the early days. Cattlemen thought the sheep business was undignified. There were many differences among men on that account, and many were divided and became enemies who were once friends. But it all worked out for the best, and now we have communities and towns of which we can justly be proud.

Annie McAulay

A watering place on the SMS Ranch, formerly the Spur, near Stamford, Texas, 1907–10.

James H. Childers

THE place and date of my birth was Murray County, Georgia, Dec. 10, 1855. My parents were John and Jane Gray Childers. Father was an overseer for a large plantation owner of Murray County. He died in 1857, and mother moved to Tennessee, where she had relatives living, in 1868. I lived with her and farmed until I was twenty-two, which was in 1877, and then I came to Texas. I came direct to Fort Worth and have lived here ever since.

When I came to Fort Worth the Texas & Pacific was its only railroad, having built into the city the previous year. At the time I arrived, I was compelled to walk over a mile to Main Street. This spot of ground where I am now living was part of a cattle ranch, as was practically all the south side of Fort Worth. There were a few houses and cultivated fields scattered through the region.

During my first year in Fort Worth, I became acquainted with W. J. Boaz, one of the early-day ranchers, and about the year 1880 I accepted the position as ranch foreman under him. His ranch was located west of Fort Worth about ten miles, where Benbrook is now located. Boaz owned almost three thousand acres of land entirely devoted to ranging cattle. In the same section were located Corn's, Winfield's, Scott's, Wooten's, and other ranches. The ranches utilized the Clear Fork of the Trinity River for their cattle's water supply.

The Boaz ranch varied greatly in the number of cattle we ranged. At times we would have over a thousand head, and then we would sell till the herd numbered as low as two hundred.

Boaz did not raise many of his own cattle, but bought and sold constantly. When he found a good buy he bought the cattle and would range the animals till he could sell at a satisfactory price.

The first year I managed the Boaz ranch we fenced the three

thousand acres, and thereafter our crew numbered about six hands. We used one waddy to ride the fenceline constantly. His job was to inspect the fence for defects and repair all minor defects, but if he found a major break, such as a broken post, broken or cut wires, he would report it, and a repair crew, with the necessary material, would make the repairs.

Occasionally we would find the wire out. The wire cutting was done by cattle thieves, who cut a gap through which they would drive the stolen stock. We were compelled to keep a close watch for thieves. One or two men were used to ride the range whose principal was to watch for thieves. Also, to attend to injured and bogged cattle.

We kept salt licks close to headquarters and near the river where the cattle could get water, and near the licks is where the cattle chose their bedding grounds. The cattle would range over various sections of the range during the day and begin to drift towards their bedding ground towards the late part of the evening. By coaxing the cattle to bed near the headquarters, we reduced the chances of having cattle stolen during the night. Our time of trouble with rustlers was during the day when the cattle would scatter and some grazed near the fence. If a thief was watching for a chance to steal some of our cattle, it was an easy matter for him to cut the fence and drive the cattle away. Our losses to the thieves were small because of the fence and the constant watch we maintained.

The man who suffered the most from rustlers in our section was Corn. A thief came very near to putting Corn out of the cattle business. For a period of time he was losing cattle constantly. In order to create an interest in catching the thief, Corn offered a reward of five hundred dollars. Corn's foreman was a fellow named Mitchell, and he stayed awake many nights watching for the thief, and during the day he put one of the waddies attending to part of the foreman's work so he could devote the time watching for the rustler. But he was unsuccessful.

Tom Snow, now deputy sheriff, was just commencing his career as a law enforcement officer, and one day a Negro came to Tom with several letters and a complaint. The fellow's complaint was that the man he had been hauling some cattle for had cheated him out of some of his pay. The Negro said he had hauled cattle from Corn's ranch, and the dispute, over pay, developed the previous day. He had hauled a large cow into market, and the weather was exceedingly hot, and because of the weather conditions the cow became overheated and died. The Negro and his employer took the carcass to a ravine east of the city, where they skinned and quartered it. The meat was sold to a retail butcher named Zimmerman.

The letter dropped out of the employer's pocket when he took his coat off and threw it on a bush while skinning the cow. The Negro took the letters to Tom Snow to disclose the name of his employer. The letters were addressed to Mitchell, Corn's foreman.

Mitchell was a man with an excellent reputation and had worked hard to catch the rustler, even to staying awake nights and laying out on the range watching, but there were the letters. Snow went to the ranch and arrested Mitchell, and when the prisoner was confronted with the letters and the story as told by the Negro, he confessed. He was tried and sent to the penitentiary. The stealing stopped on Corn's ranch immediately with the arrest of Mitchell.

This series of incidents took place before the days of the automobile. With the coming of the automobile truck, there came a change in the methods of the cattle rustler. Now, the rustler hauls the cattle off in a truck instead of driving the critters off or hauling the animal in a wagon.

An incident which took place between Wooten and Corn is brought to my mind by talking about cattle rustling. When I first came to Fort Worth, there were a few unbranded cattle to be found on the range. Also, occasionally, a stray branded critter would be found which had gotten away from some herd which had been driven through Fort Worth. The various ranchers kept on the watch for strays. One day Wooten and Corn were riding over the range region together and found three head of tip-top strayed yearling steers. Wooten suggested that Corn and he flip a coin for the odd steer and drive the steers to their ranches. This suggestion was agreeable to Corn, and the coin was flipped, resulting in Wooten winning the odd steer. Then Corn sug-

gested that they should return the following morning to get the
steers, because the hour was late, and driving the steers, as
would be necessary, would keep the men out late. Wooten
agreed to the suggestion as the two men speeded their mounts
homeward.

Corn met Wooten the following morning, as agreed, and
rode to get their steers. When the men arrived at where the
steers had been, the animals were nowhere in sight. The two
men spent about an hour hunting for the strays, then quit, thinking somebody had taken the three animals.

About a month later Wooten and Corn were discussing the
disappearance of the three steers. Wooten said: "Corn, I wonder
who got 'em."

"You know, Wooten, I never lie," Corn replied. "I just figured them critters weren't safe with you knowing where they
were. So I doubled back after parting with you that night and
drove the steers home. I made fair time and arrived home about
2 P.M."

Wooten and Corn were good men. In fact, all the ranchers
in the region were good men, and practically all ranchers I have
met were dependable men, but they just couldn't resist match-
ing a pretty yearling. A fat and magnificent yearling was just too
tempting to them, and they couldn't keep from driving the animal home.

During my early days here there were hundreds of cattle
herds driven in and through Fort Worth. Many were shipped
from here to the northern markets. Many of the herds were
driven through here to be grazed on the northern ranges of Kansas, Nevada, Montana, and other sections. They were driven to
the northern range to be fattened before delivery to the markets, and others were being shifted to a less congested range.

With the herds coming here and being drifted through, the
ranchers in this section discovered many strays. Generally, the
strays were the result of a stampede.

The worst stampede I ever saw happened just south of town.
A herd was drifting in and a terrific storm blew in from the
north, striking the cattle in the face. The herd was fretful, because of being in strange territory, and when the storm started

the herd turned and went on a stampede. The storm started just before dark and soon the darkness made it impossible for the waddies to see where they were going or where the cattle were traveling to. This stampede cost the drover about a hundred head of cattle. Of course all the strays were found later by the ranchers in this vicinity.

After the cattlemen's association was organized and developed to a position so it covered the many problems of the ranchers, the association looked after the strays of the drovers that were found by ranchers of the territory through which the herd traveled.

After I had worked seventeen years for Boaz, I quit to enter the cattle business for myself. I bought additional land adjacent to my farmland for range purposes. I fenced about eight hundred acres and in the pasture I ranged about five hundred head, on an average. I started my ranch at the bottom of the 1893 panic. The prices were low, and I bought some of the yearlings as low as five dollars per head.

I calculated on holding the cattle for a year or two before selling. I anticipated the market would be on the upswing during the following couple years. My guess was correct, and before the two-year period was up I began to sell at a fair profit.

During the panic of 1893, many ranchers were compelled to quit, because the prices of cattle were so low the stock did not bring enough money to pay the debts. The ranchers with a little money ahead were able to stay in the business by marking time, but the man who owed money on his stock found himself unable to sell the cattle for enough to pay the loan. There were some shipments made which did not sell for enough to pay the transporation cost to the northern market.

I bought close and was at very little expense ranging the herd. My range being fenced and with an abundance of grass and water, all I had to do was to meet the expense of one man. Wages were low and I paid my helper fifteen dollars per month. All we needed to do was to watch the fence for breaks and look over the herd occasionally for sick or injured cattle. With a small herd and plenty of range room, one is not troubled to any extent with sick or injured cattle. My herd did well and stayed in excellent flesh. Therefore, while the panic ruined many ranchers, it enabled me to get an excellent start in the cattle business.

By the time I was ready to sell cattle, there was a good market in Fort Worth. The packing industry had been established here in 1902, and it was then I was ready to do any great amount of selling.

I was never entirely out of the cattle business from the time I started in the business. I was elected and served two terms as a member of the Commissioner's Court of Tarrant County, and this position took me away from active attention to my cattle business. My service as a commissioner began in 1918, and after I terminated my service as a county official, I have left the work of raising cattle to others.

Sheldon F. Gauthier

Richard C. Phillips

WELL, now, to begin with, I was born on my dad's XX Ranch near Bandera, Texas, on December 17, 1884. Reckon as how that'd make me sixty-three, wouldn't it? You asked if I ever worked on the range, and I'll answer by saying that I rode hosses when I wasn't but four years old. You see, my dad's spread wasn't much shakes, and he couldn't hire much help because he didn't have so much money, and so he started me out to learning to ride just as soon's he figured I was able to sit in a saddle.

And the tough part about it was, he died just after I'd learned to ride pretty good and could climb up by myself. After he died, that left nobody but me and my mother, so I had to learn to tend to the hundred-odd head of stuff we had. She'd talk to me and try to make me feel my responsibility so's I'd go out there and do my dead level best to take my dad's place. I'd never have made it, though, if it hadn't have been for the good neighbors we all had around there. They done a marvelous lot for us and took the load in the roundups. I went on the roundups, all right, and slept out away from home during them roundups. Come branding time, and I was right in the big middle of it, tending to the irons and everything else a stripling could shake. One thing about it, though, and that was there wasn't a lazy bone in my body, and I learnt to rope and brand on my own account. I reckon I could pull it all off by the time I was eight years old. That's pretty young, but in them days a kid wasn't always hanging out in some ice cream parlor. Instead, he went about his business and tried to be some account in the world. Another thing, people weren't always yapping baby talk at him, but gave him jobs to do, and if he didn't, he wanted to the next time he was given something to do.

I was left a dogie when my mother died, and I wasn't but twelve at the time. You know, even though we had tried to get along, we didn't have much stuff when she died, and I sold out for a hundred dollars and lit out for the west. I wanted to get away from the place where I'd had so much trouble.

A couple of months later, I lit in Fort Stockton and met Tom Bailey. He was ramrodding for the Western Union Beef Company and was in town right then, looking for cowpunchers. I told him I could ride and rope, and he gave me a chance. I was told to beat it out to the ranch, and when he came out, he'd see what I could do.

When he got out there, he put me through my paces and hired me. I got fifteen dollars a month and chuck. Now the Western Union Beef outfit was a big spread, going from Fort Stockton to the mouth of the Pecos River. It was a big outfit and had ranches from below Uvalde to clean up in Montana. A couple of bankers, R. T. and N. T. Wilson, were the ones that owned the company. They ran the Alamo National Bank in San Antonio, and that's where all our checks come from.

Now, naturally, since the ranch was such a big one, and even ran two brands at the same time right on the same range, there was a lot of cowpunchers working the spread. There were a number of Negroes, too, and don't you ever believe them Negroes couldn't ride and rope to beat the band. There was old George Adams, and he could ride and rope with the best. Then too there was Tom Ganning, a younger Negro that was good. Negroes weren't allowed a gun on that spread. I said Ganning was young—well, old George was an ex-slave. He'd been a slave down near San Antonio on a plantation that had been in the Wilson family for years and years. There was one more Negro that I recall, and his name was Snow Ball. That was because he was the blackest Negro anybody ever saw. And yet, he was sure a mighty good cowhand.

About the best rider on the spread was Henry Salmon. He was in charge of the hoss ranch, and I reckon he had charge of five hundred saddle hosses at least. Besides having that many, they had to keep busting more wild hosses in to take the place of those that got killed or were too old to work anymore. Believe me, that's many a hoss and a sight to see for sure.

Then there was "Button" Clark, the trail boss. He was always in charge of the trail drives because he'd been up the trail so many times and knowed the country like a book. He was called Button because there was another top hand on the spread whose name was Buck Clark.

About the cattle, well, have you seen any longhorn critters? That's what the Western Union Beef Company run. Whole herds of them. Why, they branded ten thousand dogies a year when the spread was going great guns. The two irons they run was the 7D and the Double Half Moon. You make the 7D like this: ⅃ , and the Double Half Moon like this: ⌒. Of course the critters carried the irons shoulder, side, and hip.

Oh, yes. Jim Watts was the wagon boss when I first got on, but he was fired a couple of years later for staying drunk all the time, and Doc Coleman took his place. I don't recall at this time just how long he did work as wagon boss, but Hugh Boles took his place and stayed right on through, working for John T. McElroy of Pecos City, who bought the ranch, lock, stock, and barrel, along in '94. I had word of the ranch in '98, and Hugh Boles still had the wagon boss job.

Now I've told you about the men on the spread, I'll spin a couple of yarns about some of the work. They might sound to you like they was yarns, but if you're on the spot at one of these things, it is not so funny. Not by a darn sight! Now, you take a stampede, and they're one of the most dangerous things ever was, and yet they happen all the time on any ranch where a bunch of cow critters are rounded up into a herd. Anything will cause them, too.

There was one when I went north with about fifteen hundred head of four-year-olds, steers they was, and we was trying to hold them at Canyon City. Them ornery rascals would stampede every night, and one time they run plumb to Amarillo! Button Clark, who was in charge of the herd, trailed them there himself. After we rounded the critters all up again, the tally showed twenty-three steers gone.

Then another night they run towards Amarillo again and veered a little east just enough to run right smack into Joe Nation's herd, which put the whole kit and b'iling to running. Now that was the worst mess ever I got into, because after stopping the run, we had to cut the whole herd to get the two of them separated. Work, work, work. That's about all that trip amounted to.

The reason the 7D put that herd up there in the first place was because there was so much dry weather, and we had to get the critters to water. In one year, 7Ds had three herds around Amarillo, and Joe Nation had six.

Another reason the 7Ds put so many cattle in Amarillo was because Amarillo was our shipping point to the Montana ranges. We shipped on the Fort Worth and Denver City road to Brush, Wyoming, where they were unloaded and drove to the range the W.U.B. Company had in mind. That's the way they done business. When conditions in Texas were unfavorable for cattle, they tried to put their beef into a country that was favorable, and they owned ranches everywhere like I showed you before.

Now I've always been considered one of the best shots in the country, but I'm not going to tell anything about it. Instead, I'll tell you about some of the boys on the spread there that could really shoot as well as ever I could myself. Now there's Bob Wilson. Just a cowhand, but a darn sight better than any I've seen since I left the 7Ds. Old Bob was a noted pistol shot, and the quickest on the draw ever I seen. One day the boys decided to prank him, and one of them that was a good roper waited up a draw for him to come to the chuckwagon that was spotted right on top. Well, old Bob finally come along in a lope, whistling some sort of a tune, and this roper zizzed his lasso out, trying to trip the hoss. The rope made the hoss's front foot all right but old Bob shot that lasso in two before any pressure could be put on it. He'd had shot the cowhand himself, if he hadn't ducked behind a rock the minute he made his cast. That sure was funny to everybody but the zany that tried to throw old Bob, because if he hadn't gone to hollering, "Don't shoot! Don't shoot!, I'm one of the boys!" old Bob'd have rode up into them rocks and made a sieve out of him.

Now, I never done much hoss busting. They had men on the hoss ranch that took care of the busting, but I did do a lot of bronc riding because them ornery rascals was half Spanish and mustang, and the mustang hoss was as mean a critter as ever walked. They pitched every morning when you went out and roped the one you were to ride. And they'd pitch for fully five minutes until they got what we called "warmed up." In other words, they pitched until they got the laziness out of their bones.

Some way or other, I sure wish I could make you realize just how hard they pitched. They pitched every bit as hard and fast as these critters you see now in the rodeos, so we had a real rodeo every morning. There would be some funny sights take place sometimes, too. I recall very plain how one of the Negroes was pitched plumb over the corral walls, and they were eight foot high. When that Negro come down on the other side, he let out a big grunt that could almost be heard in Fort Stockton. Then, too, I've seen the boys pitched into mesquite trees and every other way you can think of.

What I'm trying to picture to you is that in them days a man had to be a man every day without no layoffs. Every day! You take in a stampede, now, and I've seen a hundred or more. The boys that are out with a herd must be real good riders willing to take chances with their lives. When a herd starts to running, it goes hell-bent-for-election and will run over anything it can unless its too big, then the herd will run until it runs up against something it can't run over, then it will split and go around but keep running. That's the way them ornery critters will do every time. Well, when a herd gets to running, it'll run until it runs down or gets so tired it can't run any more. The thing a cowhand has to do is to get that herd to milling, and then they'll run in a circle until they get run down. If they're not put into a mill, they'll run over some bank of a creek, or a cut, or even a canyon if there's one in the way. Then there'll be a lot of beef killed and lost, which can run up into the thousands of dollars.

Now, then, I want you to picture a herd on the stomp and realize that any human or hoss that gets in the way, that the herd will run over them and stomp them into the very ground if it possibly can. Get that picture, then realize that the only possible way to turn a herd into a mill is to get right out in front and beat the lead steer until he starts turning and trying to get away from you. That away, the rest of the herd will follow him, and the herd will then go into a mill. When you get that picture, then you'll see and understand why men had to be he-men in them days. Not now, because these fine cattle are hard to put into a stomp, and when they are, they don't run long because they're not grown for strength but for fat. They didn't grow them in the old days for strength, but, them old longhorns just naturally growed like a hoss without any help from man.

They'd hide out in the brakes, and when we were on the roundup, they'd come abusting out and try their dead level best to kill the cowhand. That was the old mossyhorns, of course, that got so testy, and there were mighty few so mean, thanks be. Others were real wild and flighty and would run away from the cowhand as hard as they could go. That was expected, though, and the cowhands would rope them and then drive them to what they had rounded up, where another hand would stay with them and keep them corralled. After a little persuasion, most of them critters would stay together in a herd.

Now, what I'm telling is what actually happened to me, and not something I've read. Truth of the matter is that I can't read nor write, the reason being because I was raised a dogie and had to hustle for my bread and meat all my life. I just want to tell about one of them stomps we had on one of the last trail drives to Amarillo with 7Ds, while it was still owned by the W.U.B. Company. I'd been standing night herd, and it'd been raining pretty hard. Whenever it goes to raining, a herd will stand up and go to shifting around, trying to get their tails and backs to the wind and rain. That's their nature, but they're also ready to run in case anything makes the least little old bobbie. Well, sir, instead of the rain getting harder, it began to lighten, and the night itself got lighter. We could see a heap better than when it was raining, and all of a sudden, we heard a shot from the camp where the rest of the boys had gone to sleep.

The herd heard it, too, and were off like a shot, running right towards me and the other night rider. We'd stopped for a bit of talk and a cigarette but was in the wrong spot at the right time. If it hadn't been that the night was pretty light, and we were able to see the leaders, we would have been stomped right into the ground. Instead, we could see the leaders, and we turned that herd into a mill in less than five minutes after it got started. Five minutes! I'll bet that'd have made some kind of a record if records had been kept, because five minutes is a wonderful time.

We had a lot of good times there on the 7D, what with our

contests we had every time we weren't pushed with the work and all, but along came the thing that spoiled it all when John T. McElroy of Pecos City made a deal with the W.U.B. Company and bought the ranch. I don't know just what kind of a deal was made, but I do know that the cowhands were given the order to round up every head on the ranch and bring it to the chutes at the headquarters for a tally. Well, on the day we were to have the herd there, there was a stranger there with McElroy. Nobody paid no attention to him, because we were all busy with the herd.

Finally came the order to shoot the chutes, and we started the cattle through. Hugh Boles made the count for the W.U.B. Company, and John T. made his own count in the middle of the chutes as the critters passed him by. The stranger made the count at the end of the chutes as the critters all passed out and into the new herd. Twenty-eight thousand head passed through the chutes in that one day, and this stranger was Segal Saunders of the Kansas City Saunders Cattle Commission Company. He bought every head that came through and paid John T. four dollars a head for every one of them twenty-eight thousand critters. Figure it yourself.

Then the real work started. Segal Saunders gave the order to have the critters road-branded, and I myself put a seven on thirteen thousand of them critters. Thirteen thousand! You see, all I had to do was put on the iron as the other boys downed them, and there were three crews working with me. It certainly kept us all busy. After the cattle were all branded, then they were roaded to Amarillo and shipped to different points. I myself left Amarillo with a trainload for Terre Haute, Indiana, to be fed out.

When I returned from working with that herd, I quit the range for good and never went back. A man could really save his money and be healthy in it, but it just didn't appeal to me no more after I got back from that year in Indiana, so I quit. I'm now living on my farm out near Springtown, Texas. Just doing nothing all summer but wait for winter, then when winter gets here, I wait for the good old summertime.

Woody Phipps

Tom Massey

My father and family came from Mississippi to Dallas when I was one year old. There was a very small settlement around one store. I've heard my parents tell of their hardships in traveling by wagon train. I can remember that in those years we didn't have a great variety to eat, but we were happier than people are now and we didn't ask "Mr. Government" for no help, either.

In 1873 we moved to Lampasas County. That trip was a great experience. My father had several hundred head of horses and driving them and moving the family was a big job. Hunters used to come in from the west of us with great wagonloads of buffalo meat, and we dried the meat, enough for a winter supply.

My father's people came to the Concho country in 1884, but I didn't come until the next year. I worked first on the Emerick ranch on Little Lipan Creek. This was the prettiest country that anyone ever saw. Grass was knee-high. We could put down a saddle blanket to sleep on at night, and the grass was so thick that it seemed like we were on a mattress. Lipan Flat at one time was covered with great mesquite trees, but a prairie fire swept over it one August when the moon was right and killed the trees. The old stumps were there when the farms were put in.

There wasn't a fence in the whole country. Cowboys rode all the time to keep stock from drifting too far. Our horses would go as far as Brady Creek. Every March, ranchmen would start out on their work of rounding up. We would organize, I suppose you'd say—decide who would be boss, wagon boss, and all the others that would be needed for good work. Sometimes as many as sixty men would start out. We'd work toward Paint Rock, then across toward Brady, through Menardville and old Fort McKavett country. After we had covered the country, each fellow would take his own horses and go in home. In May we began the cattle work.

Mat Walker, wagon boss for the Matador Ranch, on Doodlebug, famous
Matador cutting horse, 1901–10.

Cowboys were the nerviest fellows that ever were in the country. When they went to bring in a cow or horse, they stayed until they brought in what they were sent for. One Monday morning old man Bright and his boy George started out together from their place near Mullin Crossing (on the Veribest–Miles road). Mr. Bright had heard that some of his cattle were down in the Eden country, and George was going to the Loomis ranch to work at a roundup. When George reached the Loomis ranch they were not ready to start work, but he had seen about twenty head of their I.C. horses and he thought he would throw them back toward the home ranch. While he was running the horses, his saddle horse stepped in a hole, fell, and broke George's right leg in two places and knocked him unconscious.

When he came to, his horse had run off with the loose bunch, and George was left alone. He took off his boots and left them and his quirt on the ground. He took his knife, cut splints of mesquite sticks, tore up his undershirt, and bound up his broken bones. The nearest human being was four miles away, so he started out crawling to that house. The first night, a thunderstorm came up, and the next morning George found that he had traveled in a circle and was just about one hundred yards from where his horse had fallen with him. He then crawled down into the bed of Lipan Creek, crawling along the creek until he came to Dry Lipan and followed it toward the dwelling of some people by the name of Frame. As he crawled down the creek, he would pack mud on his broken leg; that kept down the inflammation. He lost his hat, his clothes were torn to shreds, and he was covered with blisters as big as a silver dollar. On Friday morning a rider heard a dog from the Frame ranch barking down the creek and went to investigate and found George. It was a long time before he got well, but he lived to be an old man. We found the boots and quirt where he said he had left them and his horse with the loose bunch, still with the saddle and bridle on.

I lived in the rock house built by Ike Mullins, who came to this country in 1868. The house used to have portholes for shooting at Indians. This old house is still in use. Below the Mullins place, R. F. Tankersley (father of Wash, Fayette, Mrs. Frary, Mrs. Lewis, and Mrs. Emerick), had built a rock house and dug a great ditch from the river in order to irrigate a small tract of land. Parts of the old ditch are still there.

There were plenty of antelope, but buffaloes were scarce. One time I was looking for some horses and about night I came to Bird and Mertz's ranch, where I stayed all night. Mr. Mertz had just killed a buffalo, and the meat was fine.

In the fall of 1888, Ab Blocker brought four herds of cattle up here and wintered them around Lime-Kiln Crossing. The next spring he trailed them to Kansas.

One spring when we were working cattle, we had three thousand head in one bunch. We got them bedded down, but a big cloud was coming up, so none of the fifteen men with the herd turned in for any sleep. The cattle were restless, and with the first hard clap of thunder they were off. They ran all night and until nearly dark the next day. We boys rode with them through the dark and rain. We could see the lightning on their horns and on the tips of our horses' ears. We tried every way to get them milling, fired our six-shooters in front of them and beat them with our slickers. When they did begin to mill, the ones in the center were crushed to death.

A lone robber held up two stagecoaches at a stage stand between Ballinger and where the town of Miles is now. W. J. Ellis was driver of one stage, but I don't know the name of the other driver. Each had seven passengers and each passenger handed over his money. Harry Bennett, a saloon keeper, was going somewhere to buy liquor. He had seven hundred dollars with him, and when he saw what was happening he stuffed his money down his shirt collar. The robber gave each passenger fifty cents to buy dinner. A preacher on the stage only had thirty-five cents and his daughter who was with him didn't have any money, but anyhow the robber gave each of them fifty cents. "Haven't you been in my congregation when I preached?" inquired the preacher of the robber. "Well, if this is the effect your sermons have," said Ellis, the driver, "I don't think much of it." The robber laughed, but the preacher didn't like it much. The robber left on horseback. He rode to the north, stopped and put sacks on his horse's feet, rode east awhile, then changed directions again. They picked up his trail twice, but in the thick grass he was hard to follow. They arrested a fellow who used to work on a ranch down the river named Jim Brant (maybe I don't remember the name exactly) and sentenced him to twenty-five years in the pen. The only evidence that they had was that Jim had several large bills which amounted to a hundred dollars.

Jim stayed in the pen about two years, then Mr. Ellis and a man at Ballinger got him a pardon. Years later a man in Chicago confessed to that robbery and other things of like nature. W. J. Ellis drove stages all over this country. He was never scared of anything and was equal to any emergency.

Nellie Cox

W. L. ("Bill") Dobbs

Dɪᴅ you say did I ever ride a wild one? Why, son, I've rode them in my time that none of these dudes here at the rodeo could touch with a ten-foot sapling! Sure, I've rode them! Why, when I was just a young fellow we all had to go out and catch them wild, right where they growed, and tame them on the spot. I practically spent my life in the saddle, and out on the open range where it takes a man to stay on the payroll. You bet! I wasn't born on the range, though. I was born June 21, 1875, on my dad's stock farm in Fannin County, but was raised on the famous Muleshoe outfit in Stephens County. My dad moved everything we had out there when I was three years old.

That's the reason I can't tell you about Fannin County and where I was born, but I can tell you plenty about the Muleshoe, where I was raised.[5] For one thing, I rode hosses when I was too little even to climb up by the stirrups but had to have some cowpoke to give me a boost so I could get into the saddle. All the cowpokes were right anxious to learn me to ride, so I got teaching aplenty, and by the best riders in the business them days, because the Muleshoe had too many cattle to just have a few greenhorns messing around. My uncle Henry Black ran over two thousand head in the Upside Down Muleshoe, made like this: ∩ . My dad, John Dobbs, ran over one thousand in the Right Sideways Muleshoe, made like this: ⊃ . My uncle George Black run around fifteen hundred in the Left Sideways Muleshoe, made like this: ⊂ . And later on there were other Muleshoe brands, as others in the family got a few head. Oh, there was a whole mess of them for awhile there. My dad died about thirty years ago, and my mother married Amos Atkins, who ran the Rail A, made like this: Ꜻ . He owned about thirty

---

[5]The Muleshoe brand was originally registered on November 12, 1860, in Fannin County by Henry Black. The history of Muleshoe Ranch is examined in "Black's Muleshoe Ranch," *West Texas Historical Association Year Book*, XLI (1965).

thousand acres in his Rail A spread in Kent County. He still owns that place, but I never did know just how many head of cattle he ran on it. He finally leased all of the Muleshoe outfit and runs it today. I worked for him myself up until 1935, when I quit to take it easy. Not that I couldn't take it, but I've saved my money, married a good woman, and we just intend to take it easy for a while.

Now I'll get back to myself. Why, I said I'd learned to ride before I could even climb up on a broomtail. Well, sometime before I was even five years old, I'd go out with old George Benson, the wagon boss, when he went out to the herd where the boys were working. I'd ride around here and there, then, while the boys were eating their dinner or supper I'd ride herd on the cattle. Yep, rode herd when I wasn't but five years old.

Now I can't give you an exact lineup on just when I roped my first calf, and so on, but between five and twelve I was taught to work with cattle just like the rest of the waddies on the place. And when I was twelve I thought I knowed a heap more than they'd ever learn if they stayed in the business 'til they had chin whiskers to their knees. And for a fact I could ride and rope with the most of them, because I stayed at it as long as I could see. Main reason for that, I suppose, was because I loved to ride a hoss and work cattle. I was really in my glory if a hoss pitched with me, or if I had some trouble with the dogie. Just anything that could happen was apple pie for me because I always wanted to show what I could do—if not to the others, to the critters themselves. From what they say, I reckon I was pretty hard on the stock, but I got a lot of work done.

My first stay away from home was when I was about twelve, or maybe a little less. I stayed out on the regular roundup for three months. You know, where there's a lot of cattle on a ranch, the critters will drift. We'd have to go into four and five counties to round up the Muleshoe stock all around the ranch and on other ranches. In that roundup, I slept just like the regular hands. Used my saddle for a pillow and my saddle blanket for a mattress. However, I had a good bedroll to go over that saddle blanket. Any man that there was anything to always had a good bedroll. The regular way we slept out would be to find a small rise and throw the flop right on top of it. Then we'd take a stick or something, our boots if necessary, and drag little ditches down away from our bed so if it rained the water would wash away from us and not get us all wet. Of course we throwed a tarp over the bed after we got it made, and that was just like sleeping in a tent.

While I was still just a young fellow, the plains had a lot of buffalo chips around, and when we couldn't find sticks to build a fire, we'd use them chips. Nowadays the chuck wagon totes a gasoline stove, and the cooky can set up and have a meal in the same time as a woman can where they have natural gas.

I always wanted to be around the gang when mealtime came, because they'd get to talking about old times and telling tales on one another. A lot of kidding went on, too, and I always liked that. Many a time I've heard my uncles talk about Indian raids when they first came to Fannin County, and other tales about rustlers, and so on, but I'll have to skip that because I don't remember the important things about them. I'll just say that the old-timers had an awful hard time when they first settled here and had to put up with things you and me wouldn't put up with atall.

One of the things that has changed since they first came out here is the hoss business. We used to, when I was a kid, go out and trap wild hosses right out on the range. There wasn't any fences then, anywhere, and the hosses ran wild everywhere. There were old mustangs that never tamed down like the hosses of today. You'd have to break them all over every morning when you caught them up. While they weren't as wild as they were when they were first caught, they were rascals. They'd pitch and snort around for ten or fifteen minutes every morning, and it'd be a small rodeo to be around if you weren't used to seeing it all the time. The only difference was when a new hand was trying one out. The boys would try to slip him a salty one, and he'd try to stay with it just to show his mustard. On most of the West Texas ranches of that day, they didn't hire you if you couldn't ride the saltiest they had the first time you tried out.

I know that was the way they tried me out when I left the Muleshoe to try for a berth on the ULA's in Foard County. It was owned by Jim Witherspoon, who ran it. I can't, for the life of me, recall the number of head he ran, but it was way up in the thousands. ULA was his brand for the stock, and Tom Benson was the wagon boss. I worked there during the spring and fall roundups, then left for the XIT's.[6]

The XIT spread was so big I reckon it took in eight counties and was cut up into about eight divisions. Each division took in a county. I couldn't call off the names of the counties, but I'd be safe in saying the XIT was in the Panhandle. I worked in the fifth division, and a fellow by the name of Hayden was the ramrod. Thomas Smith was the wagon boss, and a better rider and pistol shot never lived than old Tom. Just give him a glimpse of what you wanted drilled, turn him around two or three times, and he could turn right to it and drill it plumb center. He was so good he was a wizard with a six-shooter—a wizard for sure!

I don't reckon any human ever knowed just how many head the XIT's ran. There were ways and ways you could figure out a tally, but it was just impossible to go in there and round up all the cattle because there were about fifty thousand head in our division alone. Yes, fifty thousand; and there were eight divisions. I was on the spread a whole year and seen new cowpunchers right along that had worked there for a long time. I know for a fact that I never seen anything like a third of the cowpunchers on that spread.

I was back at the Muleshoe for the next spring roundup after my year on the XIT's. Glad to get back, too, because they put me on the payroll. That was the reason I left in the first place, because I wasn't drawing money, and I was doing the work the top hands done. I don't recollect the salary I drawed when I come back, but all in all, salary being gauged by the beef prices. I've drawed from ten dollars a month to sixty dollars a month. You see, there's been times, and recently too, that the price of

---

[6]One of the better-known ranches in Texas, the XIT, with its divisions eventually covering parts of nine Panhandle counties, was established in 1884 by the Capitol Syndicate in exchange for the construction of the state capitol building in Austin. Its more than three million acres furnished employment to hundreds of cowboys. See J. Evetts Haley, *The XIT Ranch of Texas and the Early Days of the Llano Estacado*, and Louis Nordyke, *Cattle Empire: The Fabulous Story of the 3,000,000 Acre XIT*.

beef wasn't as much as it cost to ship it somewhere to sell it. Of course, when the cattlemen lost money just on shipping beef, they naturally didn't ship it, and when they didn't have any money coming in, they tried not to let too much of it go out at a time.

I don't mean to let you think the cowmen didn't have the guts. They had the guts to do anything. My uncle George Black, I seen him get in the way of a speckled, blue roan bull that was mad and trying to catch somebody. If that bull had caught him, he'd have gored him for good and left him for dead. Now, anybody that's ever had much to do with cattle knows that when a critter is coming at you, if you'll fall on the ground and roll towards it, it'll jump over you and you can get away. Uncle George fell and rolled towards the bull, but the bull didn't jump. Instead, he started pawing the ground. Quicker than the eye could follow the move, Uncle George jerked his six-shooter out and pumped five shots in that bull's belly before you could say Jack Robinson. The bull sorta shook his head, walked to his left for about ten feet, then dropped over dead. Many an old-timer will remember this when they see it, and I know Uncle George has told lots of them that didn't see it, because he was so well known that lots of them asked him about it. It was a good show, all right.

That's something about the range. There's always something happening that puts on a show. Old Negro Cal was as good a rider as ever you'd see, and he was throwed by a hoss he rode every day for several years. It was this way: early one morning, when all the cowpunchers were out roping their hosses and saddling them, Negro Cal had his roped and saddled before the most of them had theirs. His hoss was standing by the corral fence, and another hoss bucked over to where they were. Negro Cal's hoss bucked right straight up, and Cal lit on top of that eight-foot corral fence. After he lit, he rolled off into the corral where the other hosses were trying to get away from the ropes, and he darn near got killed before he could climb that fence and make his getaway.

Now I'll tell you one on myself. That same mare, a cutting hoss and a good one at that, hadn't been used for a couple of weeks before the spring roundup and was a little stale. I ex-

pected to have to let her buck for a while and was working with
the saddle when she jumped around and kicked me right between the shoulder blades. Now, it probably couldn't happen
again in a hundred years, but she kicked me in such a way that I
went almost straight up and lit in the limbs of a mesquite tree. I
was scratched up quite a bit and went around all humped for a
couple of weeks before I got the kinks out of me again.

There's one more thing, then I'm through. I made a lot of
drives, but never made a drive like the first big drive I made.
Just before I went to the ULA's, my Uncle Henry decided to
drive five thousand head over into the Territory (now Oklahoma)
one spring, on account of the grass shortage. The grass was good
over there, and we started out. Well, I'd never seen any Indians
to speak of, and just after we got over the line there, somewhere
north of where Vernon is now, our herd ran right through an Indian village, and it was Quanah Parker's to boot.[7] Well, the first
thing I knowed about it was when I rode right up to an Indian
tepee (you know, they all lived in tepees in them days), and I
saw about fifteen Indians in that bunch. I didn't know whether
to run, shoot, or just go straight up. They didn't say anything,
either, but just stared. I can't make you feel the way I felt then,
and I just know that you couldn't have bent my hair anyway because it must have been straight up and stiff as a board. One of
the Muleshoe old-timers, old Bill Proctor (and he lives right
here in Fort Worth, now), he rode up behind me and said something to them in Indian. They never smiled, but grunted, and
everything seemed to be all right. I never did get over my scare,
though, and was ready to ride at the drop of a hat. Not towards
them redskins, either.

Then, to top it all off, about thirty Indians, Quanah Parker
in the bunch, came over to the chuck wagon and had dinner
with us. The menfolks joked around, and after quite a bit of talk,
we went on our way.

Stampedes? I've been in a hundred, I guess. You're bound
to have stampedes anytime you've got a herd gathered up. Not

[7]For a biography of the great Comanche chief Quanah Parker, see Clyde L. Jackson and Grace Jackson, *Quanah Parker, Last Chief of the Comanches.*

every time, but a lot of times you will. You see, they'll run at the least little scare. Why, a saddle can make a noise, a rabbit can jump up and run, a skunk can show up, or any little old thing can happen, and they're off like a shot out of a gun.

Anytime it rains, whether it's midnight or straight up noon, the herd will be a little skittish. Then those electric storms, for which West Texas is noted, they make the herds stomp. I can't say as I blame the cattle, because the heat of their bodies draws the lightning bolts right down to them. Why, one time I seen an electric storm in daytime, when we had around fifteen hundred head in a herd about four or five miles west of Crowell, and the bolts just skipped around over the herd, knocking four or five out, and then three of them were killed. That same time, one of the cowpunchers riding herd on that bunch was knocked clean off his hoss and unconscious by a bolt. It was a wonder he wasn't killed, because another cowpoke riding herd on another herd about the same distance east of Crowell was killed on the same day and in the same way. These electric storms are something to be reckoned with, and yet you couldn't hardly ride off and leave the herd to itself.

Now, about the first barbwire fence I ever saw: My Uncle Henry fenced a hoss pasture in Stephens County, and lots of people hollered about that because they didn't want any fence in the country. You know, they kept the Swenson and Campbell fences cut for ten years out there before they could get one to stay up. The ranchers just didn't want any fence in the country and felt that fences would ruin every cattleman.

I'm just in to see the fine cattle here in the stock show right now. I don't live here but still live on the old Muleshoe. I saved my money while I worked, at least the last years I did, and that's what we're living on now.

Woody Phipps

W. L. McAulay

My family and I had been living on a ranch near where the Concho River empties into the Colorado before we moved to Runnels County in 1879. Heavy rains often disturbed families, cattle, and stock that were located so near the two rivers. I always tried to be at home when a heavy rain came, as my wife was afraid of that location.

One day in the early spring a bunch of cowmen and I went over near Ballinger on a cattle deal. I left my wife and baby at home with a hired hand to keep things going.

The rain began to fall. My, how it did rain; we had a West Texas downpour. I knew the creeks and rivers were swelling far and wide, and I had to get to my family, so I headed home. When I came to the Colorado River I discarded my clothes with the exception of my slicker, which I fastened to the saddle. I swam the river, leading my horse, and we made it across safely, then I put my slicker on and rode a few miles to the Concho River crossing. Here the river was not so high or wide, but the water was very swift. I again attempted to swim, leading my swimming horse with my slicker tied to the saddle, as before. I was always a good swimmer, but my horse was a little shy of water. He got frightened, began to rear and pitch in the water, then pulled himself free, and at the same time the saddle girth came loose. My horse made for the bank he came from. During this escapade I lost my slicker, saddle, horse, and all. I had to walk four miles facing the cool spring breeze in my birthday suit before I reached home.

This was my most trying experience during my forty years of riding the range.

Annie McAulay

Old-style cowpuncher wearing six-shooter, "doubling," etc., mounted on his paint pony, 1910.

George Bedo

My father's name was Albert Bedo, and he lived on a farm in Sabine County, Texas, where I was born April 1, 1876.

The following year, 1877, there was a colony of folks got together for a drag out to New Mexico Territory. Among the crowd was my father's family. My father landed a job with the Jinglebob Ranch. The ranch was given this name because they marked the critters by cutting a muscle in the ears, and that caused the animals' ears to flop down and they would jingle and bob as they walked. The ranch was owned by "Cow" John Chisum.[8] Father nested on that outfit for five years. The outfit was located five miles east of Roswell, New Mexico.

The camp where Father was working was the main outfit. The Jinglebob outfit had many camps, and several in that section of New Mexico.

Father provided a shack for the family to live in, near the ranch. The only things I saw while growing up were critters, cowhands, and wild animals. What I heard, besides the voices of the humans, were the howls of the wolves, caterwauls of the catamounts, bellowing of the critters, and singing of the birds. My playing was done with a lasso, pretending I was riding a hoss and snaring the rope over the critters, until I became big enough to ride; and then I used a hoss and used critters for my play.

After the five-years nesting period Father put in at the Jinglebob outfit, he went to work for Pat Garrett. Pat run an irrigated farm, as well as a cow camp, but Father worked on the farm. I was a kid of six years, then.

While in that section of the country I met Billy the Kid, the

---

[8]Not to be confused with Jesse Chisholm, for whom the Chisholm Trail was named, John Chisum founded a vast cattle empire in Denton and Concho counties, Texas, and later moved it east of Roswell, New Mexico. See the chapter, "The Jingle-Bob King," in Douglas, *Cattle Kings of Texas*.

notorious bad man of that section in those days.[9] He worked for ranchers in that section and among them was the Jinglebob outfit. He worked there for a spell while father was with the outfit.

During the spell of time I was growing up in that section, I often met the Kid and heard Father and the other cowhands talking about him many times. Whenever I met him he acted mighty decent, and it was generally said about him that he never turned a fellow down that was up against it and called for a little help. But also the folks allowed he would shoot a man just to see the fellow give the dying kick. It was said he got a powerful lot of amusement out of watching a fellow that he didn't like twist and groan. Anyway, it was well known by all he did plenty of shooting.

Another thing I often heard chin about was that he was a dependable fellow to use in settling long-standing accounts between the ranch owners and cowhands. In those days a greener would be stood off for his pay by some of the ranchmen. Cash was hard to get at times, and when it was scarce, the settlement with the greener would be delayed at times on general principles. In some cases the accounts would run from six months on to two years. The cowhand would be paid a little along, enough to buy 'baccy and such. Some would start squawking sooner than others. In many cases, so it was told (and no one denied it as not being the fact), when a greener went to squawking too hard, Billy the Kid would be called upon to settle the account.

The settlement would be made by sending the greener out with the Kid to pull a critter out of a bog. The Kid would send the greener into the bog to tie the rope on the animal. While the party was making the tie, the Kid would load him so full of lead that the fellow would also become bogged down. Father told me that while he never seen Billy do any of the settling, he did personally see several fellows that got to squawking and suddenly disappeared. The last seen of the fellows, they were riding off with the Kid.

While we lived on the Pat Garrett place, Billy came there several times on invitation from Pat. You see, Pat had been a

---

[9]See Patrick F. Garrett, *The Authentic Life of Billy, the Kid*, for an account written by the man who hunted down and killed the Kid.

partner of Billy's before Pat went to farming and ranching. Under some sort of an arrangement, Pat surrendered and was not sent to prison. After a short spell of time Pat was appointed to a U.S. marshal's position. Some folks say that he was sheriff but I am sure that during the middle eighties he was U.S. marshal.

When Pat became a law, he sent for Billy the Kid and had him come to the farm for a talk. He promised the Kid that he would not arrest him and would let him return to his hangout if Pat's shape-up was not to the Kid's way of thinking. Pat was hankering to have the Kid give up under some sort of compromise. The Kid made several calls, and each time he called I heard some of the chinning. Garrett failed to pound it into the Kid's conk that it would be best for him to change his way of living. I guess the Kid hankered for his amusement of watching shot men kick and groan and liked his work of settling long-standing wage accounts.

I am sure Father and I heard the last words the two men said on the subject of the Kid's surrender. As my recollection has it, the Kid never dragged to the farm again. The Kid was mounted and ready to leave, and Pat said to him:

"Billy, you can see it my way I guess?"

"No, Pat," the Kid said.

"Well, you understand I have to either resign or kill you, and I am not going to resign."

"You mean that you'll try to kill me," the Kid answered while laughing, and then he rode off, saying, "So long, pardner."

It was some spell after that last call of the Kid's when Pat killed the fellow. The Kid was cornered in a Mexican's shack, and there Pat made his word good when Billy refused to surrender.

When I was thirteen years old I dragged back to Texas. I lit in the Midland section and joined up with the XX outfit, owned by John Garfor. The outfit was located in the Blue Mountain country about fifty miles north of Midland. Of all the outfits that I have nested on, that XX was the top in several ways. I never will forget the outfit. The first work I did was to help brand some critters. Garfor said, "I have twenty-five of the White Hoss critters to brand." He had worked for the White Hoss outfit, which

was located about ten miles away. The owner had died, and Garfor took the job of ranging the cattle for the man's wife. It was
agreed that he should receive one hundred cows for doing the
job, so he said.

I then drifted over to the 7D outfit, which was owned by
the Wilson brothers and located fifty miles north of San Angelo,
on the Colorado River.[10] That ranch is still running, but the
name has been changed to the Sugg ranch. I worked there a few
years ago, in 1932 to be exact, and that was the last fence riding I
ever done.

The 7D had several cow camps. The one where I nested
was the main camp and ran critters over three hundred sections
of land. When I went to work on the 7D, it was in the nineties,
and the range was fenced. My job was fence riding.

I rode and examined the fence for a distance of fifteen miles
each day for six days, and on the seventh day I rode the whole
ninety miles. When I found a piece of fence needing to be fixed,
I reported it and a crew would go out to do the repair work.
When just a loose wire, or some other trifling matter, I would
repair it. I carried a hammer, pliers, and staples to do the small
repair jobs. I had one hoss that could make that ninety-mile trip
from sun to sun. The animal weighed about eight hundred
pounds, and that hoss could easily canter all day. But, after that
drag, I placed the hoss in the pen and let it rest until the next
trip. I used that hoss for those runs for a spell of two years and he
did not seem any worse for wear at the end of the time.

The 7D outfit was sort of different from the old open-range
outfits. On the open ranges the ranchmen worked, as steady
hands, three waddies to the thousand critters, then at roundup
time extra hands would be taken on. On the open range the boys
lived behind the chuck wagon most of the time and slept in the
open. Critters belonging to several outfits would be found mixed,
and at the roundups there would be the waddies from several

[10]Established originally in Irion County in 1880 with longhorn cattle brought into
the area by William ("Billy") Childress from Atascosa County, the 7D Ranch was
purchased from Childress and Fayette Tankersley by J. B. Wilson in 1883. As stated by
Mr. Bedo, the Sugg Brothers consolidated this ranch with other holdings. Leta Crawford,
A History of Irion County, Texas, p. 13.

outfits working together cutting out the various brands. Those critters would be bunched, according to their brand, branded, and drifted back to their proper range.

On the 7D five steady hands did the work of handling several thousand head, and the waddies were in most every night. The waddies working the fenced range had a snap compared with the fellow that worked the open range.

When I was a kid and father worked for Chisum, the waddies had to fight the drifting herd and stampedes at times. There was the night riding to do that called for men with sand in their gizzards.

In New Mexico, and in Texas, the ranchmen of a section built drift fences, which helped a tolerable lot in taking care of the drifts. Before a spell of bad weather, the critters would start drifting towards shelter and keep on going until they found it, if such could be found. That called for work on the part of the waddies to hold the herd back; if the animals were not held back, they would drift for miles and become scattered. With the drift fence, the critters were held to a certain extent and the waddies could handle the herd better. After a storm, waddies would have to drag out and gather the herd, then drift the animals back to their grazing grounds.

The drift fence was built leading into canyons and other places of shelter, so when the herd started a drift, the fence would lead the critters into shelter. Some of those fences were nearly a hundred miles long.

I have seen, in the fall and winter, the critters start to drift when the weather was pretty and not a sign of a change in sight. Father would say, "Well, we are due for a spell of weather," and the spell would sure come. Maybe it would be as much as four days off, but it would hit.

I worked for the Littlefield outfit for a spell after I spent a couple of years on the 7D outfit.[11] The Littlefield had a cow

[11]George W. Littlefield is best known for establishing the LIT brand in Oldham and Hartley counties in 1878. When the LIT was sold to a Scottish syndicate in 1881, the syndicate refused to allow Littlefield to retain the LIT brand; he reentered the ranching business with the LFD brand in 1882 at Bosque Grande east of Roswell, New Mexico. See J. Evetts Haley, *George W. Littlefield, Texan.*

camp in the San Angelo section and had several camps scattered around the country and also had their ranges fenced. I spent a couple years there, working as a fence rider. After quitting the Littlefield outfit, I worked here and there, always for some stockman.

I have enjoyed the work, and that is why I have stayed with the cattle work, in some way, all through my life. It is an outdoor life and I always felt pert. Of course, there was not much amusement except what we got up for ourselves. When a greener came on to an outfit, we always had our fun breaking the fellow in.

I recall one greener that we came near losing through our hankering to show him a good time. It was on the old 7D outfit, and the boys fixed up to play the old game of snipe hunting. Of course the greener was given the best or easiest part to do, as we told him. We set him to holding the bag to catch the snipes with, off about three miles from camp. We instructed the young fellow to stay right quiet at that point, because the rest of us were going to make a wide circle, which might take a tolerable lot of time, depending on how soon we would jump a flock of snipe. As you know, the game is to go on home and let the bag holder stay put until he decides to quit, or just quits because he can't stand it any longer.

This particular night was made to order, because, shortly after we had the boy set, the wolves began to howl aplenty and the catamounts began to cry. To a fellow that is not used to such, those weird howls and cat calls will sure raise the bristles.

After the fellow had been there for the time we calculated any human could stand it and he failed to show up, we went after him, but we found he had left the stand. Well, we found him the next day fifty miles away from camp and not knowing where he was. He said that when the wolves and cats started to serenade, he just lit out, trying to get away from the animals, and never thought of the direction until later and then didn't know where he was.

That kind of hoss play was pulled considerable, and the boys had shooting, riding, bulldogging, and roping matches that whiled away a tolerable lot of time.

The best shot I know of was Ruff Young, who worked on the 7D outfit. He could ride a hoss on a dead run and put five out of six shots into a tree limb and do the shooting from the hip. The top roper was Joe Posey, who worked for the Slaughter outfit that had a ranch a piece out of San Angelo. He could handle a rope the best of any man I ever lamped do rope work. That fellow could do a loop with his foot, which I never saw anyone else do. He would put the loop over the toe of his boot, then flip it over a critter's head as pretty as you would want it done. It was seldom that a critter could hornswoggle Posey out of a loop. The best rider was Jim Miles, who worked for the Scoggins outfit in the San Angelo section. Also, I was reckoned as tops when it came to riding and hoss busting. I never was spilled but once, after I learned to ride, and I busted many a mustang.

Besides roping, riding, and the likes, for our fun poker playing was one of the main pastimes. Then there generally was at least one waddy that could agitate the catgut. Some could make the fiddle sing, and some made it howl, but the boys would take it and be pleased with the howling.

Sheldon F. Gauthier

Richard Murphy

I was born on a farm near Slapout (now Holden), Brown County, Texas, March 1, 1885. When I was ten years old, my father dragged out to Haskell, Haskell County, Texas. My father had learned the carpenter trade and followed it in Haskell.

The next year, 1896, I dragged out of Haskell for the Skillet section of Texas. I lit on the T Diamond outfit, which was located twenty-seven miles north of Amarillo, and there I nested for six years, quitting the outfit in 1902. When I lit in that section, I don't suppose there were twenty acres of land under cultivation in the whole section. It was just one cattle range, with a number of cow camps dotted here and there. The foreman on the T Diamond ranch at the time I lit there, Head White, was the owner. The regular hands were John Stockford, George White, George ("Jesse") James, Ross Parnell, and John Held, who was the belly-cheater when we were out with the chuck wagon. When we were in camp, Miss White, daughter of the big auger (owner), cooked our chuck. In addition to the regular crew, we had a few extra hands who worked during the roundup.

At the time I lit on the T Diamond outfit I was for sure a "greener"—green as an alfalfa field about cow work. All that I could do was to sit straddle of a hoss, but if it switched its tail I would go into a spill. However, it didn't take me long to get hipped about the work. I was in good hands, because practically all of the waddies were old rawhides, and top hands. It was an open range, running around three thousand head of whiteface Herefords and a thousand head of Spanish breed hosses.

My first work was riding the range, looking for strays and "bunged up" critters. My riding pal was "Jesse" James, the best rider I ever saw. he was called "Jesse" after Jesse James the old outlaw because of his riding and shooting ability. He gave me some good riding pointers, and I did a pert lot of practicing under his directions. Whenever we had time, a wild bronco was saddled, and I would try my hand at busting broncos. At first I would watch James ride them to get next to his methods; then, when I reckoned I had all his tricks in my conk, I tried to do likewise. I put a blanket roll at the front and rear of the saddle seat, which was used as a brace when I first tried to ride them. When I wedged in between the two rolls, I did make the grade of staying with the critters and was soon able to discard the rolls.

Inside of a month, I was riding with the average waddie. I practiced roping along with the riding, and before the year was up I was working as a top hand. At least, the "big auger" reckoned me a top hand, because he raised my wages from fifteen dollars, the amount I started with, to thirty dollars per month.

The TS outfit joined the T Diamond outfit on the south; it was owned by the Johnson brothers. The Q Bar was to the west of us, with George Longly as its top screw. The critters belonging to each of those outfits were mixed among our cattle, and likewise, the T Diamond critters were mixed in among the cattle of those other ranches. During roundups, all of the ranches in that section threw in together and worked first one range and then the other until the whole range section had been gone over. It took us around two months to make the roundup, and during those two months we lived in the open, and it was our hardest period of the year. We did our sleeping rolled up in a blanket, with our conks layed on a saddle. Living in the open was not bad, except when a spell of weather hit on us; then it did call for a home-sweet-home song. The rawhides nesting with the outfit were a jolly bunch of buckaroos who took things as they were and said, "It could be worse."

We were always furnished with plenty of good chuck for lining our flues, and John Held was a top chuck fixer. He was tops when it came to fixing beef and beans, and when mixing the sourdough for bread, he knew how to manipulate it.

I worked at cutting out, during the roundup, the second year I was with the T Diamond outfit. I had worked with a number of hosses in my string, to fit the animals for cutting work, and there were three of those critters that could do a jamb-up job as cutting hosses. The hosses did everything but pick out the critter and throw the rope. They were fast and could turn on a cent piece. When I was mounted on any one of those critters, cattle were put down for the iron heaters about as fast as they could burn the animals.

When the roundup was over and the herd in tip-top shape, we then went back to our routine work, but, before getting down to routine duties, the waddies always took a little spell in Amarillo to shake off the roundup fever.

Amarillo was a pure cow-town those days and run by stage. There were just a few womenfolks in the town, and they were at a premium. Most of the waddies would make the town after the roundup, and some of the boys would stay until all their money was gone. Some of the boys played the gambling joints, some just soaked themselves in the "pizen," and some went sally-hooting in the sally joints. Any kind of a joint that a fellow wanted was in the town to satisfy the waddies' wants.

I was just a kid, but the older waddies took charge of me so I wouldn't get taken in, or get in wrong, and the boys held me down to earth, but I watched and saw the op'ra.

I saw some shootings and many bear fights. Nearly all the saloons in Amarillo, at that time, had bull-pens at the rear of the joints. The purpose for which the bull-pens were built was to have a place to shunt the fellows who became overloaded where they could sleep off the load of "pizen"; also, to prevent interference from the law or meddling gentry who were looking for a chance to swipe a roll of money. The bull-pen was also used for a battle ground. When a couple of fellows got riled at each other, they were shunted into the bull-pen to cool off. The saloon bouncers would take the guns aways from the riled men and push them into the bull-pen to settle the argument, bear-fight fashion. That method saved a lot of shooting, but could not be worked in all cases, and there was an occasional shooting.

When I think of the Amarillo of those days, I recall a big sign that one saloon had in front of its place of business. It read: "Whiskey, the road to ruin. Come in".[12]

[12]This infamous sign was undoubtedly copied in many places. The original probably was in Haskell and not Amarillo, as recollected by Mr. Murphy. According to R. E. Sherrill, "Early Days in Haskell County," *West Texas Historical Association Year Book*, III (June, 1927), the sign was the creation of Draper and Baldwin, early Haskell saloon owners.

After the bunch had their fever cured, they would jiggle back to the camp and take up the routine work. We would not, as a rule, see the town except when we drove a herd of critters to Amarillo for shipment to Fort Worth, which was where the critters were sold.

At Amarillo the critters were loaded in railway cars and hauled to the Fort Worth market. Some of us waddies would go along to act as bull-nurse to the cattle on the trip. Those of us who bull-nursed into Fort Worth always enjoyed ourselves, for a spell, seeing the sights of the city before returning to the gang, and at times some would get to see more than they expected to look at.

Our routine work consisted in riding the range and watching the herd's condition and keeping an eye peeled for rustlers.

The whiteface critters gave us very little trouble; they were not bad about drifting or going on a run. Sometimes, when a real busting storm lit in on us, with sky-fire and thunder, the cattle would start running, but we could put the animals to milling in a few minutes, or half an hour at the most. The Hereford critter can't run fast enough to get a hoss warm following it, so it's easy to handle a stomp of those kind of cattle.

The rustlers were what kept the silver out of our cloud. We had a number of set-tos with the rustlers and many times re-took our stock without seeing the rustlers.

The hardest scrap I took part in took place in 1900. A party of Indians came over from the Territory (now Oklahoma), working under the direction of a white man named Rep Harrington, and took four hundred head of our critters which we had in a herd ready for a drive to Amarillo to be shipped. Harrington was a known rustler, and he used Indians to do his rustling. He gave them a percentage of the receipts from the sale of the cattle.

It took us a week to locate that herd of four hundred head. We located the cattle grazing in the Chisholm Canyon on the Red River, being herded by a number of Indians. According to reports we got, Harrington was away at the time fixing a deal for delivery of the herd. In the hunting party, besides myself, were John Stockford, Ross Parnell, and Jesse James. We sighted the cattle in the late evening. We knew that it was our herd when we sighted it, off a mile or more, because we had been tipped off that a herd of critters carrying our brand was off in that direction.

The Indians spied us when we were about a half a mile off. Ross Parnell had a spyglass and could see the rustlers' detail movements and reported to us he saw them move about. It was plain that they were getting ready to meet whatever was coming, friends or foes. We reached a distance of around a quarter of a mile from where the Indians were when they started to scatter and went to various points of shelter. That move on their part promised an ambush for us the moment we started to move the stock. No doubt the Indians reasoned that if we were not after the cattle, we would ride on, and if we were, they would warm us with lead.

We followed out our plans and opened fire, shooting in the several spots where Parnell said he saw the redskins go. Just at the moment we started firing, the Indians started shooting, but the range was too far for either party to do good work. After a few moments of shooting, James dashed towards the herd and started the animals to moving. That move pulled the Indians out from behind their shelter, but they did not stand up and fight. They would run a piece and then drop to the ground and crawl a piece towards us. We stood our ground, and there was a hot fight for a short spell, and all the while James was moving the herd.

All of us but James got nicked, and John Stockford was wounded badly. He died a few days later from the effects of the wound. We knew that one Indian was killed and possibly another.

When James had drifted the critters about a quarter of a mile, which did not take long, we suddenly gave our horses the guthooks and dashed to where the herd was. That move put us out of range; however, we faced our mounts towards the Indians to indicate we were ready to fight. The Indians decided that they had enough, because they didn't follow us. After a bit, we dressed Stockford's wound the best we knew how and let him and James drive the herd while Parnell and I rode in the rear watching for a surprise attack. Along about midnight we allowed the critters to bed until daylight and then continued our drive to the ranch, which was finished without any further trouble.

Driving that rustled herd was the longest drive I ever made, with one exception. I was one of seven waddies who went with our big auger to Old Mexico, near Laredo, and picked up a herd of seven hundred critters. The boss had bought the steers from old San Francisco. He paid $7.00 a head for the herd, and sold the lot for $27.50 a head within thirty days after we had the critters on the T Diamond range.

It took us forty-one days to drive the herd through, and we had the silver lining pulled out of our cloud many times on the drive. We drove the route of the old Western Trail, which runs west of San Antonio. We crossed Red River at Doan's Crossing and then angled northwest to our range.

We had one spell of ten straight nights that the herd went on a stomp. They were not so bad that we could not handle the critters, but the stampedes put us to working plenty hard every night to hold the herd together. White, Parnell, and James had a heap of dealings with the longhorn cattle and knew how to deal with a stampede. Them three waddies always worked in the lead during a run, while the rest of us rode the line watching for bunches that might stray from the main herd.

None of us could get it through our conks what ailed those critters. The weather was pretty and nothing unusual seemed to take place, but every night the herd would get restless and finally go to running. In spite of all that we did to hold that herd quiet, the animals had to have their run. We would ride the line, singing, whistling, and talking soothing prattle to the critters, but that did not get results. After the herd had run for thirty minutes or so, the boys would get the animals to milling; then, in about an hour, the herd would be bedded and rest for the balance of the night. The old rawhides said that they never had heard of a herd acting in the same way.

With all of these runs, we reached Doan's Crossing of the Red River without any loss, but in making the crossing we had plenty of agitation.

The river was high and the water running quite swift. To wait for the water to go down would have meant a delay of about ten days. Also, there was a herd behind us, and White was afraid that the two herds would get mixed there at the crossing and put us to a lot of trouble cutting out. Because of this situation, White decided to ford the river in the high water.

We started the remuda across first, in charge of an extra hand named Johnny Frances, and the cattle followed in charge of the rest of the crew. The current carried the whole outfit downstream a considerable distance, which caused those critters to hit against a sheer bank on the opposite side. Also, there was quicksand at the point. Johnny Frances's mount went down with him, and the other hosses piled in on him and his mount; then the critters piled in on the hosses before the rest of us could cut the herd off and head the animals further down the stream where a landing could be made. Johnny Frances was drowned and stomped to death; in addition, seven head of hosses and five head of cattle.

We had to float the chuck wagon across with the aid of a raft. Two of us tied our ropes to the tongue of the wagon, and with the rope tied, also, to the horns of our saddles, we swam our mounts across, pulling the wagon over safely to a landing.

After we had the outfit across the river, we attended to putting Johnny away. We carried him to a cemetery at Lefors, and there he was buried. We then finished our drive to the home ranch without any further trouble.

I quit the T Diamond outfit in 1902 and went to Arizona, where I joined up with the Turkey Track outfit, located sixty-five miles northwest of Tucson. The ranch was called the Turkey Track because its brand was the outline of a turkey's foot. It was owned by the McKinney brothers, and they had ninety-two sections of land in the range, most of it fenced. What was not fenced, the mountains held the critters from drifting off. I stayed with the Turkey Track outfit until 1915 and was one of the five hands which made up the steady crew. It being a fenced range, it did not take many hands to deal with a herd of four thousand.

There were two of us riding the fenceline at all times. The rest of us rode the range, keeping a watch over the herd and attending to the critters that needed attention, cutting out other brands which would break through the fence every now and then. The H-H outfit was south of us, and the TL west. A few cattle from each ranch would be found on our range, and some of our cattle would get out on the other ranges. Every once in a while the waddies of each ranch would cut out the off brands and drive the critters to the proper range.

We lived at a camp, and the supply wagon came once each month with our chuck and other supplies that the waddies needed. We had no belly-cheater to do our cooking. It was done first by one and then the other, depending on who reached the camp first. The outfit supplied us with plenty of chuck fixings. We had all the canned goods we could eat. Our cooking art was applied to the meat, beans, coffee, and bread. We couldn't yell about the chuck, but did cuss, at times, at our own cooking.

We had no rustler trouble, or stampedes, to deal with, so our work was just routine, except at branding time, when extra help would be used to help do the job.

I quit the Turkey Track outfit after my pal, Henry Ford, was killed and I became lonesome.

We were all sitting around the campfire one night, swapping yarns, and I was sitting at the side of Ford, with my right arm resting on his shoulder. He and I was singing, or rather trying to sing, the following verse:

> Take me back to my boots and saddle,
> Take me back to my hoss and blanket,
> Take me back to my spurs and quirt,
> Take me back to the open range
> Where the longhorn and buffalo roam.

We had reached about the end of the song and finished the words "Take me back to the open range" when a shot was fired from out of the darkness, the bullet passing through the sleeve of my shirt and entering Ford's head at the base of the skull. He fell forward, dead.

There had been trouble between Ford and a fellow named Henry Lewis for some time. That night, Lewis came up, unexpectedly, and shot Ford. Lewis rode away, and up to the time I left the country had not been caught.

I quit the week following the shooting and came back to Texas. I lit in the Midland section and joined the 5 Wells outfit, which ranged critters around the Shafter Lake section.[13] The outfit adopted the 5 Wells brand because there were five wells dug for water.

I went through the drouth which hit that country in 1918. That dry spell gave us one of the big jobs that we called on to do, and that was watching for critters that went to gnawing on bones. When cattle are starving for water or food, for some reason they will pick up bones and go to chewing on them. Frequently a bone would get hung up in the throat or jaw of the gnawing critter. It was then necessary to remove the bone to save the animal from choking.

I recall an incident that took place between Bob Harrington and Tom Lee. The two waddies were riding together and spotted a critter that was gnawing a bone. When the waddies pulled the bone out of the critter's mouth, a small turtle dropped out of the animal's mouth and crawled away.

Now, Harrington was rated as the biggest liar and was proud of the title. He said to Lee, "By God, you'll have to tell about the turtle deal; folks won't believe it if I chin about it."

There were thousands of critters that died during that dry spell, and it put a lot of cattle folks out of business.

I made a good piece of money as a result of the dry spell. I made a contract with Mr. Williams of the Williams Metal and Bone Company of Dallas, Texas, in 1921, to take all the bones I could gather at twenty-two dollars per ton.[14] During a two-month period I shipped twenty-three carloads of bones, each car holding around nineteen tons. My total sales were about ten thousand dollars.

I gathered all the bones from around the Shafter Lake section, hauling them to Midland by team. During the first part of my bone gathering, we could gather a wagonload in about thirty

[13]Located in Andrews County, the 5 Wells Ranch traces its beginning to 1894, when John Scharbauer purchased the lease on approximately 400 sections of state land from Colonel C. W. Wells. The ranch, which contains 125 sections, is controlled by the Scharbauer Cattle Company.

[14]For an authoritative description of gathering and selling bones, see Ralph A. Smith, "The West Texas Bone Business," *West Texas Historical Association Yearbook*, IV (1979).

or forty minutes, because the ground was simply strewn with carcasses.

With the money I made out of the bone deal I bought a piece of land and started farming, and that ended my range career.

To tell whom I considered the top waddies among those I worked with is a tough proposition. There were plenty of top men, of course, some standing out in one way or the other in the art of the work. My friend George "Jesse" James of the T Diamond outfit, was the best hoss rider I ever saw or heard talk about. He weighed only ninety-seven pounds and was as quick as lightning. I never saw him fail to handle a critter, with or without a saddle. He would snub a hoss and then grab a handful of mane and swing on its back. He could, in some way, stay with any of the pitchers. One time I watched him stay with a critter for half a day, and without a saddle. He just tuckered that animal plumb out.

John Stockford was among the best ropers. I have watched many waddies put on the show I am going to tell about, but none could beat John at it. We would put a wild hoss or steer in the pen and drive it around at top speed. While the critter was running we would call the leg for John to loop and he would do it, rarely missing it.

John Stockford could do a trick of shooting that I have never seen any other person do. He would place two posts about fifty feet apart and while mounted on a hoss, starting back around fifty feet, he would ride towards the posts. When he arrived within twenty-five feet of the posts, he started shooting. Using two six-guns, one in each hand, he could put ten out of twelve bullets into the posts by the time he reached an even line of the posts.

My best act was whirling the rope, and I was rated next to John Stockford.

Sheldon F. Gauthier

Troy B. Cowan

W<small>ELL,</small>I reckon I've rode the range! In fact, I believe I even hit the trail younger than most anyone else in history. I had just turned six when my dad took me on a trail drive from Anderson County, in East Texas, to the Panhandle.

To start at the beginning, I was born August 1, 1878, on my dad's CAS Ranch in Erath County. He run from a hundred to a thousand in that iron. The difference come about on account of him being such a dealer. He'd sell, trade, or buy at the drop of a hat. About the only thing I recollect about the Erath County ranch was learning to ride a hoss. They worked with me until I could ride pretty good. I could ride as good as the baby rider they had here in the stock show. I believe his name was Kidd; he'd been riding since he was three years old—riding in a Wild West show.

I could ride good enough that when I was six my dad took me and went to Anderson County, where he bought around fifteen hundred three- and four-year-old steers. He took on some cowpokes, and we started west with the herd. Of course I didn't do any night riding or roping. The only thing I done on the drive was to hustle the stragglers and help keep the herd together. That's an important thing on any cattle drive and keeps the cowpokes busy doing it.

Since I was so young, I can't recall any names of rivers, counties, or anything else. I do recall, however, crossing a lot of rivers, creeks, and so on. You see, this drive was in the fall, and all the rivers and creeks were up. We'd have to find a place to ford them before we crossed them. If a ford couldn't be found, then we'd make the herd swim for it. Dad never did like to make his critters swim, because there was quite a bit of danger in losing some of them. On that first drive we never lost a head, and we run it clear to Haskell County.

When we got to Haskell County there wasn't but one fence

Shoe Bar Ranch chuck wagon, hoodlum wagon, and some of the boys, 1905–10.

in the whole county. It was a drift fence and run along the south and east sides of the county. We tried to fence up some acreage for winter holding but failed. Dad fenced two sections, and anytime anybody wanted to go through, they just stomped the fence down. You see, they'd been used to going in a straight line to wherever they'd started, so when they come to Dad's little old fence, they'd have their hosses push on the fence posts until they got a little weak and bent over, then they'd tear them down.

The rest of the country was open everywhere. In fact, I don't recall but two other herds of cattle in there, and they belonged to two big outfits. One was the W Cross, made like this: w✝. The other was called the Fleur de Mustard, the iron made like this: X̃ .[15]

Now, we never did see the owners of these outfits, and I don't know that I ever did hear who they were. I just don't recall it, if I did. We did all pitch together, though, when we went on roundups. The men from both outfits came and all of us rounded all the cattle together into one holding spot, then cut out what belonged to each other and drove them to our headquarters. Of the two outfits there, the Fleur de Mustard was the biggest, because there were thousands of them there.

We all followed the same practice of branding in the spring and selling in the fall. Because Dad never did establish him a headquarters, with buildings and all, he was called a stray rancher.

In the middle of '86, or something along in the summer of '86, Dad sold his cattle to some fellow by the name of Jeff Bowdry, and we went back to Anderson County. This time, though, we went back to Erath County and got the rest of the family. I had three sisters, Lula, Bertie, and Annie. They could all ride and rope, and Dad just brought them along. My mother died while we were in Haskell County and was buried before we got word

[15]According to F. G. Alexander, Haskell, Texas, in Gus L. Ford, ed., *Texas Cattle Brands: A Catalogue of the Texas Centennial Exposition Exhibit*, p. 66, the first cattle to be seen with the Fleur de Mustard brand were twelve or fifteen miles above the confluence of the Salt Fork and Double Mountain Fork of the Brazos River in 1884. When the brand was seen for the first time by local cowboys, and in the absence of a popular name for it, one of the old cowboys said, "That must be the 'Fleur de Mustard,'" and the rest accepted that.

of it, because in those days there was no mail, telegraph, telephone, or anything else for a man that didn't establish a place for himself near a place where he could get mail.

When we got to Anderson County, Dad made the rounds, made his deals, then we rounded up the cattle we were to drive west. I don't know whether he knowed where he was going with the herd or not. I don't believe Dad did know, though. I just believe he had it in mind that he'd settle on some piece of land that looked good to him when he came to it. Now, that's how plentiful land was in them days.

I don't recall the brands Dad brought from in Anderson County, but I do know that he road-branded every head with a 3. You see, whatever brand the cattle had before, he'd brand a 3 right along with it, and that way people'd know they were his.

This time, we took a little different route, and, in about four weeks, we landed the herd in Borden County. That was certainly the most God-forsaken country I ever saw when we got there. No neighbors for miles and miles. You'd hardly see a stranger a month. That was how unsettled Borden County was then. There was plenty of wild game everywhere. Prairie chickens, which are now out of existence, were so plentiful then that they were a pest. They flew in big flocks, like wild geese.

After a couple of years, though, other cattlemen began to drive their cattle in, and the country began to settle up. Dad never did like to have so many other cattle in with his stock, and it wasn't so long until he sold the cattle to some man that wanted to go into the Territory.

We made another trip then, back to Anderson County, and dad bought another herd. This time, though, he got three thousand head, and we drove it back on about the same route we used going into Borden County. My sisters took a big hand in this drive, and I stood night herd with the rest just as I was supposed to do. I was about thirteen then and rode and roped with the rest of the cowpokes.

My sisters rode and roped with us and did all of the cooking, so they really didn't take as big a hand as they could have if they'd been allowed away from the cooking end of things.

Somewhere along in Eastland county I was standing night

herd, and the night was actually black as pitch. You couldn't see your hand, it was so dark. I have a good picture of that night, as I rode along about twenty-five foot away from the herd, singing to the cattle to keep them quiet. Then, all of a sudden, the herd jumped up and started running right towards me. Not a sound had I heard—nothing.

You know, in a stampede, there's always something to start the herd to running, some kind of a noise. This time, it wasn't raining or anything else. Everything was just as quiet as could be, then this herd just jumps up and starts running. Things could have been better for me if they'd started some other way, but they ran towards me. At first, I turned my hoss and tried to ride away from the herd, but then my better sense got the upper hand, and I turned around and tried to find the leaders of the stampede. Finally, after letting the front of the herd come alongside me, I singled out a couple of the leaders and went to one of them and started pushing and slapping him with my rope. Pretty soon he turned a little to get away from that rope, and then some more.

The result was that he started a mill, but the night was so dark that the most of the herd just ran on by. Those that I got into a mill finally run down, then laid down to rest. The next morning, we started out to round up the ones that had got away. We were four days rounding up all we could find, and when the tally was made there were more than forty head missing that we never did get.

We stayed right there on that spot for a week, looking for the rest of them, then moved on. We wound up in Howard County, and Dad made his headquarters right by the old Tahoka Lake Trail. You see, there were no roads anywhere in that part of the country in them days. If you wanted to go somewhere, and wanted something to guide you, you took a cattle trail. They all had names, and this one was the one ranchers used to get up into the deep Panhandle. It led right by Tahoka Lake.

Them cattle trails looked right queer after you'd seen roads other people used. You see, no matter how big a herd you had, nearly all the cattle followed a leader, and that made a lot of trails right together. Now, any number of herds on the trail drive passed by our place. There'd be from two thousand to five thousand head in the drive, and they'd make from two hundred to three hundred separate trails, or paths, right together where they'd followed a leader. I'm sure you've seen cow trails in a pasture. Well, just picture three hundred of them going the same way. That's the old trail drives for you.

I don't recall the year, but a couple of years later we moved to Lynn County, and Dad established a regular ranch with buildings, barns, corrals, and everything he needed. He proved up four sections of land and made it his own. The rest of his grazing he rented.

Along about 1910 he cut his place up into homesteads and rented them out to tenants. That finished the ranching business for him. And it wasn't so long until the rest of the ranchers followed suit and done the same. Today, there's only three ranches in Lynn County, and they're not wholly in Lynn either. Just a part of them.

Now there's the T Bar Ranch, owned by C. O. Edwards of Fort Worth. I reckon there's 140 sections in his spread. The Yellow House Ranch has a part of its ranch in Lynn, and the Lazy S Ranch. The Lazy S spread was owned by C. C. Slaughter, but his heirs have it now. The iron is like this: ⌄.[16]

Naturally, from living around them ranches, I got to know quite a few people from there. I got to know the Lazy S people better. There were a couple of cowgirls on the Lazy S spread that could really ride and rope better than any woman ever I seen. Their names were Ethel and Bess Andres. They were

[16]The T Bar Ranch was established in the mid-1880's by the Tahoka Cattle Company in Lynn County. William C. Holden, *Rollie Burns; or, An Account of the Ranching Industry on the South Plains*, p. 191. The Yellow House Ranch, with headquarters in Hockley County, traces its ownership from the days of the buffalo hunters (late 1870's). The successive owners were James F. Newman, the Capitol Syndicate (XIT Ranch), George Littlefield and his relatives, and a modern midwestern corporation. Haley, *George W. Littlefield*, p. viii. Known as the "Cattle King of Texas," C. C. Slaughter held more than a million acres of land and owned forty thousand head of cattle. During his career he was a trail driver, Texas Ranger, banker, philanthropist, and rancher. His contribution to Baptist work in Texas is of particular note. David J. Murrah, *C.C. Slaughter, Rancher, Banker, Baptist*, is an excellent biography of this famous rancher. Another work, Mary W. Clarke, *The Slaughter Ranches and Their Makers*, provides valuable insight on the contribution of the Slaughter family to the Texas ranching industry.

what I'd call boys in girls' clothing, because they sure took the place of a boy on the range. I'm not talking from hearsay; I'm talking from seeing them do it. Why, I've seen them riding after a cow critter and come to a place where they had to do some fancy riding, and you could see light between them and the saddle. You know, they could cut out as well as most men. Of course, they didn't ride no "buckers." They rode the gentle ones, but they rode them fast when fast riding was called for.

Now, in cutting out, you've got to ride your hoss into the herd and make a cast at the critter you want out. You don't rope it, you just do that to show your hoss what one you want, and he's been trained to chase it out of the herd to where you can lasso it and throw it. Well, while in a herd, your hoss will have to do a lot of in-and-out dodging. The rider has to know the trick of following the hoss's motion and so fixing themselves that they'll stay in the saddle when a hoss turns real sudden. The way you do that, you keep your eye on your critter, and when it turns, fix to turn that way because your hoss is going to turn that way, and if you're not already fixed to turn, you'll find yourself on the ground. Or, if in a herd, you might get stomped to death. It's happened many a time just that away.

I'll just give you an example of what happens when you don't know to watch the critter you're after. I went over to the Lazy S one day, and, to give me a good time, the foreman called a fellow out to him, pointed him out a steer to get, and told him to use his hoss to get it. Now, this man had this here TB consumption. He was out in the west to get his health back. He'd told the foreman that he could ride a hoss, and the foreman had given him a job. This fellow, who'd been a tobacco salesman before, didn't have any cow sense but was right willing to work. The only way he was ever to get any cow sense, the foreman figured, was to put him right into the work, so that's what he did. Well, on the day I was there, he decided to learn him to cut.

Now, he hadn't really handicapped him when he sent him after that steer, because he'd given him the very best cutting hoss anywhere, the foreman's own hoss. He was easy to ride, too. Well, the greener mounted him and rode him out into the herd. He slapped the critter with his rope, and the hoss took after him. Well, the hoss jumped this way and that, trying to head the steer off every time he headed any way but out, and the greener nearly fell off at every jump. He tried to watch the hoss and lean with the jump, but when you've got a good cutting hoss in the herd, you just can't follow it that away. This greener would have been in that herd yet if it hadn't been that his hoss was good enough to bring that steer out of the herd without help from anybody. We boys just roared and roared. Some of us laughed so hard at that greener that our sides were sore for a spell after that.

The cowpokes just naturally all loved to pull pranks that away. This same greener had a hard time for a spell around there, for I was over a couple of days later to the roundup, and they pulled another on him. Just before supper the greener come in, dog-tired, and laid down under the chuck wagon to rest. Out in the open like that, where the air's clean and pure, there's not much racket, and because the work's all hard, it's mighty easy to sleep. And that's what mister greener done. Some other cowpokes come in, and they saw him there. One of them decided to prank him, so he gets a saddle and takes it over to the greener. The greener don't hear him coming, but snoozes right on. The cowpoke puts the saddle right up close to the green- er's head and starts rocking the saddle from side to side, holler- ing, "Whoa! Whoa! Whoa!" That greener must have thought he was still in the saddle, because he come straight up and bumped his noggin on the reach pole. Bumped it hard, too. We had an- other laugh on him, then.

For supper that night, the cooky had roasted the smelts, tongue, ribs, and so on, over the fire. Now, the greener hadn't been out before where he couldn't get any wood, and he didn't know that when you can't get wood on the range, you used cow chips for your fire and was glad to get them. He was a little put out by the cow chips, and we could tell it. He wasn't saying any- thing, though, just looking. Well, one of the boys decided to fix him up some more. He takes a section of ribs, finds him a cow chip to lay them on, then proceeds to use it as a plate. He'd tear off a hunk, then lay them ribs back on the chip while he ate the bit he'd tore off. The greener couldn't take it. He left the chuck wagon, got on his hoss, and rode off for a piece. We had another laugh on him.

You know, when a greener hit any spread, he sure had a hard time for a while, because the cowpokes would ride him until he caught on to all the tricks. By that time there'd be another come on, and the first could join in on the fun.

Woody Phipps

UP THE TRAIL

Matador Range, Texas, 1909–10. A trail herd headed for shipment from Lubbock, Texas. The cattle are allowed to drift along fairly slowly, as they have several days' traveling to reach the railroad.

J. K. Millwee

I was born in Pinhook. Well now, you would not know that place by that name now; it is called Paris nowadays. I was born there on the fifteenth day of January, 1851, and my father was a lawyer. I went to work at a young age, and my first job was driving sixteen hundred head of cattle to Ellsworth, Kansas, and Smoky River, and we went by way of Wichita, Kansas, which then only had one saloon and a blacksmith shop. The cattle were sold to private parties on nearby ranches and not shipped. On that drive, I saw one of the biggest herds of buffalo and the boys figured that they numbered about five thousand head in that one herd. They were so thick they took up the entire Panhandle, it seemed like. We had to stop our cattle and let the buffalo have the right-of-way. We encountered some Indians too, but I never saw an Indian killed. The tribes we would usually encounter were Apaches, and they hankered after trouble. It was on account of the Indians and of course the advancing settlements that the cattle trails dropped more and more westward every year.

In 1868 I worked for the Bar X outfit in Archer County and worked for them off and on for twenty years.[1] Robert Strayhorn of Chicago, Illinois, and E. B. Harold of Fort Worth, Texas, owned this ranch, which extended over Archer, Wichita, and Young counties, and they ran about forty thousand head of cattle.

Say, I want to tell you about John Chisum. Nobody that has ever written anything about him has ever told the truth. John Chisum was an educated man, a big cowman, and a good friend of my father's. Chisum was the first county clerk of Lamar County. W. H. Millwee, my father, and he were boys together. I went to work for him in 1869 in Coleman County. Helped him

---

[1] See Jack Loftin, *Trails through Archer*, for background information and a list of cowboys who worked on the Bar X.

move a herd of cattle to his Bosque Grande ranch in New Mexico, somewhat northeast of where Roswell is now located.

Well, as I started to say, we rounded up the cattle at Bolivar on Clear Creek, in Denton County, and moved to a point on Home Creek in Coleman County, from where we started on the trail drive to New Mexico, where Chisum had built himself a magnificent ranch house about three miles northeast of Roswell on the South Spring River. His cattle brand was the Bar or Rail, placed on the left hindquarter, and the cattle were given a "jingle-bob" on each ear, which did not prove practical, however, as in cold weather the ends would freeze off. John Chisum used this brand between 1869 and 1892. He probably sold the first herd of cattle to the Matador people. His career became a rather sketchy and checkered one in later life, especially so during the Lincoln County War, which was started by Billy the Kid. However, let me say that Billy the Kid was friendly toward Chisum and he had no trouble with him.

After leaving Chisum in 1872 I went back home and attended school in Mansfield, Tarrant County, for three years. There I also attained membership in the Masonic Order.

After that, in 1875, I joined the Bar X ranch again in Archer County, about 115 miles northwest of Fort Worth, Texas. I also worked for the Circle outfit, forty miles east of Albuquerque, New Mexico, at Antelope Springs, in 1880. Then I went with Jess Hittson and drove trail for two years to Deer Trail, Colorado, for him.

Some time after that I ranched in Crosby County, about one to two miles south of Lorenzo. Here I branded my cattle the Flying M and ran about fifteen hundred head. I used this brand for twenty years, even while I was managing the Cross C.

In the year 1885 I came to Lubbock County and helped organize the IOA Ranch.[2] I had the first six wells dug in Lubbock

<hr />

[2]The chapter "The IOA Ranch," in William C. Holden, *Rollie Burns; or, An Account of the Ranching Industry on the South Plains*, explicitly referred to the contribution of J. K. Millwee as the first ranch manager of the IOA. Headquartered in Lubbock County, the IOA was established in 1885 by the Western Land and Livestock Company of Iowa. Of note was the fallibility of the chosen brand (IOA) to the ingenuity of cattle rustlers. According to Mr. Millwee, this was quickly corrected by replacing the IOA brand with the Cross C ᑕ obtained with the purchase of fifteen hundred cattle from the Brigham brothers.

County and also planted the first hundred acres of sorghum in this locality. The next year I purchased eight thousand head of Cross C cattle for the IOA Ranch, which were tally branded by putting a V on the hindquarter, which indicated that they had been purchased.

By 1887 approximately thirty thousand head of cattle were grazing on the open range, which extended over a sixty-five-mile area. At that time T-Anchor was the only fenced range.

In 1896 I went into Lynn County, where I acquired a part of forty sections of land for which I paid fifty thousand dollars. I ran around two thousand cattle and bought about a thousand head from the Deuce of Hearts, from J. L. Vaughn, in Hale County, but did not use his brand. I discontinued and wound up my business in 1935.

Did you want to know Indians? Say, I have had several experiences when I was a young boy. It was when I was helping drive that herd of one thousand cattle from Coleman County to Bosque Grande for John Chisum. We were in the neighborhood of Old Eddy, which is now known as Carlsbad, on the Delaware River, when some of the boys wanted to stop to shoot fish (you shoot fish only in shallow water). One fellow was left at the head of the herd; he was Ed Burlingham. After a little while he rode up to where we were fishing and told the boys to take their time, that some Indians had driven off the cattle anyway. He said that the Indians just swooped down upon the herd and that he alone could not give chase. Our straw boss decided to go after the Indians and try to get the cattle back, but when the boys made the bend in the creek, they counted at least fifty Indians. Feeling that they were outnumbered, they decided to let the Indians keep the cattle. Say, we never did get them cattle back.

Once while we had a herd bedded down on Seven Rivers in New Mexico, the Indians stampeded them. Five of us boys worked like everything and finally succeeded in calming and settling the animals down again. A band of Indians had caused this stampede, and Jim McDaniel and I were close upon their heels, for we had been nearest to them and had given chase on an impulse. They shot Jim's horse from under him, and as the horse fell it turned over and pinned Jim under its body. I was plenty scared and plenty mad, too. In order to keep Jim from being killed by the redskins, I kept on firing at them. We found we had killed three Indian ponies. Well, for some reason the red devils went off, and Jim and I thought that maybe they were going after reinforcements. We decided to get away, and so we went and hid in a clump of hackberry bushes, scared and expecting to be found and killed any time or to starve to death. Shortly we heard the clop clop of galloping horses, and now we were sure that it was the redskins back again. However, it turned out to be twenty of Chisum's boys. Seems that they had been rounding up some cattle and had heard shots and had also found my riderless horse, which made them think we had been killed.

Say, we sure were glad to see the boys that time.

Wyndam Robertson

H. P. Cook

I was born near Peoria, Illinois, March 26, 1861. As my father had been a soldier in the Confederate Army, after the war it wasn't so healthy for him in that part of the country, so he moved to Texas in 1866 to start life anew.

We spent the first year at Veil Station, Parker County, then in 1867 moved to Indian Creek in Tarrant County, locating about eighteen miles from Fort Worth, Texas. At that time Fort Worth was about "where the West ended." As I remember it, there were just a few frame buildings on the west side of the square.

Four years later, in 1871, we moved to Jack County and settled on the West Fork of the Trinity River about seven miles east of Jacksboro. Indian raids were so severe about that time that we lived in Jacksboro, which was then called Fort Richardson, as I remember it.

The way it was, these Indians were assigned to their reservations, but they would get permission to go on hunts, or just slip out, and go on raids instead. It was a funny thing to me, but they nearly always picked a moonlight night for these scalping parties. They would steal all the horses and cattle, too. Lots of time they would come in broad daylight. I remember once when a band of them came through in their war paint. I was out in the pasture. Just as soon as I caught sight of them, I climbed a big mesquite tree and hid myself the best I could so they wouldn't see me. Well, they went on by, and made a raid in the community and scalped some of the settlers (I don't remember who they were, now), and stole a lot of horses. I still think it was just a miracle that they didn't see me in that tree.

I went "up the trail" when I was only ten years old. It was in 1871 that I made my first trip. At that time, I was working for Hillery Bedford, who lived on Black Creek, near Decatur, Texas. He had several thousand head rounded up to take to Fort Dodge, Kansas, consisting of native Spanish cattle (longhorns), including steers, cows, and yearlings. I think there were twelve cowboys and a chuck wagon. Now, I wasn't taken along as a mascot, but as I was working for Bedford and doing regular cowboy work, he told the boss to let me go if I wanted to. I made a regular hand on the trail, too, and took my place on the shifts at night after the cattle were bedded down. You know, back in those days, lots of boys were good cowboys by the time they were ten years old. But the next youngest boy on this drive was eighteen. I don't think there was anybody else in that part of the country my age that was doing regular cowboy work on the ranches.

It has been so long ago, I don't remember so much about the details of the trip. I remember we crossed Red River somewhere about Spanish Fort and bumped right into a band of Indians the very first thing. We had explicit instructions from the government not to molest the Indians in any way, so we were going pretty careful, not knowing what might happen. Well, it was a funny thing; the bucks had sent the squaws out in advance and they were waving their red blankets and shawls, which almost caused a stampede. We soon found out, though, that what they wanted was "toll"—that is, they wanted some of our cattle for crossing their reservation. We cut out some of the scrawny beeves for them, and they gave us no further trouble. But it was a sight to see how quick those beeves disappeared. They must have been pretty hungry for beef, because as soon as the beeves were killed, they didn't wait to cook them, but devoured them raw. It wasn't any time at all before they were picking the bones.

Well, we passed through a lot of Indian reservations and saw a lot of different tribes, but they were all just Indians to me. I remember they said some of them were Comanches, some Kiowas, and some Cherokees. Nearly all of them wanted toll, and this cut our herd down some before we got to Fort Dodge. We were more afraid of the Comanches, as they were considered the most warlike of all the tribes.

I made another trip to Fort Dodge with the Bedford cattle in the fall of the same year, and over the same trail. We had a tougher trip this time, because there was almost continuous rain, snow, and sleet all the way up. We had three shifts of the guards at night, after the cattle were bedded down, and I took my place on these shifts along with the rest of them. The trip must have taken about six weeks going and returning. It was really tough, sleeping on the ground this trip, it was so wet and cold. I had just a couple of cotton quilts, and by morning there wasn't a dry thread in them, it was so wet. I used my saddle for a pillow. We would move the fire over and flop down on the ground where the fire had been, which would stay warm for a while. We were struck by a "blue norther" and the next thing it was sleeting. The wind was blowing so hard that it cut like a knife. I had to dig into the ground that night, to keep from freezing. This herd was gathered up in the counties of Johnson, Hill, and Ellis, and must have been thirty-five hundred. I heard some say it was five thousand, but I don't believe they could drive that many in a herd.

The last trip I made up the trail was in 1874. They were John Chisum's cattle and were rounded up in Denton and Tarrant counties. It was a big herd, too, at least three thousand. Some said it was six thousand, but I don't see how that many could be handled on a drive, unless it was made in two herds. We crossed Red River at Doan's Crossing and took up the Western Trail. I have heard people say over three million head crossed at Doan's in one year, but you know that's a lot of cattle.

We handled the Indians about as usual, paying them a little toll now and then to keep them satisfied. But we had a new experience when we got to the Kansas state line. We ran into a bunch of settlers. The cowboys always called them "nesters." Now, they didn't like for these trail herds to cross their lands at all, and there they were gathered in groups, armed with shotguns and clubs, to force us to narrow the trail down as much as possible and keep the cattle moving. They were afraid they would lose some of their grass. You know, later on the Kansas legislature passed a law to keep cattle from south of a certain line from being driven at all into their state. They claimed it was to prevent the spread of the so-called Texas fever. It was in June of that year that they almost came to war with the cattlemen coming up the trail. There might have been a war, too, but word came through from Washington granting the Texas cattlemen the right to drive their cattle through the Indian territory and to the Kansas market.

About cowboy lore, I don't remember so much of it. I don't talk it either, like some of the old trail drivers, because my cowboy days were over even before I came to Cottle County in 1890. I have heard about driving across the quicksand to get water for the cattle, when the rivers were dry, but on the drives I made we had more water than we wanted; they were all during the wet seasons. I can tell you one thing, though, a cow will not start across a swollen stream until she noses the calf around to the upstream side, and then the calf just rests snugly up against that mammy cow's side. Just the opposite with a mare, though; they swim across with the colts on the downstream side. I think it is because the mare is a little longer and breaks the water so that the colt has still water to swim in on the downstream side. It would be hard to say which side is the best, but I guess nature just takes care of that.

Well, we'd usually stay in Fort Dodge about a week, and of course, after coming such a long distance, the cowboys were always ready to celebrate. They'd ride around the square and discharge their six-shooters until there wasn't any ammunition left, then quit. Nearly all the cattle were coming to Fort Dodge then, and the place was full of cowboys, and they usually pulled a few wild pranks before their return to Texas. You know, the cowboy is noted for pulling pranks.

Well, we moved to Lamar County for a while, then went to Young County. I lived there about two years. As I had got married, we decided to go further west and make a new home, so in 1890 we came out here and settled in the Ogden community, about twelve miles east of Paducah. W. G. Morris and John Wilson were the only families living there at that time, so Mrs. Cook and I are actual pioneers in this county.

You know, there are drawbacks to every country. I guess the most complaint here is sandstorms and drouths, but some years we don't have either. Besides, most everybody who has lived here very long has about got used to it, even the gyp water. Even the topsoil seems to have gyp in it, and I suppose in some places more than others. I remember we once made up a batch of sorghum molasses, sometime back in the nineties, and do you know at the bottom of the vat there was at least six inches of solid gyp.

There is one happening I didn't tell you about. In fact, I didn't think anything of it much at the time. It is about Will Rogers. I think it must have been about May, 1894, when we were living in a dugout in the Ogden community. As I remember it, it was in the late spring. One morning, a dilapidated buggy, drawn by a small bay pony, rolled up to my front yard gate and stopped. It must have been about twelve o'clock, because it was just at dinner time. I could see that the driver of the buggy was a loose-jointed, bow-legged boy about fifteen or sixteen years old. As I started to the gate to see what he wanted, he hailed me and said, "Say, mister, don't you want a hand?"

Well, all the settlers were having a tough time that year to make ends meet. A long drouth was on, and nobody had raised anything much. I was hunting and trapping wolves and varmints and selling the hides in order to get money to feed my family. During some of the long drouths that occurred back in those days, many of the early settlers resorted to gathering bones off the prairies and hauling them to market sixty-five miles away for the paltry sum of three or four dollars a load, just so they could live until times got better. So I just told the boy that I didn't have a job to offer him, but to unhitch his pony and come on in to dinner. He said his name was Will Rogers, and it was, too, because I saw him afterwards in a little town in New Mexico where we both happened to be at the same time.

That boy stayed with me for a month or more. He went out with me on my hunting trips, and he helped do the farm chores. He was an interesting chap and was a big help to me. I really wish I could have kept him. After he had been there awhile, he and I began to get better acquainted. I treated him like a guest, and soon won his confidence. He told me that he had left home because his dad wanted to send him off to school, but he wanted to be a cowboy and make some money. He was anxious to get a job on a ranch. It wasn't long before he sold the horse and buggy for forty-five dollars to a man by the name of Cunningham, and then he bought a little mustang mare from Frank Easley for fifteen dollars. I could see that he was getting ready to go. He said he was going further west.

Well, the mustang wasn't broke to ride, so I roped him for

the boy and helped him saddle up. Then he got on him, and you should have seen that pony pitch. He was plunging and bucking so wild all over the place that I thought the boy would be thrown and maybe badly hurt. That "Strawberry Roan" that you've heard so much about didn't have much on that little mustang. But Will Rogers just stuck to him like a tick.

He finally told me goodbye and said the next time I heard from him he would be riding the range. I didn't see him again until that time I met him in New Mexico, like I told you, but I saw a lady who runs a hotel at Plainview who told me that it wasn't long after he left my place until he showed up there. Said he stayed at her place a little while and then got a job on a ranch out there, but didn't stay on it long. Later, I got a letter from him and he wrote me about everything that happened to him after he left my place. That letter got lost and we never could find it again. I would give a lot if I could find that letter now.

Charles R. Fuller

D. ("Doc") Larken

I was born in Fayetteville, Arkansas, on November 21, 1866. When our family first moved to San Saba in 1873, the men always went armed on account of the wild animals and Indians. If they went to church or any place like that, they'd carry their old cap-and-ball guns along and stack them all in a corner.

I was raised on a horse's back; never did learn to walk good. I began riding broncs and breaking horses when just a lad of a boy. I never had one to hurt me bad. I rode a bronc at a prohibition rally at Johnson City once that like to got me. Several had tried to ride that demon. He was sure a mean one. I rode him, but it nearly done me in; I was so jolted and sore from it I couldn't hardly walk for a week.

I helped to drive a herd (about three thousand head) of cattle from Llano to Jones County in 1889, when I was working for the H.H. outfit in Llano. It was still open range and good grass up there, and we was taking them up there to winter them. We lived outdoors all the time, on a horse and under a tarpaulin.

We had a stampede when we camped one night on White Flat in Nolan County. Along about midnight we heard the boys on guard calling for us to get up. A big thundercloud had made up in the west, and the thunder and lightning was something to make you feel uneasy.

The boss ordered us all to fork our saddles in a hurry. By the time we rode out to the herd, the cattle was getting restless. They was bawling and stamping and trying to move around. The boys was doing their best to keep them together, but just before the rain started it came a keen clap of thunder and zip, they was gone like a streak. We rode nearly all night, but they scattered and we never did get them all together. I had a small bunch in there with them, and I lost nearly all of mine.

I worked on the Pitchfork Ranch near Spur in '88, and

drifted on down to the Hittson Ranch. I helped sign the petition to get a Post Office at Jayton. I broke horses on the Hittson, Matador, CB, and other ranches all over the country.[3] I received from $3.50 to $5.00 per horse, according to his age.

It was fun to ride wild ones at first, but after a while it got to be work. It was a job I could do, though, and somehow I just couldn't stay off of them. I can truthfully say I never was throwed, not after I really learned how to ride them.

When we was out on the range with an outfit, we carried a pack horse and our saddle horse, too. There was usually from 100 to 150 saddle horses with an outfit, and they kept a horse wrangler for them. I was used to riding and being away from home some when I was a kid and I didn't mind.

We generally had two big roundups a year, one in the fall and one in the spring. We'd cut the cattle for shipping or branding and then hold them, and as a rule they'd have some branding and tally men and they'd start right in with the first bunch. They'd work in pairs; one would bulldog them and the other would mark or brand them.

Shucks, but we sure had lots of fun if we did work hard. We'd ride for miles on Saturday night to take in a dance or just to get to town. That's cowboy life for you: always ready for work or fun or whatever would come.

Fiddlesticks, I say we'd razz the green hands, but they was generally good natured enough to take it. If they wasn't we'd pour it on them sure enough. Sometimes we'd whip them with leggin's, maybe make them ride a side-saddle or put them on a jumping horse just to see them throwed off.

One old boy—I believe it was on the CB Ranch—got a job one day in the spring. Our boss told us to go easy with him, he'd

[3]Located in Dickens and King counties, the Pitchfork Ranch was established in 1881 by D. B. Gardner and J. S. Godwin. See David J. Murrah, *The Pitchfork Land and Cattle Company: The First Century*; and Margaret Elliot, "Mr. D. B. Gardner's Pitchfork Ranch" (M.A. thesis, West Texas State College, Canyon, 1945). The HIT Ranch was operated by Jess Hittson in Stonewall and Fisher counties in the 1880's and 1890's. The area is presently an extended oil field. Gus L. Ford, ed., *Texas Cattle Brands: A Catalogue of the Texas Centennial Exposition Exhibit*, p. 47. The CB Ranch, established near Lorenzo in Crosby County, was ultimately divided into smaller tracts and sold to farmers during 1910–19. Mondell Rogers, *Old Ranches of the Texas Plains*, pp. 99, 122.

had a streak of bad luck. He'd lost his parents and this was his first job on a ranch away from home, but it turned out it wasn't his first job on a ranch.

We saddled him a gentle old nag with a kid's saddle. He looked it over then took it off and asked if there was another saddle horse he could ride. There was only one in the lot, and they told him to help himself. He went and caught up a horse, which was a really mean one, and to our surprise he rode him. Well, the joke was on us. That boy had a right to get mad, but he didn't. He accepted our apology in a good-natured way. That made the boys more careful about their jokes after that.

I moved to Coryell County from San Saba in 1890, and in 1901 brought my family to Coke County and settled near Tennyson.

Annie McAulay

Matador Ranch, 1891. The Matador outfit eating at the chuck wagon at the time Murdo Mackenzie (center, with black hat and beard) took over the management of the ranch. At the extreme right is H. H. ("Paint") Campbell, who established the ranch in 1879 with a half-dugout for headquarters.

W. B. ("Wickes") Currie

I was born in Guadalupe County in September, 1870, and went with my parents to Hamilton County when I was six years old. Then we moved to Concho County in 1879. I worked for The Concho Cattle and Land Company for four or five years.[4] Most of that time was spent punching cattle. I was sent for a short period of time to Runnels County and other places to work.

My job was like that of any other cowboy of that time. I helped with roundups, branded cattle, rode broncs, drove cattle to market or to other pastures. And we all had to be able if we were told to ride broncs, too, no matter how mean. They was never considered too tough for riders to ride. I don't recall any terrible mean horses like some I've heard of, but I knew a lot of them that wouldn't be called gentle. I never saw any rider get killed by a bronc but have seen some pretty well bunged up; in fact, I came near getting a busted leg once myself. I was trying to bust a pretty tough pacer when he got the upper hand and threw me. I landed hard on my leg. I didn't break it but was laid up for a few days.

The longest cattle drive I ever made was in 1889. I helped to drive twenty-five hundred head of cattle to Amarillo to market them for D. E. Simms of Paint Rock. Bob Pierce was boss of the outfit which consisted of eleven men, including the cook and horse wrangler. We had, I guess, a lot of trouble. The herd stampeded several times. We lost the whole business of that ornery herd one night in a storm.

We had camped for the night on the Double Mountain Fork of the Brazos River when the stampede occurred. The country in them parts is awful rough and hilly. We had all the cattle bedded down, and most of us had gone to sleep when we were awakened to find that the sky had darkened and the rumble of

<hr>

[4]This early-day ranch corporation was organized by Joe and Alf Peacock in the San Angelo country.

thunder was drawing near. We were all in the saddle in less time than it takes to say Jack Robinson, and the cattle were already beginning to stir. Well, we began riding around them, trying to keep them together and talking or singing to them. The storm broke about eleven o'clock, and what a storm—wind, hail, rain, and electricity. It seemed like hell was busting wide open. It was dark as could be except for the lightning, which was blinding and didn't help much. All the odds seemed to be against us. We rode, whooped, yelled, and sang, but there was no use. Them dogies was hell-bound for the hills. We lost the whole doggone outfit.

We found all of the herd next morning—or practically all of it—but I'm telling you that was about the worst experience I had while punching cattle. I know of two others besides myself that was with that drive that are still living. Old John Henderson, now a retired merchant of Coleman, is one of them, and Phil Wright, who is chief fireman in the city of San Antonio, is the other one.

I went from Concho County to Motley County, Texas. I worked on the Matador Ranch in that county two years.[5] I then drifted to Cottle County in 1892, I believe it was; in fact, I helped to organize the county. There weren't many settlers in them parts at that time. We'd see Indians occasionally, but they were harmless. While in Cottle County I worked for the Richards Brothers' Cattle Company.[6] I was married in 1893 to Addie Brothers of Cottle County. We moved to Runnels County in 1895 and settled at Ballinger, where we have reared our family.

I never had any Indian encounters in the early days, although I've seen a few of the redskins who weren't to be consid-

---

[5] Although the Matador Ranch was established in 1879 at Ballard Springs, Motley County, it was not until 1882, under the ownership of a group of Scottish investors, that it became adequately capitalized to develop into one of the best known of all Texas cattle ranches. William M. Pearce, *The Matador Land and Cattle Company*, provides an excellent history of the Scottish-owned ranch.

[6] Originally W. Q. Richards and Jim McAdams established a residence in the southeast corner of Cottle County in 1881, but they abandoned it and moved to the area of Paducah by the mid-1880s. Later, W. Q. Richards registered the 3D brand, and his brother, T. J., registered the Stripe brand. John Hendrix, *If I Can Do It Horseback: A Cow Country Sketchbook*, p. 217.

ered civilized. But there is something I know, and that is that people had to suffer many hardships in this section of the country in the early days of my life here. There were drouths, and the houses most of them were poor. Often the people had to go without some of the real necessities of life. But after all, those were good old days. We had many good times together with the best neighbors in the world. People as a rule were honest, religious, and kind. Yes, I'm glad I was a range rider and glad too that I lived at that time.

Annie McAulay

J. F. ("Red Horse") Henderson

I was born in Robertson County in 1864, and I can hardly remember when I became a cowhand. I think I began to fool with cattle long before I was old enough to make a first-class hand.

In 1879 my father and four neighboring families decided to throw their luck together and try the wild and woolly West. Each family had a bunch of cattle, kids, and some horses. The women and children, chickens and dogs were all rounded up and the covered wagons made ready. Most of the men and boys were to go on horseback and drive the cattle, which were all thrown together in one big herd. We enjoyed the trip through and only had one encounter with Indians. They came up in great numbers one morning as we were cooking breakfast. They were friendly and only wanted food, but we were scared almost to death before we got rid of them. We had plenty of food, but there were so many of them that they almost cleaned up our supply, and any old-timer knew better than to refuse an Indian food, whether there was one or a thousand, if he had it. We always felt lucky to get off that light.

When we reached Coleman County, we really pioneered in getting located. We settled at the foot of some small mountains north of Talpa. After a sort of community camping, each family branched off and started their own little homes in the good old-fashioned way. Our first houses were crude affairs but comfortable, and by 1884 we were all pretty well established with regular ranches and a good-sized bunch of cattle.

By this time I was beginning to think I was about grown and was considered one of the best cowhands in the country. I joined up with the Concho Cattle Company and was with them a number of years. I ran cattle from the Concho country to the Rio Grande. I have been up the trail many times and didn't mind the so-called hardships of the drives. The stampede was our worst trouble, and as that didn't happen every night, I can look back on the old days with a memory of more good than bad.

Riding broncos was a favorite sport with cowboys. I remember some of the boys once had up a bet on my riding an old red horse which we called Baldy, because of his white face. Baldy was saddled and brought out and I was ready and eager to try him. Just as I mounted, he turned his head around and tried to bite me. His old walled eyes looked like new moons, and the devil was in them. Well he just stuck his old head down between his forelegs and bawled like a wild bull and tried to turn a somersault with me. As I went over his head, my new shirt caught on the saddle horn and just ripped off. I was lucky, however, to go over his head instead of under him, as the horn of a fifty-dollar saddle was broken off as he went over.

In 1874, D. E. Simms of Paint Rock and I drove twenty-five hundred head of cattle to New Meixco. That was considered a big bunch for one drive, and we were not sorry when we arrived. We only had one stampede on the way, though, and didn't lose any cattle, as was often the case where there were so many cattle and not enough hands. This stampede was not unusual in any way. A thunderstorm blew up, and the loud peals of thunder frightened them, so away they went like mad. We didn't have to run them all night, though, and when we finally got them quieted about midnight, the storm had ceased and they were unusually easy to handle. Before we got to the Barr ranch we were joined by J. F. Hinkle, who remained with the Barr outfit for seventeen years. He was then elected to the senate and was governor of New Mexico in 1923 and '24. I had not seen the old boy in fifty-two years and did not know if he was dead or alive until last summer when he saw my picture and a write-up on my range experience in the *Fort Worth Star-Telegram* and came to see me.

When I was with the Concho Cattle Company there were twenty of us boys. Now only five of us are left, so far as Jim and I could learn when he visited me. Bob Pierce, our boss, lives in Denver, Colorado; Phil Wright is fire and police commissioner in San Antonio; Harve Earnest ranches at Water Valley; Ed Harte is a banker in an Oklahoma town; and J. F. Hinkle is president of the First National Bank in Roswell, New Mexico. Last summer when Jim visited me, we managed to get these five rounded-up and we had our pictures made. I wouldn't take a herd of cattle for that group. My children tell me I should have looked natural and not tried to hold my squint eye open, but you know how it is: all the other boys trying to look and feel young as we used to.

You may know we didn't lose any time talking over old times when we all got together. We remembered so well a big drive near Salt Gap. We had the cattle all rounded up and were preparing our bacon and coffee while our Mexican helper was stationed about one hundred yards from camp to watch the horses. All at once a band of Apache Indians swooped down upon us like a cyclone, murdering the Mexican on the spot and fleeing with our saddle horses before our shots could stop them. They got away with our horses and drove four herds of cattle out of Coleman County on across the Pecos River, where we caught them. We hunted them for two days and nights after we got fresh horses and enough men to handle them. They gave up our horses without any trouble when they saw our bunch, as a part of them had taken the cattle on and we had them outnumbered. We never did get the cattle.

The Concho Cattle Company's brand was ♡ o H and read Lazy D/O/H. Their holdings covered some fifty miles square.

When the sheepman began coming in he was resented by the cattleman because of his encroachment on the grazing land. So far as I knew, there were more fistfights than gunfights over these differences.

The gun tales about the old-time cowboy are unreasonably overdone. After Indian depredations had ceased, the gun-totin' cowboy we see on our modern screens didn't exist. I was in only one bad shooting scrape throughout my whole cowboy career. It was when our boss took a bunch of us out on the plains to White Lake near Lubbock, Texas, to get a horse which the foreman of a ranch out there had been holding for a debt. We rode up to the door and the foreman came out. Our boss offered to settle for the horse and take it, but somehow they couldn't seem to get together on the terms and pretty soon they were fighting. One of our boys jumped off his horse to separate them, and the foreman hollered for a guy back in the house. This fellow came running out and took the boy for a round of fistfighting. Just when they were doing pretty well, another fellow appeared in the doorway with a Winchester and pulled down on us all. Our boss didn't take time to get his horse but broke away on foot as fast as he could run. The next shot killed the boy, and he dropped to the ground. I turned down on my horse's side, put spurs to him, and was gone. I slowed down as I passed my boss, and he leaped on behind. We made it to the next ranch, got the boys and a chuck wagon from there, and went back for our boy. He was still lying in the front yard, and not a man showed up as we lifted him to the wagon and started on our long, slow journey to Snyder, Texas, for burial. His father and mother lived near Snyder and had not thought but what he was well and happy until we arrived with the body.

We hear and see a lot about cowboy rigging and getups, but that, too, is exaggerated. Most of the boys in our outfit wore white shirts, Stetson hats (hardly ten-gallon sizes), chaps, spurs, and a kind of trousers known as California woolens. Ours was a high-classed outfit, and we would treat even a tenderfoot right until he got smart. We wouldn't tolerate any smart alecks in our bunch. We got one such number from Virginia once, so one day he got drunk and we poured sorghum molasses all over him, from the top of his high silk hat to the toes of his highly polished boots. When he sobered up enough to realize his predicament, he made for the creek and we never saw him again. If a guy kept his mouth shut and tried to learn, we all helped him every way we could.

One of the narrowest escapes I ever had was when we were branding a bunch of bulls. One big old bull broke his rope and turned on me, grazing my leg with his horn just as I sprang on my horse and made him leap the fence. That was all that saved us both.

I was at a roundup once where two big bulls got into a fight. The owner was afraid that the larger bull was going to kill the smaller one, so he rode in on the fight and jabbed the big bull in the back with a pole. The bull whirled and made a rush for the horse, struck him just behind the shoulder, and killed him instantly. As he fell to the ground, the man leaped off and barely escaped as the bull gored the horse madly, again and again.

Bob Pierce was chasing a big bull once, down on Salt Creek. All at once the bull turned on the horse like a ferocious beast, ran under his belly, lifted his hind legs off the ground and turned him a complete somersault. Bob was almost killed in the fall, and the horse was badly injured. We caught that old Devil and trimmed him. "Trimming" consisted of cutting off both horns and tail just as close up as the operation could be performed. It always took two or more men to trim one, and woe be unto them if a rope broke. We trimmed lots of the rascals, I'll tell you.

Plenty of funny things happened at the big roundups. I remember once when about 150 men were working together a guy from the North walked up to Ben Polk and said, "Well, I've been looking for you for a long time." Ben look bewildered and stammered out some kind of an answer, and the fellow said, "Here's your dollar." Ben looked still more baffled. "This dollar was given to me six years ago," said the stranger, "and I was instructed to give it to the next fellow I met who was uglier than I was, so here it is." The boys all yelled, and Ben did look bad sure enough then.

We started to Oklahoma once with a big herd and camped at Colorado, Texas. About 9:00 P.M. we got the cattle all rounded up on the bed ground, and one old boy struck a match to light a cigarette. That was enough. The cattle went wild. We ran them all night long. Each boy had his bull's-eye lantern. It is a strange fact that in a plains country one cannot see at night half so well as in a broken country. The skyline, which is plainly visible in a broken country, is entirely lost on the prairies, and if we hadn't had those bull's-eye lanterns, we would have gotten badly lost that night. We got the cattle back together next morning in time for breakfast from the chuck wagon by lantern light.

The boys all called me "Red" or "Red Horse," and I like to hear it yet. The remaining five of us who are heading for the last roundup have agreed to have a get-together each summer as long as there are two of us left.

Elizabeth Doyle

P. L. Cowan

I was born near Belton, Bell County, Texas, on December 18, 1856, and learned to ride a horse when I was very young. My older brother taught me how to ride and also how to work with cattle. My father, being a freighter, owned several wagons and teams. In the early days he used ox teams, and later, mules, to freight with. Freight was hauled from points east to Fort Concho. On some of those trips they encountered bands of Indians, and they were not always friendly toward the whites. One group killed one of father's oxen. The freighters went in groups and were well armed, as they were in danger of encounters with robbers as well as Indians at all times.

In 1879 my father moved his herd from Bell County to Llano County and sent my brother and me to look after the cattle. We worked there several years and I got some real experience which I needed.

In 1882 we had a pretty bad stampede. My brother and I and two hired punchers were holding about seven or eight hundred steers on the banks of the Colorado River. We were located in an old field, the fence still being good on two sides. There had been a lot of rain and the river was on a big rise. The cattle seemed restless and along came an old mule, stopping near where the cattle were bedded down and hee-hawing for all he was worth. We had been holding the cattle there for three or four days, waiting for the river to go down, and they were getting nervous and so were we. When that mule made his appearance the cattle began running, and we began riding. We stayed with them, and when daylight came we were four miles from home, but still had our herd, and the next day we crossed the river and delivered every one of them.

In 1887 I helped to drive a herd of thirty-three hundred head for Joe Mitchell of Bell County to Abilene, Kansas, starting from his Bell County ranch. There were about twenty men in

Some Spur Ranch cowboys resting and working around the chuck and hoodlum wagons, 1907.

the outfit. We traveled almost due north and crossed the Red River at Doan's Store near Vernon. We didn't have any trouble on this drive, but we got somewhat excited when we were passing through the northern part of Oklahoma and had to witness an Indian funeral. They had sewed the dead Indian up in a buffalo hide and swung him to a limb, high up in a tree. That was the way the Cheyenne tribe buried, or disposed of their dead.

The best bronc buster I ever knew was Iky Stevens. He could ride anything. I saw Booger Red thrown off of a heathenish horse—Booger was a good rider, too—but Iky was watching and saw him when he got thrown and he said he would ride that filly for a dollar. And he did. He rode him as clean as I ever saw one rode.

The Indians killed my grandfather on the Colorado River near Wolf Crossing. It happened just before the Pack Saddle fight. He was on horseback, alone, and they shot arrows into his back. He kept riding but died soon after reaching home. My mother said they would sneak up to the spring and steal her milk and butter from the milk house. Mother had a bulldog and a gun for protection against the redskins when grandfather was away from home. When I was about four years old, they stole some horses from a thicket where my father had them tied. Of course father and a group of men followed them, but they did not recover any of the horses.

I am now too old to ride the range or work with cattle in any way, but I still think the old days on the range were the best I ever had.

Annie McAulay

Ellis Petty

I was born in Salt Creek, Brown County, August 6, 1874, and helped make my first cattle drive when only twelve years of age. My father's outfit drove a herd of cattle from Bell County to Brady in 1886 and took me along. It wasn't a long drive, and we didn't have any serious trouble, but I thought it was a big trip. I can remember I had a grand time, but I sure got tired, and sometimes scared. The riders would tell ghost or Indian stories around the fire every night, and I wouldn't have been surprised to see a band of Indian warriors or some of their dead victims make an attack on us at any time.

When I was about fifteen I went to work for my grandmother's S 3 Bars Ranch in Brown County. She had a pretty big outfit and kept a lot of horses. The country was for the most part open range then; however, they were beginning to fence some of it. There was one good bronc buster working for grandmother while I was there. His name was Cooke. He made a good cowhand when necessary, but his trade was bronc riding. He contracted to break horses and he sure got some tough ones sometimes. I don't believe old Booger Red had anything on him. I knew another good rider, Oran Webb, for many years a cow hand and stockman in Runnels County. He was a good all-around rider and was well known in these parts for his nervy riding.

The women all rode on side-saddles in early days. My wife rode a side-saddle to her wedding and on her honeymoon trip. Some of the girls were good riders. Mrs. Coffey was about the best one I knew.

I worked for my father-in-law, J. M. Franks, for some time. His ranch was on the line of Coryell and Bosque counties. I practically lived in the saddle. I remember one drive we made from Coryell to a point south and west. We crossed the Colorado River at Red Bluff Crossing, and we were nearly a month making the drive. The cattle were thin, and we grazed them along as we went. It rained a lot on us and the Colorado and other streams got up, the Colorado staying up for many days. When it finally ran down enough that we could swim across, we carried the cattle across a few at a time.

They'd razz the new hands, especially green riders, in them days something terrible. "Toadies," one bunch dubbed them. It was the old hand's delight to get them on a bucking horse and see them get thrown off.

I was just a lad of a boy, but I can remember some things about the wire-cutting period. They had quite a lot of trouble over it in Brown and other counties in that country. It took a long time for people to live down those differences, too.

When we made a cattle drive to Brady in 1886, we camped one night right on a line fence of a feller's pasture that had been lately fenced in. We didn't know it that night, but the fence cutters came in the night and cut his wires all to pieces. We saw many places next morning where the wires had been cut.

In them days many of the small men would hire to a big stockman, and although they worked their own cattle, too, they would be drawing wages from the big man all the time. It is said that many times these little men would brand lots of the boss's calves for themselves—in fact were rustlers. Well, of course, fencing the land let them out. Many of the cutters, especially the leaders, were just such men. But on the other hand, the man that could afford it would buy up a lot of land and often fence in a small man that had improved a little place and perhaps lived on it for several years. There were good men and unfair ones, too, on both sides.

One man, a prominent stockman, got a hint his fence was going to be cut on a certain night and he had the Texas Rangers lying in wait when they came. When they attempted to arrest the cutters, the cutters began shooting. One of the cutters was killed and another wounded; also a Ranger was hurt in the fight. Bill Adams was sheriff at the time and was threatened many times because he tried to keep peace. Old Bill was a good man. I worked for him awhile in his wagon yard at Brownwood. Fence cutting, or the right to fence the land, was the main political issue at the time. Should the old open range survive or could it? Every candidate had to come out on one side, and there were some bitter arguments, and some almost came to blows. Many felt that it was only justice to the poor man to leave a large part, at least of school land, open for free range.

Annie McAulay

Henry Young

My father's name was Charles J. Young. He moved from Kentucky to Texas at the close of the Civil War, and we lived in Austin for a time. He followed painting for a livelihood.

I was born at Austin, February 24, 1865, and when I was five years old Dad loaded the family into a covered wagon, hauled by a team of horses, and started out to look for a new location. He wanted to build a home on a piece of land and rear the family on a farm. There were three of us—one girl and two boys.

We drifted around the country for about a month, then landed in Coryell County twelve miles west of Gatesville. Father settled on a piece of land and set to get him some cattle. That section was a free range, and critters were everwhere. During the time Father was getting his place, he worked for various ranches in that locality.

I was so set on getting started to work that the hankering caused me to jump Dad's corral just as I was reaching my tenth year and about the time he was ready to start getting a herd of critters together. We had a few saddle hosses and other things fixed to handle cattle.

One night I filled a fifty-pound flour sack half full of chuck and some clothes, sneaked a hoss out of the pen, put a pigskin saddle on it, and rode away, headed northwest. I was certain that Dad would trail me and fetch me home if he caught up with me, so I hid out during the day and did my riding at night. I used the north star and a forked stick to keep my bearings. That way I did not get turned around and kept going in one direction. I dodged off the trail whenever I heard anyone coming. Finally, at the end of a week I allowed I was far enough away to be safe from Dad and showed myself in a town. It was Colorado City, two hundred miles from home. The first person that I saw, from the time that I left home until I reached the town, was a party that run a livery stable there. On that drag from home

Spur Ranch, 1910. Cowboys around the hoodlum wagon (for hauling branding irons, tent posts, wood, and other supplies).

to Colorado City I saw nothing but cattle, occasionally a herd of buffalo, a herd of antelope, a flock of turkeys, and other wild game.

I started to chin with the livery stable fellow, and the first thing I said was, "Where can a fellow get a job?"

"What can you do?"

"Anything that anyone else can," I told him.

I wasn't bigger than a pint of cider, never was over 150 pounds when full grown. The fellow laughed and pointed to a double trail running west, going up a gentle rise, out of town. He said, "Follow that trail. The two run together, made so by cowhands riding side by side, to and from the CA Bar. If anyone in the section will hire you, Bill Adair will."

Pronto I lit out and landed at the CA Bar outfit late that evening. I rode up in front of the home-house—it was a big stone building—and I hollered hello! A women came to the door and said, "Howdy, stranger, what for you?"

"Is the boss man at home?"

"No, not now, but I expect him in a short time. Light and cool your saddle. Come in and make yourself comfortable. I am cooking supper, so you all will have to excuse me. My husband will be in by suppertime."

I lit off my hoss and followed her into the house. There I could smell the chuck cooking and that got my tapeworm real excited. I had run low on chuck and was hankering for chuck right smart.

While Mrs. Adair was fixing the grub, she would step in, now and then, and ask questions. She asked me what I wanted to see her husband about. I told her I was looking for a job. I could see that sort of surprised her. She asked me my name, and that I didn't want to tell her, because I reckoned keeping my name a secret would prevent Dad from finding me. I said to her, "I would rather not tell my name."

She didn't say anything for a minute, but was smiling and then said: "Why don't you want to tell me your name? You don't look like a fellow that would rob a bank."

"No, I have stole nothing, but don't want Dad to find me."

"A runaway boy, are you?" I had to admit it.

It was not long until Adair dragged in, and when he saw me he asked his wife, "Where did you get this big man?"

"He lit a short spell ago and is looking for a job," she told him.

He laughed and said, "I think he is more interested in some chuck at this minute than a job."

Mrs. Adair told us to get ready for supper. Bill took me outside, behind the house, where there was a pail of water and a washpan. We washed, then went to lining our flue. Adair said to me as we took our seats, "Generally a good worker can do a good job of eating; now show me what you can do."

That was the best-looking chuck, and the best-tasting, that I have ever stuffed into my mouth. When I finished, Adair said, "You can handle the chuck all right."

During the meal he asked for my name and where I was from. I told him the same as I did his wife. He kept after me, saying that he must have my name. "I have to call you; can't just say 'Here, fellow'," he said, but I stayed put and finally he said, "Kid, you have plenty sand in your gizzard." We agreed that I had to be called something, so must fix up a name. He named me Half Pint Emerson, and that name I had for four years.

The next morning, after breakfast, he said, "Come on Half Pint, we are going to town." We went to the pen and saddled two hosses. I suggested that I use my own pigskin saddle, because the stirrups were set to my size, but he would have none of it, saying, "We use real saddles around here." He pulled the stirrups up as far as they would go and then had to make extra holes in the straps before we could get a fit.

We went to Colorado City. The first thing he did was to buy me a pair of California pants, the kind of pants all cowhands wore those days in that section. The pants were made from heavy woolen plaid cloth. He had the pants half-soled, as we called it. That was to reinforce the seat with soft leather so they would stand the saddle wear.

Nothing had been said about work since the night before, when he said that I was more interested in chuck than work. When he bought the pants I calculated I had landed a job and was as happy as an oyster in its shell. He next took me to F. A. Bone, the bootmaker, who was reckoned next to Pete Hammersmith, of Belton, as being a top hand making boots. He bought me a twelve-dollar pair of boots then an eight-dollar John B. Stetson conk cover and a twelve-dollar pair of spurs. He also bought me a bandana and a jap silk handkerchief for a necktie.

When he finished rigging me out, he said, "Now, Half Pint, all this is charged to you and your wages started this morning at twenty-five dollars a month. I know that I have hired the top cowhand in these parts." I felt as big and as good as any of them.

That is how I got started in the cow business. He, at first, took charge of me and I rode with him. He showed me the tricks and was a pert teacher. It was not long until I could go on my own. I then teamed up with Jess Kettles, and we worked together all the while that I stayed on the CA Bar.

The CA Bar grazed critters over about sixty sections of land, running around ten thousand head. There were fifteen steady hands, and extra hands was hired during branding season. We hands lived in a log ranch house. The house where the hands lived was called the ranch house, and the owner's home the ranch home, or bull's ranch.

In the ranch house we slept on bunks, and we waddies had to take care of our dump. We had our own cooky. Dog Face is the only name I recall we had for him. He was a good cook and made dandy dough bread; was a good bean cook, too. Lots of times he fixed us bean-hole beans. That is beans cooked in a hole. Dog Face would dig a hole in the ground, line the hole with stone, building a fire in the hole, and keep it burning for several hours. Those stones would get piping hot, and then the hole was ready for the beans. He put the beans into an iron kettle with a tight cover, put it in the hole, and covered it with sand. There they would be left for several hours. He seasoned the whistle-berries with bacon and molasses. I am telling you, those beans were "fitting" to eat. Beef, beans, a few canned vegetables, and dried fruit was the chief chuck on which we lived. Half of the time we ate the chuck sitting on our hunches behind the chuck wagon.

Adair did the top-screw and was a swell fellow to work for. All the waddies swore by Bill. The second year I was there, he turned me loose to do my turn, line riding, night or day, and all other work.

During my entire stay with the outfit we never had a bad

stampede. The reason for that was that Adair kept his herd cleaned of beef critters so there never was many old steers. The herd was mostly breeding cows and yearlings, and those critters are not so quick on the run. It is the steers that are a year old and up that are always looking for an excuse to run.

In that section, at that time, were the Griffin, Hunters, and J. F. Evans outfits. The Lazy X, owned by Rob Slaughter and his brother, and the Carter outfit were among the biggest ranches. They ran around thirty thousand head. That crowd of men ran that country. They made the rules and enforced them. Them fellows were a square bunch that gave everybody a chance, but they stood their ground and backed up their law with a six-gun, and that they were able to do.

During the years of 1874–76 the price of cattle was so low that rustlers did not bother beef stock much, so I did not see much dealing with the kind. But the hoss rustler was busy because good hosses was in demand and there were lots of good animals in that section. The system followed by that bunch of men in the Colorado City section, during the time I was there, was to get the good on the rustler and then go to the fellow and tell him to stop it, pronto. When they went to notify a rustler, they went unmasked; there was no secret about their work. If the rustler continued, he would be hung up to dry or given a short course in citizenship.

I must tell about two deals with rustlers to show how they were dealt with. There was a family that had a good reputation in that section, but the two boys of the family were caught up with rustling hosses. Adair, Evans, and Slaughter went to the boys' home and told them to stop stealing. Afterwards they were seen in the act again.

A number of men went to the boys' home and demanded that they come out, but, they refused. They were in the attic of the log house, and it was dangerous to go in after them because the boys could brand everyone that stepped inside. They ordered the parents to move their furniture outside if they wanted it saved, which they did. That being done, fire was set to the house. The boys soon came running out and were shot down. That log house was replaced for the folks.

Another young lad continued rustling hosses after being notified. He was placed on his hoss, a rope was tied around his
neck, with one end of the rope tied to a limb, the hoss was
driven out from under him, and there he was left.

Adair moved his range to New Mexico in 1878. He had reduced his herd to around four thousand, and we drove these to
the foot of the Capitan Mountains. That is about fifty miles
northwest of Roswell. The herd consisted of breeding cows and
the bulls. We had several little runs, but each was easily handled. We arrived there with the herd in good shape and a very
few lost.

After the drive to the Capitan Mountain section, I quit and
returned home to Gatesville. I had been gone four years and had
increased in size from a half pint to about a quart. It was just
getting dusk as I rode up in front of the house. I followed the
custom of those days and hollered, "Hello."

I saw mother come to the door and she answered: "Hello,
stranger. What be you all wanting?"

"Can I stay the night with you all?"

"Light and come in. I have never turned a stranger away
yet and pray God will never let me," she said.

I took my hoss, the same one I rode away on, back to the
yard and staked it, then walked into the house. I kept my JB on
and sort of pulled it over my eyes. Mother placed a chair in front
of the fireplace and said, "Rest yourself, stranger."

She went in the kitchen and came back with a coal-oil lamp.
That she placed on the mantel. While she was fixing to light it,
she asked, "What may your name be, stranger?"

"They call me Half Pint Emerson."

"Where you all from?"

"From the West."

"I have a boy, Henry, Henry Young is his name. He left
here four years ago and we have not heard hide or hair from him
since. By chance you may have met up with Henry?"

When she asked the last question, the lamp was lit and she
had turned around and was looking straight at me. She didn't
wait for me to answer, but asked, "Are you Henry?" I began to
smile, and at the same time tears crowded my eyes and the cor-

ners of my mouth began to quiver. Before I could say a word, she said, "God has blessed me. It's my boy."

Dad soon came in, and he was pleased to find me back. In fact, he acted sort of proud of me. I had calculated on getting a piece of his mind and was mighty glad of the welcome home.

After telling the folks what I had been doing, Dad told me I had returned just in time for work. Captain Hal Mosby was buying in that section, and Dad was herding those for him until he had enough to make a driving herd.

I went to work gathering critters for Mosby and followed that work for five years. The last year I took charge of a five thousand herd that we drove through to the Little Powder Horn River near Miles, Montana. I delivered the cattle to Tom Traywick, a Texan, who was top-screw for Hal Mosby on the Montana ranch. It took me eighteen months to make the round trip. I was twelve months making the drive there, and my loss was 150 critters. All my loss was caused from foot-sore and those critters we had to drop. It was reckoned as a top job of driving.

The main reason for the good drive was due to the kind of critters we had. The animals were all first-class stock. Then we had fair weather during the first two months of the drive. During that time the animals became used to the drive and worked easily and continued to be less troublesome as we went along. The few scares that we had, that the critters started to run, we got the herd to milling and settled down pronto. I also had a good bunch of hands that knew how and when to do things. There were fourteen of us. I used two waddies in the lead and four men on each point. What I mean by the point is the men that rode at the side of the herd to keep the critters pointed ahead. I had two waddies as extra men to take the big end of night riding. I had a hoss wrangler and a cooky, and that constituted the crew. In that crowd was Jim Hall, the cooky, Tom Ward, Tom Smith, Jim Green, Jack Peevy, and Joe Franks that I recall their names. The others were called by their nicknames, such as Sandy, Blacky, and the likes.

We crossed the Red River at Doan's Crossing and drove through the western part of the Territory on into Kansas. We crossed the Arkansas River near North Platte and then hit into South Dakota, skirting the Black Hills on the west and then into Wyoming; from there we traveled north into the Miles City, Montana, section. By the time we arrived, those critters had learned to swim like a bunch of seals. At first we had a pert lot of trouble crowding the animals into the water, but as we went along, crossing stream after stream, they finally took to the water, when we hit a stream, without hesitating.

When I returned home after the drive I was sort of fed up on cattle work and got to hankering for something else. I was trying to make up my mind what I wanted to do and decided to jiggle over into the Double Mountain section around Stonewall County and look that country over. Tom Smith was with me, and we hit the Double Mountain Ranch for sort of a friendly call and maybe to work if they needed hands. On that trip was the only time I got an Indian scare during the whole time I was on the range.

We had arrived in the section of the Double Mountain Ranch but was lost, as far as the location of the ranch was concerned. We had spent a day trying to get our bearings and had not met up with a soul. We were off the regular trails, and that was the reason for our troubles. We had slept that night with the tapeworm yelling for food, because we run short of chuck. The next morning we run onto a bunch of critters, which showed that we was getting back where we should be, but the proper direction was still a matter of chance. When we spied the critters, the first thought that entered our conks was to line our flues. We picked out a calf that would make a nice veal roast and roped it. When the rope smeared the critter, it let out a bawl and kept it up, of course, until we had cut its throat. About that time we heard traveling hosses and looked up; coming over a rise were a bunch of Indians headed straight for us.

We never stopped to take our rope off the calf, but hit for hosses and dragged off with the Indians following us. We rode about a mile when we spied a draw, and into that we hit pronto. We dismounted and run off a piece from our hosses. We found a rock which gave us a hiding place. Each of us took our cartridge belt; those we placed in front of us and got our six-shooters ready. We calculated on getting all the Indians we could before we went down.

When we left our hosses, the Indians went into a huddle. They were gesticulating and pointing towards where we were. Of course we reckoned that they were trying to decide on the best move to get us without getting branded themselves. Finally three of them started to ride towards us and one of them had a rag tied on his gun holding it in the air. That indicated they wanted a parley, and we let the three come up to us.

The Indians were Tonkawas, and of course friendly. One of them could talk enough English to be easily understood. He told us they were a hunting party camped over the hill and that when they heard the calf bawl they thought it was a wolf pulling down a calf. When they saw us run, they realized that they had scared us from our meal and wanted to catch up with us to tell us they meant no harm. We returned for our rope, and they directed us to the ranch. I stayed at the ranch three days and returned home, but Smith went to work.

What I have said about covers all my dealings with the range. A short spell after that I went to work railroading, and that I followed the rest of my active life.

There is one more thing I want to mention, and that is the rigging the cowhands wore, especially the bandanna. I have been asked time and time again about why the cowhand wore a bandanna around his neck. Some folks believe it was wore as an ornament of dress. Well, the bandanna was not worn for looks. It was a useful part of our rigging and we used it in many different ways. When the cowhand was away from the ranch house it was used as a towel. After washing at a stream, we would wipe on the bandanna and then hang it on the nub of the saddle to dry, and there it would dry pronto. In a pinch it was used as a tie string or bandage in case of a wound. It was used to protect the eyes from the sun glare; by pulling it close around the neck during a rainstorm the bandanna keeps the rain from dripping down your neck and chilling the fins.

Some of the boys wore a handkerchief for dress purpose. That was what we called, those days, the jap silk. It was used as a necktie, because it was easily washed and dried and would not wrinkle all out of shape. It met the cowhands' needs in that it could be kept clean easily by him and looked good.

The big hat is the proper conk cover for one living outside in this Southwest country. During the summer when the old heater gets to shooting its hot rays, the head needs the protection that the large brim and high crown gives. The chaps, of course, were worn mostly in the brush country for protection of the legs.

Sheldon F. Gauthier

HOSS STINKS

The LS outfit at the chuck wagon having dinner in the shade of a tree, 1908.

Brook Campbell

I came to Tom Green County from Independence, Missouri, with my family when I was a lad of twelve. I used to come to San Angelo with my father when we had to camp in the wagon yard where the Woolworth building now stands.

One Sunday morning we had been in for a few days, and Tom Ketchum was hanging around the yard.[1] He was on the dodge then and was trying to get to his brother somewhere in another part of the state. He kept his horse in the wagon yard and seemed to take a liking to me. On Sunday morning he asked me to take his horse out and exercise him. I imagined that his horse would be as wild as I thought he must be, but he was gentle and I sure enjoyed riding him. When I had ridden awhile I took him down to the Legal Tender Saloon, where Tom was gambling. I went in and told him his horse was out there. He went out and petted him awhile and said, "Come on, kid, let's see how many 'splitters' (nickels and dimes) we can find." We went upstairs and he raked off a handful and gave them to me. I was tickled to death, for mother made me go to Sunday School every Sunday when I was where I could, so I had more money for the Sunday School that morning than I had ever had before.

After I got out of Sunday School I rushed back to the wagon yard hoping to get to ride the horse again and earn some more "splitters." When I got there his horse was in the yard all right, but Tom was pacing around very restlessly. He looked at me and said, "Kid, I think I'll exericse Streak this evening." He was soon off, and I never saw him again. I suffered a lot of boyish grief over that, but not like when Mr. Charley left.

[1] Raised in the Christoval section near San Angelo, both Ketchum brothers ultimately died as outlaws in New Mexico—Sam of wounds received from a posse after an unsuccessful train holdup in 1899, and Tom ("Black Jack") by hanging in 1901, also for an unsuccessful train robbery. Albert W. Thompson, *They Were Open Range Days: Annals of the Western Frontier*, p. 181.

A kid would naturally have many unusual experiences around a wagon yard in those days so I was always having my share. Charley Pierce was an outlaw trying to turn straight. He belonged to a gang somewhere in the north and had come to West Texas to start a new life. He joined up with the 4 Cross L's a few miles west of San Angelo.[2] I happened to be out there that day, so he sent a telegram into San Angelo by me explaining to his boss that he was going in for cowboy life. His hands were soft and white and his boots glistened. Adapting himself to the rough ways of earning of living as a cowboy was not easy for him. He tried it earnestly for several weeks, and I can see now that he put up a pretty good fight. He had taken a great fancy to me after I took his message into town, and like any boy I enjoyed being noticed and stuck around him a lot, especially in the wagon yard. One day I thought he seemed unusually quiet and sort of blue like, so after a while he looked up at me from where he sat marking on the ground and said, "Kid, I'm going away from here."

"Where to, Mr. Charley? Won't I get to see you again?"

"Back to the old gang, son," he said, "where I can lick my finger and pull cards and get the money one way or another, a little faster than we get it here. Here are my spurs, keep them and I will come back to see you sometimes."

I cried myself to sleep that night. To a young boy, kindness and attention mean more than anything else in all the world, and I could not think of Mr. Charley as being bad in any way. He was my hero, and my boy heart was crushed, but not as it was several weeks later. Rome Shields was sheriff here then, so one day he brought a picture to my father and asked him if he knew it. "Yes," said father, "and Brook is down at the wagon yard; let's go down and see if he knows him." I shall never forget my feelings as I looked upon the bullet-ridden likeness of my friend. His shirt had been thrown back, and the bullet holes were plainly visible over his chest.

[2]Located in the vicinity of Sherwood, Irion County, the Four Cross L Ranch was owned and operated by the Comer brothers. They began to sell the ranchland to Sugg in 1897 and 1898.

"Know this fellow, Brook?" questioned the sheriff.

My knees seemed to be crumpling under me and my throat felt dry as I answered, "Yes, that's Mr. Charley."

The report was that he was captured in a dugout and shot on sight. It took me a long time to get over that, and I still have the spurs.

My first real ranch work was on the Billy Holmsley ranch. Our brand was an A on either side, and we were located some thirty-five miles west of Angelo. Everything was pretty wild and woolly, even then, and that hasn't been so long ago as some of the ranching days of this area.

We drove a herd into San Angelo one day and were to see Booger Red's Wild West Show. It was plenty wild all right—one white man and two Mexicans were killed.

We were all out around the show, and several of the boys were sitting on the fence. A fellow walked up to me and said, "Brook, gimme some tobaccer." I handed him the tobacco, and just as he put it into his mouth an enemy shot him down. The brawl was on. Men, women, and children shouted and screamed and ran pell-mell over each other. When the law arrived and cleared things out a bit, one white man and two Mexicans lay sprawled upon the ground.

The white man ran a saloon in San Angelo, and the shooting was the result of an old feud. Just how or why the Mexicans were killed was never known, but it was supposed to have been by stray bullets. This all slowed up the show for a few minutes until the bodies were removed, but Booger Red rode his bad horses, furnished his usual entertainment, and the show went on. I don't think I ever saw an uglier man but one of the most jovial fellows and the best rider I ever saw. He could ride any way he hit, backwards or forwards.

After the show we went back to the stock pens where our wagon was, got a bunch of cattle we had traded for, and went home.

The next year I made a change to the Barr ranch and re-member so well an old boy we called Cedar Handle. He had made some kind of a mess putting in a cedar pole for an axe handle and had acquired that name. I believe he had less nerve than any man I ever knew. He was afraid of his shadow. We had all made our beds down one night, and polecats had been the subject of discussion before retiring. One of the mischievous fellows had caught a little rabbit, so he slipped it in old Cedar Handle's bed. Well, when he crawled in and felt that rabbit, he went wild. He wouldn't have shrieked or cut up any worse if a bed of rattlesnakes had piled in with him. Cover flew in every direction, and old Cedar Handle's eyes looked like saucers. When he threw his bedding to the winds, the little rabbit of course ran off. The old boy never knew but what there was a polecat in his bed. We could hardly persuade him to go back to bed that night, and when he did he lighted a lantern and kept it right by him the balance of the night.

Our outfit went to Sherwood for supplies, and once when three of us had gone in, one of the boys sent for socks. On our way back we pulled off our dirty socks right there on the stagecoach, put them in the bundle, and each of us put on a pair of his clean socks. We could hardly keep our faces straight when we handed him the bundle. I guess he was like the rest of us—needed the socks pretty badly—so he sat right down to get into a pair of them. When he pulled out those old dirty socks of ours, I believe I could have lit a match on his face, and the more we laughed, the madder he got. It went on so far that one of the boys agreed to go back to town and get him some socks when the next stage ran, which was next day. We made up the change and got him all fixed up next day, but he never did like for us to joke him about the socks.

My main job around camps was to break wild horses, and I feel sure that is why I am in this invalid's chair today, even though many have done the same thing and are still going. I rode one old outlaw horse once, and instead of hearing the usual sound of my neck apopping, it was my back, and I'm sure some part of my spine was injured in a way that doctors have not been able to aid, so far, and I have been to some of the best. Riding this chair is the hardest riding I've ever done, and I was considered good. My friends ask me how I keep so cheerful and comment on my perpetual smile. I always tell them that I've got to play the game through, with my chin up. I wouldn't be a first-class cowboy if I gave up now, for a real cowboy always has grit.

We had lots of funny nicknames in the old outfits. For the smallest reasons sometimes a fellow would acquire the most ridiculous name, which would stick to him for life. "High Pockets," "Handsome Harry," and even more comical ones were always in order. Mine was always Brownie because of my brown eyes, hair, and skin.

The cowboys carried guns sometimes, but not as is reported on them today. I have carried a Winchester on my saddle to kill deer more than any other kind of a gun, and many other cowboys did the same. This is never shown in the spectacular gunplay on our modern screen.

My pet horse was named Kid. He was the smartest horse I ever saw and could have been trained for a circus. I could put his bridle on him and he would follow the wagon a thousand miles. As far as he could hear me whistle, he would nicker. Any of the other boys could make every attempt at imitating my whistle and he would pay no attention whatsoever. We all got a big kick out of that, and I thought that was one of the cutest things he did. He was an all-around cow horse, good anywhere we wanted to use him. He was as good as the old white horse named Chicken was mean. I rode Chicken three years and didn't even tame him, much less gentle him. It was a fight every time I got on him, and I had to ride him down every morning before he was worth a dern.

I was just talking last night about a bunch of us gathering up a lot of old poor bulls down on the Suggs' ranch.[3] The boss wanted to go off somewhere and left a boy in charge. He kept trying to turn an old bull and couldn't do anything with him. I loped out to try to help him, and about that time he threw his rope around the old bull's hips. It slipped off and hung on his tail. Just then I caught him by the head and hollered at the boy that if my rope broke, he would certainly have the bull by the tail. My rope did break, and away the old bull went again. The rope must have been very tightly looped around that old devil's

[3]With the closing of the Indian lands (Oklahoma) to cattlemen at the turn of the century, Sugg moved from the land of the "big pasture" to the San Angelo country. E. C. Sugg and his brother J. D. Sugg established in Irion County the three-hundred section OH Triangle Ranch from land purchased from the Southern Pacific and the Houston and Texas Central railroads. Leta Crawford, *A History of Irion County, Texas*, p. 40.

tail, for he made a leap at the boy's horse and knocked him down. The other end of the rope was tied to the saddle horn, and when the horse fell, the girth broke and the boy jumped off. The loop was still holding, so that let the old bull loose with the saddle tied to his tail. Three of us boys were after him by this time, and across the creek we went. Just as we crossed, one of the boys made a grab at the saddle, wrapped it around a tree, and that jerked the old bull's tail off. That fellow was known as the Bobtail Bull forever afterwards.

Stampedes were hardly ever funny, but in one instance I had a lot of fun. We had run sixteen hundred head of cattle all day trying to water them. That night the moon was shining brightly and the old thirsty cattle would not bed down. They would just walk and bawl, walk and bawl. The guards couldn't do anything with them, so I made up my mind all to myself what I'd do. I said, "Jake, them cattle ain't agoing to quiet down. You get on that point and I'll get on this one." When I got over on my point, I was far enough away from the others to get down on my hands and knees, run into them, and jump up suddenly, popping my leggings together. That was enough; we ran them all night long and didn't get them corralled until about noon next day; our boiled beef and beans tasted good, too, when we got to it again. The cook would yell, "Chuck," and shake the tin dishes in the old wooden box, and we would stampede. If we had a newcomer in the crowd, we would always stand back until he got hold of the coffee pot, then holler, "Sucker at the pot." The poor old guy would have to pour until he gave out.

On one occasion I drove five thousand sheep to the 101 Ranch in Oklahoma.[4] I stopped them in a field near a little Indian schoolhouse awhile before I reached the 101 Ranch. The teacher and a few little Indian kids came out, viewed the mass of sheep in great wonder, and the teacher asked me how many there were. I told her to guess. She started off by guessing five

---

[4]The Miller Brothers' 101 Ranch of Oklahoma, established in the early 1870's of 101,000 acres, enjoyed recognition and fame as the largest diversified farm and ranch in America before falling victim to the Great Depression. Its Wild West show complemented the efforts of Buffalo Bill Cody and Pawnee Bill Lillie. See Ellsworth Collins, *The 101 Ranch*, for the history of this colorful ranch.

hundred and on up to twenty-five hundred. When I told her there were more than five thousand, she couldn't believe me. Pictures were made several times along the route, and on one occasion a scene was shot for the movies. Later the picture came to San Angelo, and one of my neighbors said, "Brook, I saw you at the show the other night."

"Nope, not me," I says, "for I haven't been to town in a month." Then he told me about the picture and I was sorry I missed it, but even in the days of the first movies, communication and newspaper service was not so good as it is now, and I didn't know the picture was coming.

On this 101 Ranch in Oklahoma were thousands of buffaloes. The night before I was to get there, I was camped with my sheep, and over a hundred buffaloes came by my camp. Men soon came looking for them, and as they can not be driven, they had a time getting them back. They just had to sort of work them in a certain direction and finally got them back.

One fall when Ford cars first came into use, six Mexicans and I took eleven hundred head of mustang horses to Mexico. Gathering and selling these wild creatures had become a right profitable business with me. One of the Mexicans and I would lead the way in our Ford while the other five rode horses and drove them. As we went out of San Angelo, we were stretched out down Chadbourne Street about half a mile. All traffic was stopped, several pictures were made, and the local paper gave us a big writeup. Several pictures were made along the route, especially in El Paso, and always we were promised a picture. To this day I don't have one picture of those horses except the dim snapshot I cut from the newspaper.

I have plenty of time now to live over my cowboy days in vivid memories, but with so many good friends trying to help me lighten the way, with correspondence, scrapbooks, postcards, and other various acts of kindness, I manage to get more happiness out of life than folks would imagine.

Elizabeth Doyle

George T. Martin

I have lived in Texas since 1870, when my father moved his family here from Atlanta, Georgia, where I was born on July 11, 1865. We settled in Dallas, Texas. My father labored at any kind of work he could get to do when we first lit in Dallas. The Civil War sort of tore things up for father back in Atlanta, so he came to Texas calculating on getting a new start. Soon as I was able to go on my own, I lit out to find a job and dragged up to Denton County, which contained a tolerable lot of small cattle ranches back in those days.

In 1880 I landed a job with the Red Robinson outfit located eight miles north of Denton on Denton Creek. There I got my learning of the cow business. I nested with that outfit for four years then went on my own in business.

I was a greener of the first water when I landed on Robinson's outfit. The only thing that I could do was to sit in a saddle, but to ride a hoss was out of the question, unless the hoss was an easy saddle.

After I had been there for a couple of weeks, my brother Jack dragged in. He was a greener, too, so each of us lads learned and broke into the cow business together.

The range life then didn't stack up with home life, with a good bed to bunk in and a mother to fuss over fixing the chuck to suit, and such we hankered for, but the work got into my blood and I couldn't leave it. I stayed with the cattle and hoss business so long as I was able to work.

The Denton County range was a brush country, and that kind of a range is no picnic to work. It takes better roping, riding, and more gizzard gravel to stay with the brush range. It is harder to herd critters and easier for the rustlers, and because of that it took more watching.

Robinson's brand was RR, but he had many different brands besides his own on the range, because he did a lot of buying and selling all the time. The brand condition on the RR made it a good spot for the brand artist to work.

The RR was not a large outfit; it run around two thousand head, more or less, according to Robinson's selling and buying activities. Robinson worked from five to ten hands, depending on the season. Negro Joe was the cook, and there was my brother, myself, John Muson, and Joe Jones which made up the steady crew.

We slept in a ranch house and ate in a cook shack most of the time. During the roundup, and occasionally other short spells, we slept in the open and ate our chuck squatted on our haunches around the chuck wagon.

Our chuck run strong to beef and beans. The beef was not considered as costing anything, because the country was full of cattle, and when some beef was wanted, a waddy would rope a fat yearling and never look at the brand. That was a fact; generally the best-looking yearling carried the brand of some other ranch. Besides beef, we would have wild game whenever the cooky took the notion or one of the waddies would decide to vary the meat deal by going out and shooting some game. Our bread was biscuits, sourdough, or corn pone. We had some vegetables which came in the can, dried fruit, and all the black coffee we called for. The cooky would regularly fix up something for our sweet tooth, such as fruit pies made from dried fruit, pudding of some sort, and once in a while a cake.

Negro Joe was a good belly-cheater and knew it, but the boys used to hoss-play him a lot, all in fun, and he would hoss-play us back. We generally got the worst end of the play, because he would load some dish we hankered for with red pepper or some sweet dish with salt. Once he made a cake with cotton strewed through it. To try and eat that cake sure put sadness in your heart, but we had a tolerable lot of fun about it when we discovered the cause of our eating trouble.

During my breaking-in period was when the boys put on the opera several times. After I had been with the outfit about a month, I got to thinking that I was a pert rider. I did catch on fast, but not fast enough for the bunch, or as fast as I calculated. The old rawhides ribbed me up about my riding ability, getting me ready for the show. One morning Jones told me he wanted to surprise the waddies by having me ride a hoss that the other waddies didn't think I could ride. "I want you to show them, and I will win some money which I'll split with you," he chinned to me. That swelled me up like a carbuncle.

The bunch saddled a hoss from the remuda and trotted it out. I was ready and lit in the saddle. The hoss elevated when I hit the saddle and then started back to the ground but forgot to take me along. I was left so high up that the birds had time to build a nest in my pocket before I hit the ground.

After that experience I figured that I needed a couple more grades of schooling in hoss riding, and that I got before I had spent many more weeks there. Jones gave me some pointers which fixed me up.

One time the boys sent me out to get a "wouser" that was supposed to be in the creek bottom, because they feared that it would get some of the critters. My instructions were to stay after the animal until I located it and got a shot at it. The boys said, "If the animal is shot at it will leave the section pronto, but kill it if you can." The animals was described as having a body like a calf and a head similar to a wolf. I left to locate that wouser early in the morning and stayed with the job until dark, but nary a glimpse did I get of the critter. I came into the camp sort of ashamed of myself because I had fell down on the job. I reported how I had watched and sneaked quietly here and there. While I was telling the tale, I noticed that all of the bunch was mighty interested and noticed some smiles. It then came into my conk what had been pulled on me. I then sure enough was riled for a bit.

After about three months, I had gone through all the rackets and was a real rawhide. I was able to ride, rope, and do all the other jobs tolerable well. I got to be a real brush rider. Riding in the open range, with no brush, is sunshine on a winter's day compared with working in the brush. When a rider is high-tailing it through the brush, it is necessary for him to swing from side to side, dodging limbs, trees, and brush. Then when a waddy can ride in the brush and, at the same time, smear a loop on a critter, that waddy can call himself a cowhand. To smear a

critter running in the brush, one must be able to handle a loop
from any position.

We were compelled to keep close watch for the rustlers,
and they were hard to keep up with because the brush gave the
varmints plenty of hiding spots. Robinson did his own top-
screwing, and his standing orders were to make buzzard food out
of any rustlers that we knew for sure was rustling our critters.

The RR Ranch was located about twenty miles north of, and
among, the biggest rustling outfits in the country—the "hidden
pasture," which was owned by Sam Bass.[5] During my time on
the RR we never found that the Bass outfit bothered any of our
critters. Sam's long suit was hosses, and that was what he ranged
on his place. He called at the ranch many times, and I met him
often while riding the range, but he never seemed to be bother-
ing critters. Sam was a sociable fellow, and I always enjoyed to
meet up with him. The fellows that gave us the trouble came
from other sections of the country. We had a number of scrim-
mages with the rustlers, and some of those never rustled any
more critters—unless it was done on the eternal range.

One day a couple of fellows were spied in the Denton Creek
area of our range, and a party of us waddies went in after them.
We surrounded the boys and then closed in on them. We demanded an explanation for their presence there. They were not
working in that section of the country and had no pumpkins in
that creek bottom. They gave us a spiel about jiggling through the
country and wanted to camp and rest a few days. That sounded
likely, but we decided to investigate after we parleyed about the
matter, so we took the boys and their hosses to the camp where
the strangers could be watched. There were line riders on duty
night and day, so watching was no trouble. They could not leave
with their hosses without the line riders spying their move. That
night the two strangers left on foot, leaving their hosses, saddles,
and all other rigging. Therefore, we calculated that two rustlers
got away.

[5]Originally a cowboy, Sam Bass became an outlaw and robbed stagecoaches and
trains. He was betrayed by one of his associates, wounded by Texas Rangers, and died on
July 21, 1878. He is buried in Round Rock. Noel Grisham, *Tame the Restless Wind: The
Life and Legends of Sam Bass.*

That affair caused a shooting a little later on. There were two more fellows found in the bottom, and they put up about the same kind of a spiel, only them fellows said they were hiding out, but not for any cattle rustling business. Jones wouldn't accept that chinning and was for hanging them up to dry, but my brother, Jack, was plumb set against the drying process until the boys were investigated. Jones held that we were fooled by two rustlers that gave us a likely chinning, and he wasn't for letting two others do the same. My brother held that being we had no more on the boys than that they were in the bottom on our range, where it was out of place for them, we should look into the matter before putting them up to dry. Them two waddies got plumb riled, and one word followed another. Finally, Jones said, "To hell with you," and pulled his gun and started to shoot the two strangers. My brother drew his gun and shot Jones's gun out of his hand. The rest of us then grabbed the two waddies to keep them from cracking down on each other, and while we were busily engaged in that matter, the two strangers made their mounts and high-tailed it out of that section. Robinson ordered that from then on all strangers we came upon like that, they should be brought to him for a decision of the issue.

There was a young lad whose father had a small ranch a few miles west of the RR outfit that we all hankered to hang up to dry one time. That young fellow caused one of the worst stampedes I ever had to deal with.

It happened during the dark of the moon one night when we could not see well. The critters were the longhorn breed and could run about as fast as a hoss. They were full of running notions, especially when fretful because of weather conditions or lack of water or feed. That herd had all the water and grass it could take, and the weather was pretty. The herd was bedded down, chewing on their cud and as contented as any bunch of critters could be.

My brother and I were night-riding at the time when we suddenly heard a strange noise off a distance. It steadily came louder, and we could tell it was coming our way. Finally it was passing us. It was that lad, with a cowhide dragging at the end of his rope behind his hoss. He had found a dead critter somewhere, skinned it, and was taking it home, but doing it, as a boy, will do, the wrong way.

The herd rose, as a flock of ducks do leaving the water, and were off. They went at top speed through the brush. When that herd hit the brush, it sounded as trees do when falling. Riding orders were given to all hands, telling them to get going, but with all of us working it was impossible for us to do anything with that herd. For one thing, it was dark and we could not see where we, or the critters, were heading, and, in addition, they had been scared loco. So all we could do was to try and hold the critters together.

It was a hard job for us waddies to keep in touch with each other and work together trying to keep the herd from scattering. In doing that, we didn't know whether we were with the herd or a bunch scattered away from the main bunch. To let the others know where we were, we would shoot our gun twice. The first shot would attract attention, and by looking in the direction of the sound, the fire flash of the second shot could be seen, which would enable you to tell where a rider was.

The animals slowed down for a spell but kept going until daylight, and only about half of the herd was together. The whole crew worked two weeks picking up strays. We found some up in Wise County, some in Dallas County, and some in Tarrant County. Part of the crew worked a whole month picking up strays, and when we quit hunting there were still a hundred critters missing that never were located.

That night my brother got with fifty stray critters which strayed from the main herd, and he stayed with that bunch. It was about one in the morning when he got the bunch milling, and the animals finally settled down. He didn't know where he was, so he just had to wait until daylight before he could herd the critters back. He was younger than I, but for a kid, as Robinson said, he showed he was made of the stuff needed to be a cowhand. He stayed there until daylight but spent most of his time sitting on the limb of a tree. The wolves got to howling, and that put pimples on his back. So, kidlike, he staked his hoss and went for a tree. When daylight came, he then drove the bunch of fifty critters into the camp and was the only one of the whole outfit that came in with strays. Robinson bought the kid a ten-dollar John B. Stetson conk cover for doing that job, saying, "You are a kid and a greener, but bested the old rawhides. You came in with a bunch of strays, which is the important work."

My brother and I stayed with the RR outfit for four years, and at the end of that time I was a real hoss wrangler. My brother and I decided to go into the hoss business.

Our first venture was to get two hundred wild broncos from the west, bust those to the saddle, and then drive the hosses to Little Rock, Arkansas. That was my first experience on a drive. All the time that I nested with the RR outfit, Robinson never made a drive to market. He sold all his cattle to them that did make drives, or put his herd in with some drover that was driving to the market.

After my brother and I wrangled the two hundred hosses, we started to Arkansas. We sold about 50 as we passed through the cattle country and had 150 hosses when we landed at Little Rock; those we sold off in two weeks. We received around forty dollars a head for the hosses, which was around ten dollars more than we could get for a saddle broke bronco in Texas. We used a crew of six waddies on that drive and averaged about thirty miles a day.

We made a nice piece of money out of that deal. The hosses cost us only the time and expense of catching and busting them, which we calculated cost around five dollars a head. Our net profit, after paying all expenses of the drive, was about thirty dollars a head. That put us in the hoss business right. We wrangled wild hosses until the animals couldn't be found handy, then dealt in tame stock.

I became a hoss trader in later years, operating in Dallas, and my last years in the business was in Fort Worth. My brother and I would trade or sell anything that had four feet and looked like a hoss. We learned to know hosses so well that when we were bested in a trade it was an accident.

We had many incidents, during our hoss-trading days, that tickled our innards. As a rule, the talkative, bragging, and smart buckaroos were the hardest squawkers when they got bested in a swap. It always put my gizzard to shaking to have one of the smart gents come back squawking. My brother was the gent that handled the squawkers. I want to tell of a couple of funny deals he pulled which gets me to laughing every time I think of the way he handled the howlers.

We had a fair-looking critter that a fellow was wanting to trade for, and my brother kept telling the man, "My hoss don't look good but is a good work hoss." We made the trade, and that fellow was bested aplenty.

We knew by the fellow's actions that he was a squawker, and sure enough, he returned howling blue murder, saying, "That hoss is as blind as a bat."

"Sure," my brother answered, "Didn't I tell you the hoss didn't look good?"

We swapped a hoss once that died the next day after the trade. The critter was a fine-looking animal, but it took frequent spells, which indicated a bad heart, and was, of course, likely to kick the bucket any moment. We made a trade of that hoss, and the squawker thought he had put it over us aplenty, but the next day he learned different and came back ahowling his head off, saying, "That hoss died a few hours after I got him."

"That's funny," my brother answered, "Why, that hoss never did that before."

We were hoss traders, and in the business to make a living. The fact that we were making a living should have indicated to all folks that we knew our hoss-trading business, but the people were bent on beating the socks off of us and would come to us for a trade with that intention. Then they would howl when we bested them.

Well, I had heaps of fun and made a good living out of it, but all that I can do now is enjoy thinking about the past days.

Sheldon F. Gauthier

Avery N. Barrow

I reckon that I am an old-timer. I was born in Jasper County, Texas, on the first day of March, 1865. I have lived in Texas all my life, and the early part of it, after I was sixteen years old, I earned my chuck and bunk on the range.

The year following my birth, my folks moved to Beaumont, Texas; my father operated a ferryboat on the Sabine River. There were a lot of cow and hoss outfits in that country then, and I naturally seen lots of the critters and cowhands. The work appealed to me, and I would go without a meal rather than miss a chance to straddle a hoss.

When I reached the age of sixteen, I calculated that I had all the schooling I could ever use and pestered my folks into allowing me to quit school and become a cowhand, and they finally told me to go and get my fill of the life.

I was a good rider then because I had tackled everything I could get a chance at. Handling hosses came natural to me, and a hoss ranch was the kind of a outfit I hankered for. I hit out for what used to be calculated as the biggest hoss ranch in the country them days. It was the Tonk Baker outfit. I don't know what his proper first name was, but everybody called the ramrod Tonk. The range was an open range and located in McLennan County. The number of hosses that he had running on that range has slipped my mind, but it was over a thousand. There were fifteen hands employed all the year round, and sometimes extra hands was hired. The brand was the shape of a Jew's-harp branded on the critter's jaw.

I landed at the outfit a real greener, as far as the work is concerned, in 1876 and hit Tonk up for a job. He eyed me up one side and down the other and sez, "Have you worked on a hoss ranch?"

"No," sez I. "But can ride 'em."

"We need hoss handlers on this outfit, son. I am sorry I can't use you."

Bronc rider for the Bar Diamond Bar Ranch riding a sunfisher, 1905–10.

Well, that took my feathers down, and I sez to him: "I have dragged clear from Beaumont way to join your hoss outfit. Let me nest here. I don't care what you pay me."

"Kid, you must hanker after hosses," he sez. "I hate to disappoint a kid so bent on being with the critters, so I'll see what you can do."

I stayed on the outfit for five years, and when I quit there I could ride a hoss with the best among the rawhides.

There were about fifteen hands, all old rawhides, with the outfit and they took charge of me. They saw that I was shaped up to a bunk and got me all set for work on a hoss ranch.

I could not get to sleep that night for thinking about the morning when I would start out as a sure-enough hossman. Morning came and we had chuck, as the boys sez—put the feed bag on. After chuck the top-screw showed me my string of five hosses that I would work with along with my own hoss that I had rode to the outfit. Blacky Smith, he was the top-screw, sez, "Kid, let your hoss rest and mount that black critter for today." I could tell by the glint in his eye that they were reckoning on some fun watching me ride that hoss. I felt sure of myself and was anxious to get straddle of the critter.

We snubbed the hoss and I lit in the tree. Now, the saddles those days were not like the kind used now. They were not a great deal better than the bare back. Just as soon as I hit that tree, that hoss elevated high. It hawg-rowed and sunperched for about a quarter mile, with me a-fanning its ears with my sombrero. When it settled down, I jiggled back where the crew were watching me on my act. I sez, "Blacky, I am ready to get going; tell me what to do." The ramrod was a-standing there too, and him a busting a gut laughing at the top-screw and the others, because they got fooled on the greener kid's riding ability.

The ramrod sez, "Kid, you rode one of the pitchingest hosses that we are working in my remuda. You sure enough have a nest with my outfit. We'll make a real hoss wrangler out of you," and they did.

All them hossy stinks took pains, from that morning on, to show me all the tricks they knew, and in a month's time I was wrangling with the best of the outfit.

The range was an open one, and it was a prairie country except for brush along the creeks. We had to keep riding the line
fairly well to keep the critters from roaming off too far. There
was night riding to do, but it was not like riding with a bunch of
cows. With hosses the stampede is something waddies do not
have to fret about. The animals will not stampede except in extreme cases, such as a prairie fire or the likes.

Hosses have the habit of grazing far into the night and don't
bed down like cows. Long after midnight they will lie down for a
spell. Because of the nature of the hoss, it was not hard to keep
the animals bunched at night. Two hands would work together
and the night was split into two shifts.

On the hoss ranch we hossy stinks hit the bunks most every
night, except at times when we went a distance hunting strays.
Our hardest work was when we wanted to cut out a bunch.
Those wild critters could run and would give us a chase, and
some of them a hell of a chase. We would have to work in relays
and wear them down to catch some of the stallions.

I enjoyed the work and was among a great crew. All the
hands were sociable fellows and made life interesting for each
other.

At night, sitting around the camp, there always was some
one pulling something for amusement. The night of my first day
at the camp I was arrested. The hands had what they called a
prairie-dog court. There was a sheriff, judge, and the court's
mouthpiece. There was a set of rules which they read to me all
concerning the conduct around the camp and how we waddies
should treat each other. There were fines for breaking the rules.
I was charged with deceiving the stinks, because I did not act
like a greener and take a spill off the black hoss. I had a right to
select someone to defend me. I selected Murray, because his
name caused me to reckon that he should be able to talk and do a
fair job of chinning in my behalf. Those mouthpieces, as they
were called, stayed at it an hour arguing the case and hearing
the evidence. To hear them waddies one would think that I had
commited an awful crime. Of course I was found guilty and fined
a round of drinks, to be paid the first time we dragged to town.

Storytelling and agitating the catgut, also a little singing, was other means of passing the time. Murray was one of the best storytellers in the bunch. He use to tell one that I had never forgot because it struck me so funny. I will try and tell it as he did:

I was working down near the Mexican border for a cattle outfit several years ago. In that country there were a lot of javeline— you could see them everywhere. They are liking unto our Texas wild hawg, but not worth a hoot for chuck, because their meat is as tough as a piece of rawhide. You can tell a javeline from a wild hawg by the fact that a javeline does not have a tail.

One day a tenderfoot from the East dropped in with lots of jack that he wanted to invest and hankered to put into critters.

The tenderfoot and our ramrod, whose name was Murphy, agreed on a price for the critters and closed a deal, and the tenderfoot was taking charge of the outfit and he noticed the large number of javeline nosing around. The animals were so plentiful that they were a nuisance. The tenderfoot sez to Murphy: "Whom do all those hawgs belong to?"

"They belong on this ranch, but I plumb forgot to prattle about the critters, so I suppose that I will have to move the herd," Murphy sez to him.

"How many of those critters are there on the place?"

"I reckon about three hundred. I do not bother about branding the critters with an iron, but I just cut their tails off; that is my mark."

"What will you take for the herd?" the greener asked.

"I don't know just what to ask. They are worth, perhaps, around two dollars. What will you offer?"

"I'll give you one dollar a head and accept your word as to the number."

"Call it two hundred and the deal is closed," the ramrod came back at the tenderfoot.

Well, sir, he paid off and was happy over getting over two hundred hawgs for two hundred dollars.

We waddies were present while the deal was made but kept our trap closed, because it was too good to bust and we did not want to take the silver lining out of his cloud.

A day or two after the deal was closed, the new ramrod took a jiggle over the range to see what he had bought, and when he returned he sez to us waddies:

"I surely made a good deal for those hawgs. I am sure I saw around five hundred of the critters."

"Yes," we said, "Murphy never paid much attention to those animals." We waddies were hard put to keep our face from slipping, but stayed put on the matter.

The greener was a sociable fellow, and about a week later took a jiggle over to Mason's ranch to get acquainted and do some chinning. At Mason's place he sees a lot of javeline and sez:

"I see a lot of my hawgs on your range."

"What hawgs are you referring to?" asked Mason.

"Those with the tails off. Those are mine, that is my hawg mark. I bought it from Murphy."

"Oh, I see. I have been wondering where them critters belong. I would be quite pleased to have you take the critters. I sure don't want your stock."

"I'll see about getting the animals tomorrow," he promised.

When the new ramrod returned to the ranch, he told the top-screw to give us riding orders to have those critters fetched from Mason's place over to his range.

That was below the dignity of a cowhand, so we all quit. I never did hear how the tenderfoot came out with the javeline.

One other pleasant thing about the Jew's-harp outfit was the camp cook. We had a good one; Dutch Meyers took pride in his work. To get him doing extra touches, all we had to do was swell him on his meals. He would raise like a boil and take extra pains fixing the chuck. Murray used to say, "The belly-cheater became very arduous if you gave him fair chinning."

Dutch made some of the best sourdough bread I have ever ate. Bread, beans, stewed dried fruit was what we lived on. The cooky would fix the beans different ways. He could fix a Boston baked dish of beans that was fitting to eat; also fried pies out of the stewed fruit. When it comes to broiling steaks, Dutch had the knack down pat. He would get his campfire hot and slap the steaks into it for a minute, which seared them on the outside. Then he would pull the meat away and let it cook slowly. Of course the beef was off a fat yearling—a good meat to start off with.

Sometimes when talking about the good beef we waddies had on a hoss range, people will ask me where we got the beef. The facts are, for the most part it was tit for tat. The hoss men found beef on their range, and cowmen found hosses on their range, so 'twas tit for tat.

When we needed a yearling and saw one that looked like the kind we wanted, it would have been too much trouble to drag all over the range country hunting for the man that owned the brand. That way we hossy stinks had beef.

After the first six months I did nothing but wrangle hosses. Tonk sold hosses all over the country. We would bust a bunch then the crew would drift the herd to places where an order was to be filled.

On the Jew's-harp range there was a mixture of hosses; saddle hosses, work hosses, and also jacks were bred.

I wrangled many hosses in my day and never failed to bust one if it was not loco. I got ahold of a few loco animals, and those animals would pitch until they were pitched down. When they gathered a little substance, away they would go again. If a wrangler stays with one of those critters long enough, the animal would stay pitching until it was wrung out and worthless. When we looped one of those critters and it threw its ears back, also turned its eyes inward until you could see nothing but the whites, then look out. As a rule it is a waste of time and the critter would brand you if it had a chance. If such a critter puts you into a spill, you want to draw a gun the first thing, because nine chances out of ten it will be coming at you and paw you to death.

The regular Texas cow pony was bred from the original Spanish hoss and mixed. That critter could never be stopped from bucking at times. That critter could be gentled to where it would come to its rider when called, eat out of the rider's hand, and in fact be a regular pet, but it had to pitch at times just to be pitching.

My ways of wrangling was the short route. After the hoss was roped and saddled, I would mount it and start fanning its ears with the first jump. If a wrangler keeps afanning a critter, it will be discouraged and quit pitching sooner than if you lay off of its ears.

I rode any of the pitching animals and had the reputation for being the top rider of that section. What cinched my reputation was because I rode a hoss one day in McGregor that had a notch in its tail. In the forenoon of the day the hoss had pitched a Negro, Tom was his name, and Tom was a top rider. He went into a spill and the fall killed him, because he fell so hard he had his neck broke. I saw the hoss pitching, and I reckoned that I could ride the animal. I told the crowd that the hoss could be busted, and they dared me to ride it.

As a rule, a hoss will be more stubborn after it has put a rider on the ground. So I expected some real pitching and got it. That animal rocked and jarred my fins aplenty. If one knows how to handle a sombrero, you can sting the ears aplenty. That hoss pitched with me until we were a mile from where we started. He had a real bump, and I could not see head or tail, but I was reaching its ears with my sombrero every landing. The critter finally decided that it was fighting a lost cause and settled down. That act gave me a top standing in that section.

After a spell of five years on the Jew's-harp outfit I quit and dragged out to Shackelford County and joined up with Hardy Roberts's hoss outfit. His brand was the letter R. I nested there for two years. I don't know how many hosses he had. They were all over that section, and when we wanted any we just cut the number out of the herd.

I wrangled there and the work was about the same as on the Jew's-harp. About the only difference was we had to watch our gentled stock close against Indian rustlers. They would rustle hosses if they had a chance, but we never lost any that we knew of.

The best rider that I had ever watched on a hoss was a Negro named Bob Sanders. A hoss just couldn't put that Negro off the leather, and Bob could play while the hoss was doing its best. There is where Bob had the best of me. I had to tend to my knitting, while he could do funny work. However, I saw him leave the leather one time. It was after a heavy rain and the creek was up. Bob was busting a wild critter near a sheer bank, and that critter was acting loco. It was elevating plenty high and sunperching. The animal went up one time and when it came down it was over the edge of the bank and landed in the water. Bob quit the critter pronto and swam for shore.

After I quit the Roberts outfit I dragged back to the McLennan County section and joined up with the McDermott cattle outfit, whose brand was MD. The outfit was a good-sized ranch, and we lived with the chuck wagon most of the time. We were supplied with the same kind of chuck as was furnished on the hoss outfits.

There was a good crew of boys with the outfit. John Goodie, Bob Smith, my brother Bob, and others I can't think of the names. We drove a lot of cattle to Young County, where the same outfit had another range.

While on one of the drives I saw and worked one of the worst stampedes that I ever witnessed. We were about twenty miles away from our home range the first night. We had drifted the critters hard as usual the first day to get the animals a good distance from the home range. The weather was quiet with lots of stars in the sky, and we could see quite pert. The critters were bedded down, and all looking peaceful. I was on the first night-riding shift and was feeling real sociable about how pretty everything was shaped up.

Suddenly, I heard a critter snort and sez, "Trouble is sure acoming!" I had no idea that it was going to be like it was. As a rule on a clear, quiet night it is easy to get the animals put into milling and then stop moving. With that snort five hundred critters jumped to their feet and were off like a bunch of race hosses. Those animals acted plumb loco. I saw critters run into trees and be knocked down and be stomped to death. They were running so fast and would not stop for anything. It was either them or the object. If a rider went down he sure would be buzzard food.

When it was over with we had lost so many, some being stomped and others strayed, that a party of waddies had to go back to the range and get some more critters.

The snort of that one cow put the scare into those critters. What it said with that snort is hard to tell, but it must have been plenty. Now it may have been scared by some varmint. There was lots of wolves in that country then, and it may have been a wolf that run into the herd. Anyway, all that we know about what started the herd was the snort of that old cow.

Hunting wolves was one of our pastimes. The ramrod had wolf hounds, and some of the waddies also owned hounds. When we had time, we would hunt wolves and bet on each other's hounds. Those hounds knew their wolf business, and I have seen some pert fights. No one hound would be able to best a lobo, but two or more would team up on one. While one dog was after the wolf from one side, a hound would come in from the opposite side and in that method would slash the wolf until it was down. Quite often we would shoot the wolf before the fight was over to save the dogs, but not until after the wolf was about in. We wanted to see all the scrapping we could.

After about eighteen months with the outfit I quit and went to my old love, the hoss ranch. I joined the Bonham outfit owned by Mason. It was like the other hoss outfits and nothing unusual happened there. It was not a large outfit, and the hands consisted of June, Bud, Bob, and Frank Mason, sons of the ramrod. Then there was Jim Patterson and myself as steady hands. After a year or so with the Mason outfit I quit so that I could get married.

Among all the waddies I worked with and seen do their stuff, the best rider was Negro Bob Sanders. Now in the shooting line there were so many good shots I can't say which was the best.

One story about roping that Sandy Smith told us waddies while sitting around the camp one night and that will end my chatter. He sez:

> While rattling about roping one night sitting in the bunkhouse of an outfit up in Colorado, I was telling the waddies that I could rope any animal that walks on two or four feet. Now, as you know, roping a critter means to a cowhand that you not only loop it but control the animal.
>
> One of the crew spoke up and sez, "Smith, I'll put up some jack that you can't rope a grizzle bear."
>
> I thought for a moment and then sez: "How much jack do you want to put up to sez that I can't?"

He came back at me and sez, "Twenty-five bucks of Uncle Sam's money."

I took the bet and had it written out on paper, that Smith bets twenty-five dollars that he can put the loop on a grizzle bear and control it.

Now, as all persons know that has any acquaintance with the grizzle, no human this side of hell can rope and take control of a grizzle bear. It is said that four or five waddies can do the job. So the boys thought that I had gone loco, and they were thinking right, except for one part of the bet.

In the mountain section of that country grizzle bears were not hard to find. After the bet had been set on paper, we all started out to find the bear, and that did not take us long, and I went in to do my stuff.

I rode up to roping distance, and the bear was running trying to get away. I put the loop on it and it then saw that it was cornered, which caused the bear to change its mind. That critter made for me quicker than a flash of sky-fire. Of course you boys know that I did not dare to start the horse because the bear would pull the hoss instead of the horse pulling the bear down. It had the rope in one paw and its teeth cleared for action. Again you know what power the bear has in its front legs. I guess the boys watching were saying, "There goes Smith to the eternal range." Well, I just pulled my .44 and put two shots into the bear's head, hitting it between the eyes. I then rode up to the crowd and sez, "Boys, there is the bear all roped and under my control."

They all looked sort of cheap and said that thereafter they would get a lawyer to write the bet of understanding made with me.

Sheldon F. Gauthier

William A. Preist

THE place of my birth was Guadalupe County, Texas, on the farm owned by my father, Dan T. Preist. The event took place June 4, 1877. I was reared on that farm until I was sixteen years old.

My father farmed and engaged in cattle raising, as practically all the farmers in Guadalupe County did during those days. In fact, the major industry of the county was cattle raising. The farmers were compelled to fence their cultivated fields to keep the cattle out of their crops. Outside of the scattered fields, the entire county was an open range upon which cattle grazed.

Father raised corn, wheat, cane, cotton, and vegetables. We consumed practically all produce of the farm except cotton, which was sold, except a small amount which we used for making clothing. The amount of wheat raised was sufficient to supply the family's flour needs. Flour was obtained by taking wheat to the gristmill and having it ground. The miller was paid for the grinding out of a portion of the flour.

The town where we did our trading was San Antonio, a distance of 25 miles from our farm. Therefore, going to town was a special occasion. The trip to town was made on hossback or riding in a wagon pulled by a team of mules.

My father and grandfather, Tom A. Gay, were associated together in the cattle business. When driving herds out of Texas to the northern markets began, father and grandfather were among the first men to drive a herd. When they started driving I was not yet born, but they were still at it when I became old enough to understand something about what was going on. My first recollection was when they were driving herds to the Fort Worth market.

Most of the cattle which the two men drove to the markets were bought from other ranchers, because our herd was not large enough to supply a sufficient amount of cattle for driving herd. Our whole herd numbered around three thousand head, and that was the usual number father would gather for a market drive. It cost about as much to drive fifteen hundred as three thousand. The crew always consisted of a cooky, hoss wrangler, trail boss, and nothing less than six pointers, which was the least number a driver would be safe in using. With a herd of three thousand to thirty-five hundred, ten pointers can easily handle the herd.

I never went on a drive while on father's farm. However, I grew up in the saddle and began doing some work on the range when I was twelve years old. When I was sixteen years old I could ride with the average fellow and do my share of the work on the range.

We did no night-riding on our range, which was the custom followed by all the ranchers in our region. Ranchers cooperated in looking after cattle. All of the ranchers had men riding the range and doing what was necessary, such as attending to the sick and keeping watch on bog holes for bogged cattle. Twice each year a general roundup was held, and then each brand would be cut out and separated into the respective herds and be driven back to their home range.

Most of the cattle in a herd will graze in the vicinity of its water and salt licks, provided the grass is sufficient. However, a few would drift off and become mixed with other herds. Each spring and fall it was necessary to separate the cattle, and of course in the spring the calves were branded.

During the late seventies after ranchers in the Guadalupe County section began to drive their herds westward, only small herds were left. I was anxious to work with a big outfit, so I followed the cattle west.

I went to the Pecos River region in 1895 and took a job as hoss wrangler on the W Ranch, which was owned by Lee and W. D. Johnson. W. D. Johnson now lives in Kansas City. Lee Johnson died at Fort Worth recently [1938]. The camp of the W Ranch was located on the Pecos River. The cattle ranged over 125 miles of territory, which included the range from Carlsbad, New Mexico, to the Horsehead Crossing on the Pecos River in Texas. We did not maintain a permanent headquarters. Our camp was generally located somewhere about the center of the range and on the Pecos River. During the summer months we lived in the open, using our saddles for a pillow. In the winter months we lived in tents.

Two chuck wagons were used most of the times during the summer months, and the waddies divided into two crews, which was necessary in order to cover the amount of range we worked. The number of cattle carrying the W brand was up to seventy-five thousand. The brand was made thus: 𝗐 , and we placed the brand on ten thousand calves during the spring of 1896.

There were about thirty steady hands employed on the W outfit. Bill Morehead was ranch foreman. We had two cooks named Mack McAdams and W. Birdville. Some of the old raw-hides who worked on the W outfit were Charles Brown, Red Ruley, R. Connley, William Nickles, Bill Newell, and Henry Slack. These were the steady hands. The others in the crew were shifting all the while. Some would work only a month or two, and others perhaps a year.

Our chuck was the usual range food, which was beef, beans, canned vegetables, black coffee, dried fruit, and bread. The bread was sourdough and corn pone. The chuck was cooked well and the amount was plentiful.

My work was wrangling hosses. The W outfit kept about two hundred hosses in its remuda. I helped to wrangle one hundred hosses each year. Out of the hundred about seventy-five would prove up to standard as top hosses for range work. It took about seventy-five hosses each year to replace the worn-out and injured hosses. A hoss with an injured leg or foot, or any fault which would slow the animal, was not used, because at any moment the rider might be called upon for top speed. The range hoss traveled over rough ground which contained holes and it was a frequent occurrence to have a hoss injured. Pulled tendons and broken legs were the most frequent injuries.

The system used on the W outfit to break a hoss was to rope and snub it. Then put the saddle on the animal and then mount it. The hoss would start pitching pronto and continue until one of the two following things took place: the hoss either threw the rider or became tuckered and convinced it could not throw the rider. When the hoss learned that it couldn't throw the rider, it would submit to being handled and soon responded to commands.

There is a vast difference in the way hosses would pitch. Each hoss has, more or less, its individual moves, and the waddies had names for the different kinds of pitching. For instance, the hoss which jumped first to one side and then to the other was called a fence rower. The hoss which jumped to only one side was called a sunpercher. The hoss which made a straight forward jump was called a pigeon winger. The toughest pitchers, which were rare, was the wigglers. The wiggler jumped forward and up and landed on its front feet with its rear end in the air. While in this upright position it would wiggle its rear end. The rider who could stay on a wiggler had the staying ability of a leech, because keeping on balance is the secret of riding a pitcher, and a wiggle is the hardest move to balance against. There were a few riders which could ride a wiggler, but not many.

I am amused at rodeos while watching the performers riding those pitching hosses. It is considered a ride if the rider stays ten seconds, and he knows beforehand what the hoss is going to do. The old hoss wrangler mounted a critter without knowing its movements and had to stay in the saddle from then on. If he couldn't stay with the critter, he was no wrangler.

Right now I want to relate my experience with a hoss as an introduction to my work on the old W outfit. The morning I started to work, the foreman pointed out a sleepy-looking critter for my mount to use for riding out to the hoss range. I saddled the animal, and while I was doing it the hoss never moved. I thought the foreman had put off a plug on me for a joke. When I hit the saddle, the critter went into the air, landed on its front feet, and with its rear about straight up in the air. While in this position the hoss did a shimmy movement, and I went to the ground. When I gained my feet, I saw the animal standing still with its sleepy attitude and about ten cowhands splitting their sides with laughter. That riled me, and I was also a little cocky about my riding ability, so I decided to ride the critter or else burst an innard trying. I tackled the hoss again. My second attempt ended as the first, except I lit a little farther from the hoss and hit the ground some harder. The hoss changed my mind about riding it. No amount of laughter or taunting would change me to tackle the hoss the third time.

I was somewhat ashamed of myself, and to keep out of conversation, I picked up a new rifle the foreman had bought and was pretending that I was examining it. I was watching, out of the corner of my eye, one of the old waddies who was starting to mount the critter. When the fellow started to swing into the saddle, his foot slipped through the stirrup and caught. The hoss pitched and started to run. Instantly I saw the danger the waddie was in. I took aim with the rifle and shot the animal. The hoss tumbled to the ground, and luckily to the opposite side from the rider. The waddie untangled himself quickly and was none the worse for his experience. The foreman said to me, "Well, you killed the hoss but saved the waddy."

"No," I answered boastfully, "the hoss is just creased."

I didn't think that the hoss was creased. In fact, what I aimed to do was hit it in the brain and drop it pronto. Well, sir, I missed my aim. The bullet went too far back, but the hit was a neat crease. I was surprised, but acted nonchalantly about it, and the crew doffed their conk covers to me as a top rifle shot. The foreman patted me on the back and said, "You may not be able to ride a wiggler, but you sure are a pert rifle shot."

That chance shot initiated me, and I was recognized as a pure rawhide.

On the W outfit we did night riding to keep the herd intact and watch for rustlers. Night riding was done in shifts of four hours' work. Night riding was pleasant work except during inclement weather. For instance, on a bright night with the moon shining, a herd which was bedded down was a beautiful sight to see. But on a night with a cold, drizzling rain the job was a tough one. Then if the herd started on a run, it was hell.

The worst stampede I ever worked with was three thousand steers from three to seven years old. The herd was ready to be driven to Amarillo for shipment to market. About midnight something scared one or two of the animals, and the fear spread to the whole herd like a flash of lightning, and the whole herd raised and started at the same moment. This bunch of steers were the worst bunch of scared animals I ever saw, and what scared the animals was a mystery. After the animals started to run, trying to stop the herd was useless. The old steers became furious and bowed their necks if a hoss ran into their way. After two hosses were gored and one rider stomped to death, we gave up all efforts to turn the herd and just let the animals run. This herd ended their run when they became tuckered out and scattered among other cattle.

Johnson had contracted to deliver the three thousand steers, so the next day we had to cut out again. Stampedes were frequent at times, and then for weeks at a time the critters would not stomp.

Rustlers gave us trouble in streaks. For a spell we would have no trouble, and then the gang would set in and keep us jumping. The greatest haul rustlers made on a W ranch herd was 225 critters in one night. The rustlers came to the Pecos region from Menard County. They rode up to two night riders about 3 A.M. and pretended they were lost. While a couple of the rustlers were in conversation with the waddies, suddenly several of the rustlers pounced on the night riders and bound them with rawhide ropes and left them lying on the ground. The rustlers then cut out the critters and drove the animals off.

When the boys failed to show up at chuck time that morning, a party of waddies started to hunt for them, and they were found late in the evening. It was too late then for trailing. The following morning the foreman and six waddies started out to follow the trail. The trail led to the east and ended in Menard County. Of course we didn't follow the tracks the entire distance, because we lost the tracks about fifty miles from our range. The number the rustlers had taken was too many for them to keep under cover, and we were able to follow the cattle from information. Folks, here and there, would tell us that a herd of about three hundred critters with the W brand was seen going east.

When we arrived in Menard County, we notified Dick Russel, who was then sheriff of the county. The sheriff joined us with a number of his deputies. The sheriff was quite certain who the rustlers were, and the herd was located where his suspicion directed us.

I shall leave the rustlers' names unspoken, because some of them, and some of their relatives, are still living and I do not wish to cause embarrassment.

When we located the herd, we surrounded the camp, and then the sheriff went to the camp and told the fellows they were surrounded, so had better come with him without any fuss, which they did. They were tried and convicted and served a term in the state penitentiary.

Law and order was making its appearance when I went to work for the W outfit. Therefore, the gun battle between rustlers and ranch outfits was coming to an end. The officers had things fairly well under control.

The Pecos River outfits had things in hand. All the ranchers had riders riding the range and cooperated with each other in looking after the cattle the same as they did in the general roundup. Those were the W, HH, LFB, Turkey Track, and JAL and a few other small outfits ranging in the Pecos region. During the roundups, crews of all the outfits united under one superintendent. Now the fence riders cooperated in watching the range fence and the rustlers. In fact, during the past few years more men are on duty watching the rustlers than were used during my time.

The range covered during the general roundups extended from Roswell, New Mexico, to the Rio Grande border of Texas. Each roundup crew consisted of about a hundred men with representatives from each outfit. Each crew worked a specified section under a range boss. The roundup lasted about three months, and I shall estimate the number of cattle handled at four hundred thousand.

After the roundup work was finished, our work reverted to the regular duties and drives to market. Amarillo and Clarendon, Texas, were the points we shipped from. The distance of the drive was approximately six hundred miles, and we allowed about sixty days to complete the drive.

We never had any serious trouble on the drive. We had an

occasional stampede, but we were never bothered with Indian raids or other depredations. The days of the Indian troubles were past when I made the cattle drives.

I reckon Burney Riggs was the quickest on the draw and the most true shot in the section during my days in the Pecos section. He was a wizard with the gun. To give you some idea of his ability, I shall sort of describe the man and tell about one of his shooting affairs. He was six foot six tall and rawboned. A man that was cool as a cucumber at all times, and one may as well as try to excite a hippopotamus as to fluster Burney Riggs.

There was a feud existing between Riggs and two other men. Bill Ahart and John Dawson were their names. The two men went gunning for Riggs and declared they would shoot him where and when found. In Pecos was a bar called Number Seven, and Riggs was at the bar at the time of the event I am relating. His adversaries learned where he was and went in to kill him.

When the two men entered the bar, one of them said, "Riggs, you are through!" and each man was drawing his gun while the words were being spoken, but they did not succeed in making one shot. Before either man could shoot, Riggs had drew his gun and shot each of them.

I speak of them men as being tough, but they were tough in a different sense than the so-called tough men of today. Outside of a very few, such as Billy the Kid, the tough men did not kill for money or shoot their adversary in the back. Neither did they sneak up and cover their opponent without giving him an even chance. They calculated that if you were not willing to match shooting ability with them, then you had no business taking part in a difference with them. However, they would not intentionally take undue advantage of anyone. Them men lived a rough and hearty life and were rough and ready in their ways.

I shall relate the nature of a contest held, as told to me. Now, I do not vouch for the facts of this story, but it was told by a responsible Fort Worth businessman following a business call in Pecos city during the early days. He was asked how he found conditions in Pecos and told the following:

I arrived in Pecos late the day of July 3, and engaged a room at the hotel. I requested the clerk to not disturb me in the morning until the last call for breakfast. He said, "Well, stranger, we're celebrating here tomorrow and the first doings starts at 6 A.M., so I can't say as you won't be disturbed!"

Long before 6 A.M. the noise was so great I was unable to sleep. I dressed and went out to watch the entertainment. At 6 A.M., four mounted cowboys were lined up and with the sound of a pistol shot they dashed off.

About the time the cowboys left, the hotel proprietor announced breakfast. I, with others, went in to eat our meal and could hear the people arguing the merits of their respective favorites and betting money on them.

Shortly after I had finished my eating, one of the contestants returned, and the others followed with their appearance shortly. Each of the men had a wildcat and a rattlesnake. None of the snakes were less than five feet long.

There was a tub of gyp water setting in the square, and each man rode up to the tub and dismounted. They immediately started to whip the animals until the cats took a drink of the gyp water. Of course the man who first made his cat drink was declared the winner.

I learned that this contest was just a warming up exercise and that the real contests were to follow. I feared that things may become a little rough, so hired a livery rig to drive me east.

Now this Fort Worth citizen may have exaggerated a trifle, or he may have taken a supply of Fort Worth liquor with him and overindulged, but the waddies enjoyed rough play. I shall relate some playing incidents which I can vouch for, because I was present.

Occasionally tenderfoots would visit the section with the object of investing money in land or cattle and sometimes both. The range looked so much the same in all places that a tenderfoot would easily become lost. When a tenderfoot desired to look over the land, one or two waddies would accompany him to assure his safe return.

On one occasion an easterner started out with two of the ranch waddies, and when at a short distance from the camp, the rawhides became engaged in a heated argument. There was one waddie on either side of the tenderfoot, and at the high point of the argument each waddie began to shoot at the other. The tenderfoot spurred his mount to get away, but the waddies spurred their mounts and kept the fellow between them until they had emptied their six-guns.

When the waddies reined their mounts to a stop, the fellow returned to camp at top speed. That tenderfoot was shaking like an aspen leaf in a heavy gale when he dismounted, and he had changed his mind about looking the territory over. Of course, the waddies had feigned the quarrel and had shot blank cartridges. Feigning a quarrel and shooting blank cartridges with a greener between two men was a favorite trick with the waddies on the W outfit.

When I quit the range in 1914, I was still employed on the W Ranch, which was nineteen years after I started to work for the outfit. During those years I held every position, even to being a cowpoke, except that of foreman and belly-cheater. I was wagon boss at the time I terminated my range career.

Cowpoke is a term applied to a man that travels with a trainload of cattle. Sometimes they are spoken of as bull-nurses. The cowpoke's job is to keep watch over the carloads of cattle and poke the animals up if one gets down. The animals are loaded so compact that if one gets down, it can't get up without assistance, unless room is made for it, because of the crowding from the other animals. When shipping cattle, the animals must be loaded compact; otherwise the critters would be knocked down from the jerking of the train.

I made many trips as a cowpoke to Kansas City, but the only part of the trips I enjoyed was the few days' time we could spend at Kansas City after the critters were delivered. Poking critters is a hard and dirty job. It is necessary to keep a close watch, because if an animal goes down, it will be shortly stomped to death.

At the time I quit the W Ranch, Means and Everman were the owners of the ranch. The Johnson brothers had sold out to them new owners in 1910.

After I quit the range I was elected sheriff of Winkler County and have held the office continually since, with the exception of eighteen months.

Sheldon F. Gauthier

Victor R. Scoville

I was a cowboy back in the days when they didn't have no fences everywhere you looked. In fact, when I was a kid, they didn't have a fence nowhere near my dad's place. That was way back in the 1890's, though.

To begin with, I was born on my dad's ranch, December 17, 1889. The ranch was known as the Cloverleaf and was located in Frio, Zavala, and LaSalle counties. Headquarters was in Frio County about fifty-four miles south of San Antonio, Texas. Dad had over fifty thousand head in the VA and Cloverleaf irons. The last iron wasn't really a cloverleaf design but kinda looked like one. It was made with two S's, one of them a straight S, with the other made in a horizontal way without leaving an opening in the first S.

I can remember, now, how anxious I was to be a cowpuncher and how I'd ride everything I could get on until I was able to ride anything that run on four feet and could get to a snubbing post. I rode yearlings until I rode them down, and I rode every hoss that I could saddle until I really did get good at it, for sure. My dad wanted me to be a good rider, so he helped me along by giving me a hoss, now and then, and pointing out my faults. When I was four years old I could ride real good. Of course, I couldn't ride no wild hosses, but I had several spills from broncs on frosty mornings when they kinda wanted to stretch out. You take any bronc, and he'll do it in spite of anything you can do. I've seen them whipped until the blood run, but they'd buck again as if they'd never been whipped for it. A regular cowpuncher takes that in a day's work and never gets mad about it, because he knows the bronc wants to limber up.

Now, I don't mean to brag when I tell you about riding wild hosses, but some people are born with the knack of handling some things good and others not at all. I reckon if you was to ask me to push a typewriter, I couldn't get to first base in ten years;

A rodeo contestant riding a pitching horse at the San Antonio rodeo grounds, 1920–30.

on the other hand, if you was offered a job wrangling hosses, you might do the same as I would in pushing a typewriter. Of course you can't never tell about those things, but I do know that few people can handle hosses as well as some can.

Now, about wild hosses: why, I was riding them when I was eight years old, and my dad would bet money that I could ride any hoss, anywhere. Tell you another thing: I was never throwed after I was eight years old. I rode in rodeos, too; rode man-killers that had already killed several men. One of them I rode was named North Fork Blue. He killed six or seven men before I got the chance to ride him at the Elko, Nevada, Rodeo in 1915. I rode that hoss and won the contest. All the papers told about the men he'd killed and said that I was the only man that ever rode him. I knew he was a bad hoss, because of a couple of cowpunchers told me about what the hoss had done before. I didn't care much, but I was extra careful.

The reason I was able to put on such a good show for them, in the rodeo, was because I was always picking out bad actors on the home ranch. I had hosses to fall on me, roped critters from green hosses and had them jerked out from under me, and roped critters too big for any hoss to hold. Speaking of roping big critters, I roped a one-thousand-pound steer in a rodeo at Falfurrias, Texas, in fifteen seconds, flat. That was in 1904. That same year two famous hoss riders put up a bet that each one could best the other. It was Clay McGonigal and Eddie McCarrol. They put up five thousand dollars, with the winner to take the entire gate, too. It come off at the ball park in San Antonio. Dad took me with him into San Antonio and let me stay to see the whole thing. It was to last four days, and plenty people come out to see it.

The first day, Clay's roping hoss bucked and lost that day for him; the second day, the same. So I went to him and asked him to use my hoss. I had a good one, one that I'd trained myself. He told me to bring him out for a trial, so the next morning, bright and early, I was there. I say, "Clay, let me show you what he can do without the bridle on him."

He say, "Strut your stuff."

I took the bridle off, pointed the critter out to the hoss, and

wc had it roped in short order. Well, Clay decided to use the
hoss, and he won the contest. After the doings was over, Clay
offered me two hundred dollars for the hoss, but I wouldn't take
that. It wasn't long after that when some other kids and myself
was out hunting. We'd tied my hoss up at the camp and was off
in the timber. When we come back to the camp, my hoss was
down with a bullet in his shoulder. I walked and ran all the way
back to San Antonio, fourteen miles, for a veterinarian. He came
back with me in his buggy and whipped the team all the way,
but we were too late. He cut a .22 bullet out of the hoss's shoulder.

Another thing about the ranches: they always kept two or
three spoilt hosses on hand to try out new hands. You'd get on
them like you would a plow hoss, and no telling when he'd come
unbuckled. That was lots of fun. Sometimes a fellow would get
hurt a little, but we was always on hand to help him out of a
tight spot.

I remember one greenhorn that come out to the place,
looking for a sixteen-foot hoss that'd been genteeled. Well, you
wouldn't ask for a better setup for some fun than that. We led
out an old, brokedown-looking hoss for him to try, and he almost
turned the hoss down on account of its looks. We told him to try
it, so we'd get an idea what he meant by a "genteeled" hoss.
Well, he got on and was throwed off in less time than it takes to
tell it. He never did try another hoss, under no circumstances,
no matter how much we talked, but it was worth it. The cowpunchers was fit to be tied, and there wasn't no work that day.
They kidded the greenhorn until he left the place. The main
giveaway was when he asked for a sixteen-foot-high hoss. He
should have said a sixteen hands high, and that's a big hoss.

The way we got our hosses for the cow work was to catch
wild ones out on the range. We had native Mustangs, and we'd
turn a young Cleveland Bay or a Kentucky Blackhawk stud out
with them. We'd have to hunt out the old studs first, though, or
they would kill the young ones, because they would be on the
young ones before they would know anything about what was
going on.

The way we catched them up was to let Blackie Edwards, a
crack shot, crease them. The way that was done, we'd raise the
herd and chase them for a day, sometimes two or three days,

according to the spirit the stud had. You see, the stud always led the mares to the water holes, or everywhere the herd went, and if he had lots of spirit, or was extra cagey, we'd have to chase them until they was plumb run down. After we'd run them until they was too tired to be cagey, we'd run them past Blackie, and he'd shoot the ones we wanted right in the muscle over the neck—the one on top. That would numb them, and they would drop like they was dead. It wouldn't last but about five minutes, but that was just long enough for one man to hawgtie them, and we'd go on until we got all the hosses we wanted.

When we had all we needed, we'd go back to each one, untie him, and one of us would ride him until he was partly broke; then, we'd go on until we had them all part broke, then head for the regular hoss corral, or remuda. There was a regular hoss wrangler in charge of the remuda. His job was to break the hosses and tend to them all the time. I liked that job pretty well, but I liked to get around over the range too well to stay put for a wrangler, so I never held the job very long at a time.

I was about ten years old on my first trail drive. Some folks wouldn't call it much trail driving, because we didn't run the herd very far, but it was done just like a long trail drive, so I just call it a trail drive. We only had two trail drives, and they was both to San Antonio, a fifty-four-mile drive.

The rest of the cattle that was took off the place went by rail. The railroad put a spur right up to the ranch headquarters, so it was easy and saved a lot of money by going that way. Then, too, there was lots less danger of stampedes that way, so it saved money that way, too, because you can figure on losing from a dozen to a hundred critters anytime there's a stampede. They'll either run off a cliff, canyon, or some of them will fall and the rest of them will stomp them down. When a stampede gets under way, you'd better figure on stopping it and stopping it quick. The quicker it's stopped, the less beef they run off, if some of them ain't killed, too.

The way a stampede is stopped is to have a rider get in front and turn the leader. You see, the herd follows a leader, and if he's turned, you keep turning him until the herd is milling around and going nowhere. They'll soon get tired, and one of them will bawl. Talk about a nice sound! The first bawl is certainly welcome, because that means that the herd will be stopped still in less than five minutes. That's kinda like a wild hoss. If he ever bawls, you've got him licked. Of course the bawl is different from a squeal. When he squeals, that means he's still fighting mad, and you'd better not give him a chance to stomp you or you're a goner.

On account of having a bad stomach, a leftover from the fracas overseas, I'm really as old as an eighty- or a ninety-year-old. I get such pains at times until I'll do anything to anybody, if they cross me. That's caused me to forget lots of things, and I don't remember so much because of it. After I left the ranch, I was an oil-field boomer, working in first one field then another. Everytime I got a chance, though, I'd enter a contest. Besides riding at Elko, Nevada, I rode here in Fort Worth for nine straight rodeos. Then I rode at Mineral Wells, Texas, and Rawlings, Wyoming. I rode and roped at these rodeos and made pretty good money at it because I pretty nearly always finished in the money.

Since the war I've worked here and there at different things, but not for long at a time because my stomach goes to tripping me up, and then I have to quit. My main way of making a living, now, is a throwback from my hoss riding days. My knack of handling hosses helped me to train a mule to do anything a mule could be taught. I work for advertising people everywhere with that mule. About the main thing we do is to work for beer companies. I fix up in a clown suit and walk down the street with the mule. He'll bow to one side, then another, and by the time we reach a beer joint that handles the beer we're advertising, I holler, "Hey!" at him, and he turns his ear to me. Then I act like I'm whispering something in his ear, and I'll point toward the joint. He'll shake his head up and down, then we'll go inside. This attracts the crowd inside, and we go right up to the bar, where I'll order two bottles of the kind we're advertising. Just set his bottle on the bar, and he picks it up in his mouth, holding onto the neck with his teeth, then empties the bottle. Likes it, too. I'd hate to have to pay for all he could hold, because he can sure outdrink me.

Woody Phipps

MINORITY VOICES

Negro cowboys with mounts (posed in connection with a fair in the interest of interracial relations, Bonham, Texas (?), 1910–15.

Will Crittendon

Do I know anything about the range? Why, man, I made a trail drive right through Fort Worth when it wasn't even a whistle-stop and I was only nine years old! I learned to ride a hoss on my pap's stock farm at Cedar Grove, Texas. I was born on December 12, 1868, right after Pap came to Texas from Alabama, where he was a slave of Governor Crittendon.

It was while he was a slave that he got his love of good hoss flesh from the governor. He always had a good surrey team and used Pap to drive it. When freedom came, one of the governor's sons had already taught Pap to read and write, so he came to Texas to start a hoss ranch and to get himself a school to teach. We did all right about the school by getting one at Cedar Grove. He was the first teacher in the county at that time. He didn't do so well about the hoss ranch. He only got around twenty to thirty head and forty to a hundred cattle critters at a time.

While he was teaching school, I learned to ride a hoss and rode herd on all his critters. I sure hankered to be a cowpuncher, and it wasn't any trouble to get me out and working the critters. There wasn't any fencing in those days. The critters ran everywhere just as if it was a big ranch with all the critters belonging to the same man.

The roundups were handled as if all the critters belonged to the same man. All of the ranchers gathered together in the spring, and we'd round up every critter in sight that wasn't under fence. The different cowboy crews herded their critters to the community roundup grounds. With all of the critters together, the cowboys would go to cutting out the stuff they wanted to brand.

The regular cowboys wouldn't let me cut out, but I'd get to run the branding iron after the critters were thrown and tied. That was my regular job at the roundups—"brand man." I'd watch the cutters circle through the herd, chase a cow out, rope it, then throw it, and I'd be on the job with the irons before I was called. If it was the fall roundup held in the late fall, the fat critters were herded off to themselves. I'd move them to the sale herd after using the iron so the boys could get back on the job quicker.

That's the way it was after I was five until I was about nine. At the fall roundup when I was nine, a man from a West Texas ranch wanted to buy all of the saleable stuff. The ranchers agreed to sell. Well, after the herd was cut out and worked over, he didn't have enough men to drive the herd. I wanted to go, so after Pap agreed to let me, I signed up. The man's name was Alfred E. Rowe, and the Wire Ranch at Paducah, Texas, was where we were headed with the trail herd.

I'll never forget how my mammy ganged around me and cried about me going off with the herd. I kept telling her I wasn't going to stay, but that didn't help her feel better. I finally broke away from her and went to tell Pap goodbye. He didn't smile none but said, "Well, son, you wanted to get out; now be a man wherever you go and you'll always end up right by doing so."

After the herd got started, I forgot all about my folks and went to riding herd. We had a couple of stomps before we got fifty miles away. One of them was when a hoss stumbled in the night as the rider got real close to the herd. The noise made by the saddle started them off, and I thought we'd never get them stopped. I'd never been in a stomp before and was a little skittish; however, I tried not to let on like I was.

When the stomps were on, I got real busy around the remuda and kept the hosses quiet while the other cowpokes were busy trying to stop the stomp. That was a good job, because if the hosses went, too, the cowpokes wouldn't have nothing to gather the critters up with again. It was always important to watch the saddle stock so as not to be left afoot, and I sure didn't like walking none at all.

I reckon the real starting place of the trail drive was at Muddy Cedar Creek, located about halfway between Wills Point and Elmer. That's where we burned the Turkey Track brand on the critters. It was the same brand Rowe used on his Wire

Ranch. After we got started, we worked on and on and finally reached Fort Worth. On account of so much work and all, I don't recall how many days it took us to get to Fort Worth. We drove the herd right through some of what now is the business district about where Twelfth and Fourteenth streets are now. The herd went west of the fort, which is where the Criminal Court Building is now.

When we got down to the river, I nearly lost a hoss because I'd never swum a river before. Since the Trinity River was up on a fall rise, the place where folks usually walked critters across was over a hoss's head. The trail boss had the chuck wagon floated across by tying logs onto the wheels up under the wagon bed and had several cowpokes on the other side pull on ropes while we got the wagon started out on this side. One of the cowpokes' hosses on the pulling end got bogged up and nearly fell, but he made it as the wagon swung out into the stream. As the wagon went downstream, the boys pulled it to shore, and after the wagon struck gravel on the other side, the boys untied the ropes, hitched it onto their hosses, and dragged the wagon right out.

The critters in the lead of the herd saw the wagon stock and hosses on the other side, and it wasn't so hard to get them to take to the water. After the leads took to the water, we boys all hollered and slapped our hats against the critters' sides until they got to crossing. After about half of the herd was over, I decided it was time for me to go. I rode my hoss right out into the water, and he swelled his sides to go to swimming, but he couldn't swell because I'd forgot to loosen the saddle straps. I sure like to have lost that hoss before we could get back to walking ground. One of the cowpokes came over to me and says, "Say, fellow, don't you know to loosen your saddle straps?"

I loosened the straps, and after two or three tries I got my hoss to take to the water again and we went on across. That was a good lesson for me, because I crossed many a river after that, and after remembering how big that hoss swelled, I always loosened the straps. Did you ever watch a hoss when he starts swimming? Watch one sometime and see how big his stomach swells.

Well, we got across and drove on. After crossing several more rivers and some hills, we finally arrived at the Wire Ranch at Paducah. After seeing the critters spread out on the ranch, I got my money and started home. On the way, I just had me a good time. I wasn't scared of Indians at all, because my folks taught me that the Indians wouldn't bother a Negro. And that's right, too, because I dealt with them later on and they never hurt me.

I followed the trail back that we used to drive the critters up, and all the way I'd study the places we passed that I didn't have time to stop and look at. I recall how the reeds and weeds at one crossing was still the same as when we fixed the place. You see, we'd come to quicksand and make a crossing by throwing a lot of weeds and reeds into the place, and then ride the hosses back and forth until we had a solid crossing.

Another place was where it was a long way between water holes and the critters all got dry and thirsty. I don't recollect how many miles it was, but when the critters first smelled the water, they stampeded for miles to get to it. There was no beef lost in this stomp because the first critters were so far in advance of the drags that they had drank and gone aside to rest in the shade while the drags also drank.

After I got back home, the folks threw a party for me. We all had a good time. I settled down to be the world's best hoss buster. I rode every hoss I could get a chance at. One thing I want you all to record is that I've never been throwed from a hoss at any time. Of course, you can ask any hoss wrangler and he will tell you the same, that some hosses won't "bust." You can ride them and ride them, ride them until they ain't got the spirit to lift their head. Still, after they've had a chance to rest, they're as wild as ever. When I couldn't bust a hoss, and I knew nobody else could, I'd shoot him in the head and go off and leave him lay. It was a regular custom among hoss wranglers to shoot them when they couldn't be busted, unless some rodeo would use them for pitching shows.

I got together all of the hosses I could to sell. When the cowpokes and me weren't "busting" Pap's stuff, we'd go to the hills and waylay a hoss herd. These wild hosses all had one stud for a leader. He was the only stud in the herd and acted like a rooster does around chickens. That is, he'd lead them to water and feed and keep jiggers on danger. Any hoss hunter will tell you that it's might near impossible to slip up on a herd before the stud gives a warning neigh.

The only chance a hoss wrangler had of catching wild hosses was running them until they were all tired out and then driving them into a hoss trap. For that job, we cowpokes all took as many extra hosses as we could wrangle and still take care of the catching job. Knowing that the wild hoss herd runs in a circle in order not to get far away from his stomping ground, we'd station our hosses in three bunches in a circle around where we figured the herd would run. The hoss trap was made in a blind canyon, a canyon that had two walls and an end where the hosses couldn't get out by jumping and climbing. At the front of the trap we'd put a bunch of poles and posts at the side so the hosses wouldn't notice them on the way in, and after they were in, we'd hurry and fix a corral fence higher than we figured they could jump.

Since I was such a good shot, I was always stationed right at the corral fence as soon as the herd went in. When the lead stud found out that he couldn't get out at the end, he'd turn to go back, and he'd call the mares to follow him. They always did without even looking around when in a tight place. They just followed him. Since the lead stud was always the best hoss in the bunch, he could sometimes jump the fence. When he came over, he'd seem to float or soar. It was always an easy thing for me to crease them as they came over.

I'd crease him and all that followed him. We'd hurry and tie them all up before they came to. After they were tied up, we'd untie one at a time and ride him until he was rode down. We'd have a rodeo all by ourselves. It was worthwhile because the wildest hosses buck the most. After riding the roped ones, we'd ride inside and snake one out, ride him, and then go get another.

I had quite a reputation as a hoss buster in those parts, and cattlemen from all around would come to me with the hosses they couldn't bust. I'd bust them at so much per hoss, and when I couldn't bust them, I'd shoot them.

When I got to be fifteen, I'd got fifty mules together and set out to make my fortune. I traded those mules around and busted hosses on the side. Among the places I busted hosses was the Tom King ranch at Greenville, Texas. Tom King had thousands of critters. Jim Harris, a banker at Terrell, Texas, had a ranch in West Texas but bought his hosses at Terrell and always had me bust them for him. Charlie Harris, his brother, ran the CH on the Saline river with about four thousand head. I busted hosses for him, too—the ones his boys couldn't bust. Jim Lancey, at Wills Point, had me bust a few for him from time to time, and Anderson that ran the JIM brand at Egypt, Texas, had me bust all his hosses. He was a cattle dealer who bought and sold from one to two thousand head at a time. The Manning hoss ranch had me bust all his hosses. His place was close to Terrell, and I'd contract to bust forty at a time. Many a time I'd have the money gambled off before I'd busted half of what I'd contracted for.

It was on this place that I roped something I didn't want. I was riding along one day, twirling my rope, when a panther walked right out in front of me. Well, I'd had several bears come up to my campfire, smelling my frying bacon, and I'd shot them over. I'd had several close calls, and my rope had brought me out of them, so I just lassoed the panther. Lord! Lord! After I'd done roped him, I saw what a big mistake I'd made, because he turned and started towards me. There was a big post by his path, and he leaped upon it in order to make his jump down on me. Well, I was quick on the draw, and a straight shot, so I just up and shot mister panther.

Don't you believe that I couldn't shoot straight, either, because I can still shoot straight and fast today. My years haven't slowed my hand, nor dimmed my eyes. I know that all old duffers like to sit around and tell what all they have done, but I can still do mine. You see that calendar on the wall? It's about thirty feet, ain't it? And the light's dim, ain't it? Well, if you'll go up close, you'll see that the pretty girl ain't got any teeth, and you'll see that the lips ain't touching. I shot that last night, and all of these boys here will tell you I did it. I ain't given up to going around and shooting, but they kidded me so much that I brought my sixer over and showed them what an old duffer can do. Up until last year, I ran a bunch of hounds out at Lake Worth and had bankers and businessmen for customers. They wanted a good shot and some good hounds in the party.

The last man I worked for busting hosses was Lindsey, at Elmo, Texas. He was a big hoss man and ran a regular hoss ranch. He'd gotten a big order for so many head of hosses, and I was hired to round them up for him. Well, I rounded his hosses up for him, but I cut back a few for myself, and after the sale was made, I went back and got the stuff and took it to Abilene, Texas, and sold it.

While in Abilene, I ran into a fellow named Jim Sullivan. He wanted to sell whiskey to the Indians, and because I was game for anything, I took him on. In 1900 we set our whiskey wagon on Choctaw Creek, at Savoy, Texas. We kept the wagon hidden and went across into the Territory to make our deals. No matter how good or sorry a hoss was, we paid one quart per head. We got some fine hossflesh, too. Indians would trade their souls for a little "firewater." We got along fine on our first trip and made a pocketful of money out of the hosses.

On our second trip we hired a man to go with us and watch the wagon while both of us got out and made deals. Some way or other, the Indians got together and were waiting for Jim and me to show with the whiskey wagon. After pitching our spot, I made off to a tribe I knew. Before I got over the hill away from the wagon, I heard shots. The Indians had come over on the Texas side and was shooting up the wagon. I rode back as fast as I could, but when I got close, I saw that Jim and the other fellow was dead. The Indians were lifting the whiskey out of the wagon and loading it on their hosses. One of them saw me coming and shot at me. The bullet passed through my right leg and killed my hoss. After they saw it was a Negro coming, they left me alone. I got Jim's hoss and rode away. After I got to town, I got taken care of, and then went to Fort Worth and ain't been away since.

Woody Phipps

Maclovio Lucero, Mexican bronc buster of the LS outfit, bulldogs a big steer, 1907–1909.

Elario Cardova

I was born on November 3, 1861, at my father's farm seven miles east of Nacogdoches County. So far as I know I have remained in the state the remainder of my life. Whether or not I have done wisely and have remained in the best state of these United States, I cannot say. Because I don't know anything about the other states, except what I have learned reading the papers, using the phrase the late Will Rogers used.

My parents were born in the Nacogdoches section. My grandparents came to America from Spain. My grandmother's family, on my mother's side of the family, came to Texas from Barcelona, Spain, at the time Spain ruled this section of America.

The Spanish government made a grant of land to my grandmother, Rachel de los Santos Coez, and her three brothers. The grant consisted of eleven leagues of land in the Nacogdoches section. Later, as the records will now show, one league was surveyed and conveyed to Casanero Cardova, my father, by the de los Santos Coez people.

The de los Santos Coez family came to America as agents of the Spanish government. Part of their duties was to learn the Indian language and customs and then deal with the Indians in behalf of the government. The family first stopped at Coahuila, which was then the seat of government for this Spanish territory. Their stay at Coahuila was for the purpose of studying the Indian language. After completing their study, the family then proceeded to the Nacogdoches territory and lived on the land of their grant. On this tract of land my father and mother were born and reared and lived until their deaths. There I was born, reared, and lived until I was in my tenth year.

The date of my father's death was July 3, 1862. My father died eight months after my birth. My grandparents were dead, except grandmother de los Santos Coez, and she then lived with my parents.

I was the youngest of all the four children. My oldest brother was about fifteen at the time of my father's death. He and mother managed the cultivation of our farmland.

My recollection starts with a scene during the Civil War. The scene was a herd of cattle being driven past our home by a party of Confederate soldiers. They were traveling east, and my guess is that the cattle were being driven to some point for the army's supply of beef. Seeing them soldiers and the herd of cattle is the only thing about the Civil War which happened that registered on my mind.

For me to say my family suffered any deprivation or not, after father's death and during the Civil War period, I must base my statement on guesses and what mother told me. So far as I could learn, we had plenty to eat and wear at all times. When I became old enough to retain impressions, I know then we had all the food and clothing necessary to live well.

Our farm consisted of about fifty acres under cultivation and about fifty acres in pasture for our milk cows and work stock. In addition to our farming, we owned longhorn cattle which ranged on the unsettled land. Farms were all fenced and were situated far apart, leaving great tracts of land for the cattle to graze on. To tell you how many cattle we owned is impossible. The number may have been five hundred or a thousand. We didn't give the cattle any attention. The cattle bred and multiplied at their will and found their own living on the range where it suited their taste. All we did to hold the herd was to provide salt licks in the section we desired the animals to make their bedding ground. When we needed a little beef or made a sale, we held a little roundup and cut out the critters desired.

In the spring of the year we worked over the whole section of the range, branding all calves with a cow carrying our CC brand. Others did the same thing, and, therefore, the cattle were almost all branded. While doing the branding, we would encounter cattle of various brands, and frequently a brand would be seen that did not belong to anyone in our section. Perhaps the critter belonged with a herd a hundred miles away. No doubt some of the cattle of our section would stray the same distance away.

As part of our farm work we raised hogs, using the same method we employed raising the cattle. The hogs bred, ranged, and obtained their living in the woods. The only feed we fed the hogs was a little corn once each week. We did this to hold the hogs close to the farm. They ranged a distance of ten miles away at times, but stayed within a distance of five miles most of the time.

The hogs were always in good flesh condition, and in the fall the beast would be very fat. The animals lived on what we called mast, which was nuts, herbs, weeds, and grass that the woods produced in abundance. Hogs so raised and fed grew into tasty meat, due mostly to the amount of nuts they consumed.

All the settlers raised their hogs the same way we did, and each owner adopted a mark with which their hogs were marked. The hog's ears were the place used for marking, and the marks were generally made by slitting, clipping, or punching holes in a certain manner in part of one or both ears.

Our work stock were the longhorn steers. When they were hitched together, the horns of each would extend over the neck of the other animal, and while they were being driven, one could hear the horns bumping and clashing as the beasts walked or trotted on their way.

We kept a few mustangs which were used for riding. If one desired to travel to some place, hossback was the means of loco-motion. If the whole family desired to make a trip, the reliable ox team hitched to a wagon was the means of traveling.

I, as all other boys of those days, learned to ride a mustang at an early age. I could ride a gentle hoss at the age of five and could handle a ordinary mustang, for all general purposes, at the age of ten years. My mother married the second time when I was ten years old, and then I left home to make my own living. That I have done ever since.

The cattle range was about the only place a young farm boy could secure employment. Consequently, I went to the open-range country where large ranches were established, and I chose Goliad County as the place to find work. I was successful and was given work on a ranch owned by the Hughes brothers. That was in 1871.

I traveled from Nacogdoches County to Goliad County on a

mustang given to me by my mother. I did not try to secure a job until I arrived in Goliad County because I was enjoying the scenery and desired to travel. By the time I had arrived in Goliad County my supply of food was too low for comfort, and then I began to ask for work.

I was no precocious child in size or ability, but I was above the average ten-year-old boy in size. I told the folks I was twelve years old and could easily pass myself off as being that age. I, not having ever been away from home, was somewhat verdant, and my experience handling cattle was limited to what I had learned assisting my folks to handle our cattle.

The Hughes outfit ranged their cattle adjacent to the San Antonio River, and during a wet period bog holes became numerous. The outfit needed someone to keep a watch for bogged critters. The work did not require a top hand or one with the strength of a man. I could meet the requirements, and there began my career as a cowhand.

My mount did the hard part of my job, and that was pulling bogged critters out of the holes. When I located a bogged animal, I put the loop around its horns, with the rope tied to the saddle horn, and the hoss then did the hauling, pulling from the saddle.

I did bog work for about two years, and during that time I had an opportunity to learn much about all the various range work. The old rawhides taught me the finer points of handling the lasso, riding a pitching hoss, and other techniques of the cowboy's work.

I was paid fifteen dollars a month at the start of my cowboy career and at the end of two years was receiving twenty-five dollars as my monthly pay.

During the two years I worked pulling mired critters out of bog holes, I slept in the bunkhouse every night, but I was away all day. After breakfast I would place a piece of meat, bread, and a canteen of water in my saddlebag and ride away and return about dusk. When I returned, I could do a man's job at the table even if I were only a slip of a lad. We were fed well on plain food, consisting principally of meat, beans, canned vegetables, and corn bread.

I graduated to the regular general cowhand's work after the second year, and then I lived behind the chuck wagon about half of the time. The general spring and fall roundups kept us busy about six months of the year, and during all the roundup period we slept in the open and ate our chuck sitting on our haunches. Then, frequently between roundups we would be away from headquarters to round up cattle and cut out critters for sale.

The Hughes outfit made a few drives but sold almost all their cattle to drovers who came through the country buying cattle to make up driving herds. The Hughes outfit ranged around ten thousand head, and when they made a drive to market, it was necessary for them to buy other critters to complete a herd to be a paying drive, because their herd would not supply from three thousand to thirty-five hundred without cutting into the breeders.

The roundups were participated in by all the cattlemen of the section. The different brands would be separated and the strays driven back to their home range. The roundup crews worked from one section of the range to another, and when the roundup was completed, all the cattle would be on their home range. Then again, from time to time a few would stray off, principally during storms, so by the time the next roundup was held, the various brands would be more or less mixed.

The branding of the range cattle was done during the roundup. The branding was performed by a branding crew. The cutting crew would call out the brand to be applied as the calf was being dragged to where the irons were being heated in a fire. The cutters would note the mother cow's brand and yell to the brand man. For instance, suppose they called for BH, then the brander would answer, "BH," and then the checker would repeat the letters. The BH brand would be applied and noted in the record book. At the end of the roundup, each outfit was given a record of the number of their calves branded.

In the morning the cooky would be up before daylight preparing breakfast. It would generally consist of broiled or fried steak, sourdough bread cooked in a Dutch oven, gravy called sop, syrup called lick, and black coffee. Breakfast over, all the riders whose job was to ride the range and gather in the cattle would mount and ride off on what was called the swing. Perhaps they would ride ten or fifteen miles before arriving at the place where the gathering work for the day was to be done.

The morning swing was always a race. The waddies always rode the best horses in their string, and it was a contest for the lead and not to be in the rear. All waddies took pride in their mounts, and each tried to ride the best mount on the range.

The waddies would saddle their mounts while waiting for their chuck, and as soon as the meal was eaten, they would mount and wait for the range boss to give word to be off. While waiting for the signal, some of the hosses would be pitching with their riders cussing, some would be prancing, and some standing quietly. When the perhaps twenty or more waddies were all mounted, the boss would yell, "Let 'em go!" and away the mounted crew would dash. They would spur their hosses, and the animals would dig their hooves into the ground to attain the best speed, traveling over varied terrain. They travel over hard ground, then sand, and next it may be a rough, rocky way, but to be a worthy cow hoss, the animal had to have ability to travel over any kind of ground.

The rider who was left behind was the object of all kinds of jibes, such as, "You should change that cottonwood stick-hoss for a piece of oak," or "Why don't you do the running and carry your weak brother?" The swings were always enjoyed, especially by the participants.

The time when the swing would return with a herd of cattle depended on the distance they had to go, the nature of the country, and how badly the cattle were scattered. Frequently the swing would return in the fore part of the evening. The herd would be turned over to the holding crew, and the swing boys then would relax until the next morning. After resting for a little while, more or less of the swing crew would engage in various kinds of sports. Hoss racing, shooting, roping, or some other pastime would be engaged in.

My career on the range was during the period when there was a great deal of conflict among the ranchers of the Goliad range territory. I happened to secure a job with an outfit which was not only called rustlers, but were classed as one of the leaders of the rustlers. However, they maintained that they were defending the rights of the small ranchers against the impositions of the large ranchers. Bud Brookings's ranch was another place classed as a haven for rustlers by the large ranchers. On the other side were what people referred to as the "Pures," and almost all were large ranch owners such as Buck Pittes, Faint, and the Ragglings. I never learned of any stealing done by the Hughes outfit, but their cowhands branded unbranded cattle wherever any were located.

During the Civil War and for a period after the war ceased, branding was neglected by many cattlemen. Also, very few cattle were sent to market, because the market was cut off from Texas. The lack of sales resulted in a large increase of cattle. Therefore, the two conditions produced thousands of cattle which were unbranded.

A few years after the war ceased, railroads extended west into Kansas, and markets were established within driving distance of Texas. Then the prices went up which resulted in a scramble to brand those cattle without a brand. Naturally, ranchers maintained they had a superior claim to the unbranded cattle within the section which they called their home range, and any unbranded cattle grazing with the cattle carrying their brand. This claim was generally accepted as proper, but there were some folks who did not confine their branding strictly within their territory. Branding cattle in territory claimed by some other rancher led to trouble and many killings. The conflict developed two contending parties.

The small fellows claimed that the Pures were claiming too much territory, for the purpose of excluding the small ranchers and to take undue advantage with the unbranded cattle. The small ranches, and some people who never had a herd, ignored the Pures' claims to territory and branded cattle where found. Some of the Pures paid a bonus to their cowhands for each unbranded animal they branded, and that method created too much branding activity to develop in some of the waddies. These conditions started arguments, which progressed into quarrels and ended in many shootings and killings.

The Pures organized vigilante committees which operated

secretly and set out to clean out the rustlers. In the section were some thieves, but when the vigilantes began to operate, they classed many cattle branders as rustlers, and many men were run out of the country who were not real thieves.

John Baker, who has lived in Fort Worth during the last few years, was served notice to leave Goliad County because he worked the Brookings outfit—also several others who worked for the outfit. Some of the waddies working for the Hughes outfit received notice to leave.

The system of giving notices was to place a notice on the lintel post or send it through the mail, telling the party to be west of the San Antonio River by a specified time or take the consequences.

Hamp Davis, who worked for Hughes, received a notice to leave. About the same time, Jim Simpson and Adire Miller, who worked for Bud Brookings, also received their warning to leave. These men were just a few of the many to whom notices were sent. After receiving a notice, it was unsafe for one to go off of his home range unless he was traveling to cross the river within the specified time. Many made the mistake of doing otherwise.

Hamp Davis made the mistake of going off of his range territory without sufficient company. As it happened, he was ready to get married and continued to carry out his wedding plans. Hamp married and was traveling in a buggy with his bride to visit some friends after the specified time he was given to be west of the river. The vigilantes caught him at a lonely spot in the road. He was taken out of the buggy, from the side of his bride, hanged to a limb of a tree, and shot full of holes. I know that Hamp didn't steal any cattle, but he did brand cattle with the brand of the Hughes outfit.

John Baker's uncle, Bob Baker, from somewhere north of Goliad County, came after John to save him from the vigilantes. John later went to the Double Mountain section of Stonewall County. Jim Simpson left the country. Adire Miller refused to leave, and his body was found in the river with a stone tied around his neck.

During this period of strife I remained close to the home range. If one desired to go somewhere, he had to go with a party of several persons who were ready to swap lead. A person was quite safe with a crowd, because the vigilantes did not attack except when they had the drop on their victim.

The matter was eventually settled by the Rangers and other officials taking a hand in the matter, and the unbranded cattle finally disappeared, which removed the main cause of the strife.

After all the unbranded cattle disappeared from the open range, the conflict among the ranchers ended, but there remained the rustlers, and strife continued between the rancher and rustlers. Both cattle and hosses were the object of rustlers. The rustlers, as a rule, would cover up their depredation by changing the brand. Some of the rustlers did an artistic job working a brand over. Usually the rustlers worked in company of two or more. Each would register a brand which would be similar to a brand of a large rancher. To illustrate, we shall presume an OX brand existed. The rustler would register his brand as XOX and then the OX brand could easily be changed to XOX by adding an OX, or the rustler could register OX and then he could change the OX brand by adding a bar through the cross of the X.

The most shrewd rustler brand I have ever heard of was what was called the terrapin brand. It was made in the outline of a terrapin thus: ⌒⊃. When this brand was placed on a critter, it blotted out all other marks and left only the terrapin brand showing.

A part of our range work was watching for rustlers. The rider rode from one point to the other using a spyglass constantly. When any strange mounted men were seen, an investigation followed. The rancher who did not keep a constant vigil would find his cattle count short. If a buyer bought such a herd, accepting book count, in a short time he would be singing one of the old range songs:

> Oh, he said that he had 'em, but damn him he lied.
> Damn him he lied, damn him he lied.
> He said you'll sure find 'em with my brand on.
> Damn him he lied, damn him he lied.

However, even range count didn't always keep a buyer from singing, "Oh, he said that he had 'em, but damn him he lied." A number of sales were made at which some of the cattle were counted twice or more. The most spectacular event of double counting was at Buffalo Gap. The Gap is a narrow passageway between two buttes, and between the two buttes was where the counting took place. Waddies drove the cattle up to the entrance, and as the animals were counted, they were driven on through to the opposite side. At the opposite side of the hills other cowhands were stationed, and they drove the counted cattle back to where the uncounted cattle were being held. Thus, the counted critters joined the procession of uncounted cattle and were recounted.

During the later part of the eleven-year period I worked for the Hughes outfit, the country began to change from open to a fenced range. Settlers were developing farms, and the result of this change was a westward movement of the cattle ranchers to the plains section, where the open range was still existing.

I foresaw the elimination of the open range in Goliad County and calculated I would be working on a farm unless I followed the westward movement of the ranches. This situation caused me to return to Nacogdoches County and engage in farming, which I followed for a number of years. In my middle life I discontinued farming and entered the mercantile business and I have followed the business up to date.

Sheldon F. Gauthier

James Cape

I was born in South Texas a long time before the war. I do not know exactly when except it was over one hundred years ago. The place I was born was in Gonzales County, Texas, on the farm of Mr. Bob Huston. He owned a hoss and cattle ranch, too. I was fully grown before the war with the Yanks.

You see my mom and pop were bought by Bob Huston. My father told me that he was born in Africa, and he was brought to this country and sold to folks in Virginia. Then Mister Bob took him to Texas.

I was so young when I learned to ride horses, it seems like forever. The first work I recall was riding hosses tending to the critters and horses on the ranch. There were about ten hands working for Mister Bob attending the horses. We all lived in the bunkhouse and had a special cook. The chuck was meat, beans, corn bread, and black coffee. Sometimes the cook made us fried pies, but that was not too often. It was only when he could get his hands on dried fruit that he could make pies.

Our job as hands was to watch over the herd and bust them. Sometimes Mr. Huston had as many as a thousand head of horses. He was buying and selling them all the time. On the ranch he raised lots of horses and also bought many from Mexico. There were many times we would go across the Rio Grande to fetch back horses for the ranch. On those trips there would be six in the crew—the cook and five riders. We didn't have a chuck wagon with us, so everything was toted on pack hosses. When night came, we would sleep on the ground and rest our heads on the saddle. When we were coming back with a herd of horses, part of the crew had to ride the line every night. Riding the line means riding around the herd in order to keep them bunched.

It was never hard to drive the horses because they are not skittish about going on the stomp like cattle. Naturally, if a busting storm comes in the face of the horses, they will try to run in the other direction.

The worst time I saw with a herd of hosses was when we were bringing a herd of two hundred horses back from Mexico. These were fine-stock horses, with racing blood, and Mr. Huston was awful particular about the critters. Because of the kind of horses they were, we were awful careful about losing them. It was a hot day, awful hot. All the horses were wet with sweat and just moping along. The driving boss was named Rogers, and he said, "Gosh for mighty, boys, we are going to have a pert spell of weather, and we'll have plenty of riding to do to hold these critters." Just as he predicted, the wind came, but that was all right because we hands held them. But then the hail came, and that wasn't all right because we couldn't hold them anymore. No sir, those horses went plumb loco and like a bunch of soldiers began going helter-skelter running away from the storm. There wasn't any woods nearby, so there really wasn't anyplace that offered shelter from the hail. When hosses go on the stomp, there is only one thing to do, and that's to work the leaders. I was always the one put in the lead when a herd got the "runs," because I was the best rider of the whole crew. I headed for the lead so that I could give the herd a leader. Hosses follow a leader always. We shouted to Rogers, "Don't worry about the crew's safety, just save the horses." However, it's a little hard not to mind hail when it's busting you on the back, legs, and arms. Our big hats saved our heads—without them, we'd have been knocked loco. Well, we kept riding because there wasn't anyplace for shelter, and we'd might as well keep riding as stand still. I stayed in the lead, and the other riders rode on each side in order to keep the horses from scattering. Well, the hail lasted about ten minutes, and I'm sure in that time the horses ran about ten miles. Everytime a hailstone hit a horse, it would try to run a little faster. As soon as the hail stopped, I began to circle the herd, and they settled down soon. In spite of everything, we lost a couple of horses—yes sir, they were knocked down by the hail and the other horses stomped on their bodies until they were dead. All the other horses had bumps all over their bodies. We men had the same. For a week we squealed like a pig when we tried to move fast, because of the sore spots. Some of the hailstones were as big as baseballs, but they felt as big as two baseballs when they hit.

Mr. Huston busted horses for the saddle, and he sold them in many parts of the states. We hands took horses to different places in the East and North.

Now, hoss busting is the work I best liked to do, and once I learned to ride them, there wasn't any horse that could put me on the ground. I could stay on the pitchers until they were plumb tuckered out. Mr. Huston used to call me the "riding fool" because I was not afraid to ride any hoss, and I never gave up.

When we were ready to bust a hoss, we'd put a loop on it and then we'd snub him. Next we would put the blinders on and saddle him up. We would climb in the saddle, take the blinds off, and then the rocking starts. Some hosses are worse pitchers than others. some are just natural pitchers and can do the hootchy-kootchy while in the air. Now, a hootchy-kootchy horse is not going to be ridden unless the rider is an excellent hoss breaker. I can ride them, but sometimes a horse like that will make stars come right down in front of you, while it is still daylight, too! Many times, when the horse quit pitching, my nose was leaking blood. The nosebleed is caused by the many times the horse hits the ground, and when I say "hit the ground" I mean hit hard!

In the spring of the year we would break two hundred or more horses. It would take two or three months of work. Breaking horses was done after the roundup was over. After the horses were busted, we'd ride them at least five or six times a day until they were ready for a sale.

As far as care of the horses on the range, there wasn't much to do about watching them. Horses are not like cows. The horses stay on the range unless something drives them off. What waddies had to watch for mostly were the cripples or horses infected with the misery—like if a horse gets cut and screwworms get in the cut. Then we'd have to put a loop on the critter, flop it down, and put a salve the boss made in the cut in order to kill the worms. Mr. Huston also ran cattle, and we had to do the same for those critters when screwworms got in their cuts.

Cattle on the range were allowed to run where they pleased. The riders just started the herd back when they drifted too far off. It was more riding watching cattle than horses because they would drift off if not watched.

In the spring and fall, the cattle were always rounded up. The branding and counting was done in the spring. In the fall the cattle were again counted and those that were not the boss's were cut from the herd.

I worked on Mr. Huston's ranch until after the Civil War started. One day the boss came to me and asked, "Jim, how would you like to join the army and look after the horses for the general?" Now I didn't know nothing about the army, so I asked Mr. Bob Huston, "What does the general do in the army?"

He told me, "The general is a big boss. He dresses in fine clothes and rides awful fine horses. He has music and lots of fun."

Well, I liked to work with fine horses, and I liked music and fun, so I said I'd like to join the army.

I was still a slave, so there was some sort of arrangement between my owner, Mr. Huston, and a Dr. Carrol so I could go. I left Mr. Huston and never went back to him.

I got in the army around Saint Louis and Kansas. It went well for a short time. I tend horses for the general and the sergeants and the captains, but there wasn't much music or fun of the kind I liked.

After a while, tending the horses wasn't all I had to do. Then there was lots of music, but of a kind I hated. We got in a battle, and I was told, "Do some fighting—fight like you've never fought before." You see, they had been teaching me army drill just in case there was a need for me to fight the Yanks. Well, that need came up some place around Independence, Missouri. We fought for three days and nights. There was plenty of music—it went whiz, whiz, bang, boom, and bang!

We fought hard when we were not retreating. We did more running than fighting, and that suited me just fine. Retreating was one thing I could do better than anyone else. The Yanks killed lots of the soldiers, took lots of them prisoners, and captured guns, horses, and everything. We just left the stuff and ran.

See the scar on my left shoulder? Well, that's where I got shot when I was fighting, and I didn't even know it until the blood wet my shirt. I was just too excited to feel the bullet when it hit me.

After the battle, we ran fast and far from the Yanks before we stopped to rest. The doctor fixed my shoulder, then he said,

"If the bullet went three inches to the right, it would have cut your jugular vein and then I wouldn't be needing to tend this wound." I told him that if the jugular vein had been cut, I wouldn't need him to fix my wound, either!

While I was waiting for my shoulder to heal, I thought a lot about what Mr. Huston told me about joining the army. I felt very resentful toward him. I thought to myself, "You sent me to join the army for fun, but I sure didn't enjoy the ways they play in the army—it is too rough. The Yankmen don't play nice."

There was another time when we fought for two days and nights. The captain-man put a gun in my hands again and said, "Fight for your life." That time we were fighting what was called a "rear action" (that's when some are fighting and the rest run away). I like to do the running better than the fighting, but there I am, so I have to listen to the music again.

After a while, we come to a river and we have to swim it to get away. Before I got across the river, I was sure that I was going to Gloryland. Well, I made the swim, but lots of the soldiers didn't. If I'd had to go one more foot, I would probably be in Gloryland myself now. The "runners" are now on the other side of the river, so they protect us, the "rear action" men, while we are doing the swimming.

That was the Battle of Saint Louis—but the Yanks stopped us and sent us back faster than we came. Sometimes we get even with the Yanks. One time we were over in Tennessee, and we stopped a train and took rations, money, and some other stuff.

After the war, I am sent back to Texas and I go back to Gonzales County. I was in town, and Mr. Ross comes up to me and said, "A person told me you are a good cowhand!"

"Yes Sir, that's all I know how to do," I said.

"Come with me if you want to work on a ranch for fifteen dollars a month," he offers. I take him up on it.

We ride many miles before coming to the camp near San Antonio River. There are twelve hands working, and we sleep in a tent. There was a cook and chuck wagon and the same old eats. That was meat, beans, molasses, corn bread, and fried pies made from dried fruit.

Mr. Ross gave me the job of riding the lines and busting

horses. There were not too many horses to bust—just those for the use of the hands and maybe one or two more a month. Mr. Ross gets the wild horses that no one owned. We would go to where the wild horses were, catch them, and bust them right there.

Mr. Ross sometimes had a thousand head of cattle, then he sells them until he had maybe five hundred left. There were cattle coming and going all the time.

Mr. Ross, with four or five hands, was gone most of the time. They would leave and be gone from one to three weeks, and they would come back with a small herd of cattle. I thought, "Mr. Ross has a lot of money because he doesn't pay any mind to raising critters, he just buys and sells."

One time Mr. Ross and his crew were away for about two weeks, and when they returned they had no cattle with them. That night I heard them talking about the one who didn't come back. He was killed by the folks that chased them. They talked about how the rest of them got away.

That night when I turned in for sleep, I thought over what I had heard them talking about, and wondered why Mr. Ross and his crew was chased and why the chasers killed one of them.

When I worked for Mr. Huston, there wasn't anything ever said about stealing cattle, but I remembered that about the only thing Mr. Huston ever said about hoss stealing was how some fellows get hanged. I realized suddenly that I was in deep trouble. Now I knew why the herd was made of such fine steers and why the hand had been shot. Still, I had no idea of how they were doing the stealing.

After that night, I tried to hear what the men are talking about every chance I have. I act like I'm paying no mind to what they say, but have my ears wide open. Then one late afternoon I hear Mr. Ross talking about the dark of the moon on such and such a night, and how it would be a good time to get some cattle from such a such a place. I'm now sure that Mr. Ross is a cattle stealer.

From that time on I worry about what Mr. Huston had said about hanging the fellows for hoss stealing, and how to get away before the hangers come for the stealers on Mr. Ross's place!

I thought long and hard on how to get away from Mr. Ross, and I decided to tell Mr. Ross that I'm lonesome to go back to "Marster" Bob Huston's place and be with my own. It wasn't a good enough story—Ross said in a threatening voice, "James, when I'm ready for you to go, I'll tell you, and if you try to leave before them, I'll put daylight through you!" Well, I was certainly scared after that; if I left, Mr. Ross would shoot me, and if I stayed maybe the hangers would get me! Every time I saw someone coming to the camp, I could feel the rope around my neck and see myself hanging from the limb of a tree, the buzzards flying round. It seemed to me that the army would even be a better place for me now.

After some time studying the situation, I come on a scheme. I knew Mr. Ross often had cattle drives, and I decided to try to get to go on one of his drives and make a sneak when we were far off. When I asked him, however, Mr. Ross only said he would think about it. About a week later, he told me, "Jim, I am going to gather a big herd and drive them way up north. You said you were a good driver, so I'll take you along." On that drive there were thirteen other men besides me. There was the cook and twelve riders; I was the horse wrangler with about fifty horses to tend. On a drive, riders change horses often, and we always had extra in case some got hurt or died.

We drove slow all day to let the critters eat while they drifted. We only hustled the cattle when we were trying to reach water before camping for the night. During the night there were always four men riding the line, the crews taking four-hour shifts. Riding the line was done to keep watch over the critters, because at night nearly anything would put the fear in them and they'd start on the run.

We drifted through rain and mud, across streams, and through dry country. The most trouble we had was when we were far between water. When the critters could smell water, even as far away as ten miles, they'd rush to get there.

We also had to cross many wide rivers on the drive. After crossing a couple of streams, the cattle learned how to cross without trouble. The problem came when the streams were running swiftly, because the current could carry the cows too far downstream for them to make the landing. The riders had to fight against this drift, so they would swim their horses by the side of the cattle and wave their slickers or anything available to force the cattle to swim against the stream. Of course as the horse tender, I had an easy job crossing any river. All I had to do was ride one hoss in the lead, and the others would follow the leader.

We had some stomps, but I never was called on to help except one time. There was an awful stomp, and one of the riders was killed that night because the horse he was riding stepped in a hole and the rider was thrown in front of the cattle herd. The sky that night was full of fire and thunder. Mr. Ross called the cook and me and all the other sleeping riders to get going and keep the herd from scattering. The only way we could see the cattle was when the lightning flashed, so we did our best to keep track of them when the flashes came, and could once in a while see another rider. Mr. Ross had told us not to try to stop the run until the storm stopped, but to watch the bunches of cows that separated from the main herd. It was a prairie country, so all we riders just strung out alongside the herd and headed back any cattle trying to break away. The storm lasted about thirty minutes, and when it stopped, we shot off our guns in the faces of the leaders, and soon they settled down and started circling.

After days of drifting, we came to Kansas City. When the herd was in the pens, the boss said to us riders to rest for a couple of days and then start back. I said to myself, this is one hand that is not going back. To Mr. Ross I said, "Sure, I'll be on hand." He gave me ten dollars and said to have a good time. I knew I was going to use that money saving my neck from the rope.

I went off by myself and sat down in front of a saloon, figuring what to do next. A fine-looking white man came up to me and asked me what I knew about tending hosses and cattle. Of course I told him what Mr. Huston had said about me being a "riding fool," and the man said he needed a good hoss man on his farm in Missouri. I knew this was the job for me and went with him. He told me his name was James and that he had some fine horses that he wanted good care taken of.

There were about fifteen fine horses on the place and cattle as well; all I had to do was tend the stock. He paid me twenty-five dollars a month and gave me extra money lots of time. I stayed on his place for three years. I got lonesome for Texas, though, and that's why I quit Mr. James's place. Before I quit I learned he was the Jesse James that is an outlaw, but he was a fine man to me.

I came home to Texas and landed in Fort Worth, and here I stayed. I started working for local stockmen until the stockyards were built, and then I worked in the stockpens until ten years ago.

Sheldon F. Gauthier

WOMEN ON THE RANGE

Four cowboys and a cowgirl in front of a house, 1901–10.

Mrs. Ben McCulloch Earl
Van Dorn Miskimon

M<small>Y</small> father built the first frame house in Whitesboro and Grayson County. I was born in that little house in 1862. The very next year we moved to the country. My father, being progressive, had the first orchard in that area. We had a ranch of one thousand acres on the Red and Little Wichita rivers, and six large farms. We also had access to the open range for cattle and horses to roam.

One day during a roundup the cowboys found a fawn; it was so cunning they brought it to me. This was my favorite pet; I would sleep and eat with it. I was about eight years old, and we had great romps together. When spring came, my fawn had grown and was very destructive to the orchard. One morning father said, "Ben, I'd like to swap you out of that deer."

I said, "What have you got?"

He said, "I'll trade you that little speckled heifer for him."

I agreed, of course, because I thought I would get to romp with the deer anyway, but no, father sent me away for a few days, and when I returned, my deer had been killed and most of it eaten. The next morning I went out to the haystack, and my heifer had a little calf, the blackest little devil you ever saw. This was how I got my start in the cattle business.

I was a fruit peddler, and I wasn't but nine years old, either. Old Judge Harris was my helper. I would gather the fruit and carry it to the courthouse and he would help sell it. Can you imagine Judge Stovall (our present county judge) even buying a peach from a little stringy-head country girl, let alone help sell it?

I kept saving my nickles and dimes, and every time I got enough to buy a dogie, I bought, because it took dogies to make cows. I just kept this up until I got a start.

When I was a little girl about twelve years old, me and my sister were carrying about four hundred dogies from Jack

County to Stevens County. We rode along and began to get hungry. In them days we had to find a place suitable to stop our cattle before we could stop and eat. We unmounted our ponies and made a fire and put our coffee in a skillet to parch; it sure was smelling good. I heard a noise, looked up, and yelled, "Stampede." We sprang on our horses and galloped around and around until we got them under control. It was like the old tale, Gingham Dog and Calico Cat: there was no sign of fire, coffee, nor skillet left. The remainder of the journey was very pleasant.

I kept adding to my herd, riding the range, and cutting out cattle until I had a nice business. When I was seventeen years old, I bought and sold cattle like a man.

Jim Loving was secretary of the Cattle Association. He had a lot of friends and often gave entertainments. We would ride fifteen miles to his house to a dance. The fiddlers would get better all the time, and many times we would gallop home in early morning.

When I was nineteen years old I married W. A. Miskimon. I had property and cattle, too. We lived in Jack County seventeen miles below Jacksboro. We had a mighty hard time, loss of cattle, and dry weather. My husband wasn't no cowman; I tried to teach him about cows, but he never could learn, not even to feed one. At last God gave me a boy. We would have to stay by ourselves on many instances. Once my husband went to Missouri on business. The severe drouth had caused all the water holes to sink and all wells to dry up. I strapped the baby on my back, papoose style, and would walk a mile or two for water. The wild hogs rooted in the low places, and water would come up in small holes. With my baby on my back and a teacup in my hand I would dip water here and there until I filled my buckets and carried the weary load home. The people of today demand water in the house or will not rent. I didn't stay out of the saddle long. I began riding the range again when my baby (papoose, I called him) was quite small.

We started to Tom Green County on September 1, 1889. We had about one thousand head of cattle and three hundred head of horses. I had five cowboys to help; as I've said, my husband was no cowman, couldn't ride nor cut out cattle, so he wasn't much help. The boys laughed and told me they could track my route by my hair hanging on the bushes. I had rode through them Indian hills, corraling the wild mustangs to tame them. I tell people that's why my hair looks like this now. We got as far as Graham City when the rain poured down. We spent the night and went on all right. When we neared the Brazos River, I told my husband to see if the river was up too much to cross with the horses. He went and came back and told me to go see, since he didn't know nothing about cattle. I sent my husband on with the horses, and he crossed and put them in the corral. Me and the boys were to hold the cattle. We drove them down to the river and camped with intentions of pushing them across the next morning. The cowboys were from the malarial country, and when they got cold and wet they took chills. I got on my horse and logged the wood up, built a fire for the sick boys and made blankets down, the poor boys with high fever and me with the cattle. That was one awful night, trying to hold the cattle all alone, with wolves howling and panthers screaming and boys sick. I stayed on my horse, rounding the cattle, keeping them down. The boys were better next morning, and we pushed the bellowing herd across the swollen stream. We came to a shack where my husband had camped. He was on the porch washing his face. We got breakfast ready and ate and stood around the fire until we dried out, as we were submerged in the Brazos. We continued our journey on to Tom Green County, which was comprised of several counties then. We came to Red Creek, which looked very desirable for camping. There was plenty of water and fresh fall grass.

Mr. Miskimon's mother lived here, and he went straight to visit her, leaving me and the boys again. He always trusted the boys with me, as a real cowboy can always be trusted under any circumstances. We herded the cattle on that area until the fence was built and ranching started. In the later part of 1889 we built the old ranch house that now stands on the corner of Randolph and First Street. I traded a little old red bull calf for that lot. I have the house divided off into two apartments, and it stays rented.

Ranching business looked fine; my herd had increased so

much and water was plentiful. I bought old man Seymour's cattle and horses in 1893. We had such a great herd I sure enough did have to ride, rope, and cut out cattle, but they never got too tough for me.

In 1894 a severe drouth came. Cattle were starving for water and food. They died by the hundreds each day. There was no rain for nine months. I knew something had to be done.

I was pretty much of a businesswoman, as well as a cow-puncher. I really had a credit rating with Dun and Bradstreet, as good as gold. I wrote in and had supplies sent down to open a dress and millinery shop. I got my goods on a ninety-day plan, and I did a good business right where the Guaranty State Bank stands today. In those days we had certain restricted districts where the women were not allowed on the streets. I managed to contact them with my little Negro boy. He would take their orders. I would send pictures and scraps of material like my dresses were, and they would choose what they wanted. The Negro boy would fill their order. They bought hats the same way, by pictures. Their money was as good as anyone else's, and they had a lot more money. I kept the ranch out of debt, and that was my motive.

I sold my business and had five hundred dollars in cash and three hundred dollars in merchandise that I sold to an Ozona merchant. The drouth was over and our ranch out of debt. I went back to the ranch where I belonged, to roam and ride with the cows and horses. I never could teach my husband to be a cow-man, and somebody had to do the work.

I had to go back to town (I operated the old Nesbitt Hotel); my only daughter was born there. Again I was successful in business, came out with money. I'm a better businesswoman right now than most young people.

I got our ranch business going pretty good again. My husband had to go away on business, and I donned my riding habit and went with him as far as Abilene to help get the horses started. It was late in the night when I got back, and I was so tired I lay down on the porch to sleep. Bang! I heard a noise and got up and a man was trying to break in the back door. He knew my husband was gone. I rushed in and got my shotgun. I went through the house to the back door, and I recognized the old sneak. At the point of my shotgun I told him to get going. I had no ammunition but bluffed the coward. He had driven his wagon near my house and put his little girl to sleep under the wagon. He rushed back and put the mules in a high lope.

I told him if he stopped before I heard him cross the four-mile hill, I would follow him and kill him. He really went on over the hill in a hurry. Ever afterward this same man never passed my house, but would circle away around, with his shotgun between his legs. He was never seen without that gun for fear my husband would kill him. Revealing his name now would startle the social public of today. The little girl that was under the wagon asleep is a very prominent woman of today. He also had a good wife that lives here now; that's why I have kept silent. I must make this statement for the sake of our dear cowboys; the man who tried to attack me was not a cowboy, for any woman was as safe with the old-time cowboy as she would have been with her brother.

After we got established again, we began to gather stock around us. Our ranch was well known and we enjoyed helping cowboys; our house was always open to them. Boiled beef, red beans, and good black coffee brought many a cowboy our way. They showed their appreciation by rounding up my cattle anytime they found them on the range, and returned them safely.

I continued riding the range. In that Seymour bunch I bought I found a frisky little horse. I called him Ned. I put a hackamore on his nose and mounted him. He made a paw at the sun and fell backward in the cow disposal that was about knee-deep. (It was easy to slide off at the side, since I rode a side-saddle). I did the same act three times, and the fourth was a successful attempt. I rode old Ned until I thought he would fall for punishment. This really made a fine pony.

We had another fine horse we called Silk Stockings because of his nice stocking legs. The owner of his mother once said, "She's as fine as split silk." We watched this horse two or three years before I decided to ride him. I caught him and saddled him up. The cowboys held him while I climbed on. He bucked some, but I rode him. His worst trouble was pawing and fighting when he was being saddled.

One morning I wanted to ride Silk Stockings. I knew I couldn't mount him by myself. I carried him to the wagon yard (where Hemphill Wells now is) for the cowboys to hold while I mounted him.

I was riding with my new sidesaddle, hand-made, that cost me near a hundred dollars. When Silk Stocking leaped for one of the boys, he threw the hackamore at him, and it wrapped around my waist just as I was trying to mount. Well, that horse pitched me as high as the courthouse and ran through a fence. He tore my fine saddle into strings. From then on I rode a man's saddle.

Now for the cows. The worst cow I ever saw, I had to milk her, of course. (I was a little dare-devil.) She was an old brindle cow and would hardly let me come near. I wore my old black bonnet, and she hated it, I guess. I always had to tie it on to keep her from kicking it off. We finally sold that old cow.

One day a great big black sow came to our house, and I penned her. The next day she had fourteen of the prettiest little pigs that ever was born. There was no such thing as advertising in the newspaper. We posted signs on the bulletin board in the lobby at the courthouse. Well, I carried my sign and began getting results. Every day the ranchmen would come. I would ask them if she was branded. "No," was their answer. I just said, "Well, she is still my sow and pigs." The wealthiest oil man that Texas has produced was a poor man then and worked every trick possible to get his paws on her. There are three of San Angelo's most prominent men that can tell you about this old sow. They tried to claim her.

One day the owner finally came. Mr. Kirkendall rode up said, "Mrs. Ben, does that sow have a K on the right side?"

I said, "Yes."

Then he said, "Let's look under her hide and see if she has some buckshot. I had an old sow that looked like that and I shot her several times for eating chickens." Sure enough, her hide was full of buckshots. He didn't want the sow but took two of the pigs and gave the remainder to me.

I've had many trials and tribulations, but I own a good country home now and lots of chickens and stock, four lots in Westland Park, and all the west end of block P, on West College Avenue. My one daughter, her husband, and children are here with me. I am about as happy as most people of my age. The general public knows me as "Flapper Fannie" as well as "Ben." I'm still working hard as a cowman for my husband, because I've tried for fifty-four years to teach him, and he has never yet learned. He never will as long as my name is Ben McCulloch Earl Van Dorn Miskimon.

Ruby Mosley

Mrs. C. C. West

Wʜᴇɴ we heard of the wonderful climate and free range of West Texas, we thought surely that must be the place for everyone to go. Mr. West thought if we could only get here with our sheep and baby boy that we would never want or need for anything else.

In 1889, equipped with covered wagon, a few supplies, an ordinary team, and a bunch of sheep, we started out from Stephens County. Our sheep had no water for three days, and our own supply was running very low when we came upon some water holes, where we camped from one hole to another for several days.

When we reached Schleicher County, water was still the problem until my husband got help and dug a well. I cooked all around that well for months, and the few passers-by never failed to stop.

We camped under a big live oak tree for six months before we got a tent. The tent looked like a mansion to us, and we certainly thought we were getting along then.

Our sheep were doing well, and I have taken the old family dog and my baby and herded them for days while Mr. West would be away on business. We would sleep in the wagon then, and always the wolves seemed to howl more and louder at those times.

There were a few bad Indians left then, but somehow we managed to escape them. I spent many sleepless nights, however, in horrible fear of them.

While we were living under the big tree, Easter was approaching, and the little boy had been told the story of the rabbit's laying for him, and so on, until I thought it would be disastrous for Easter to come on and that child without an Easter egg. I had one old Dominecker hen, and she hadn't laid an egg for weeks, but the day before Easter I was prompted to go to her coop, and she hadn't failed me. Lying there, all bright and shiny, was a big white egg. It all sounds foolish now, I know, but I was a fond young mother in a strange land, and to me that egg was a beautiful sight. Eagerly I snatched it up, ran into the house, and began coloring it with my quilt scraps. That was the prettiest Easter egg I have ever seen, and of course I have seen every kind since then. The rabbit had been under a tub for days, so we all had a very joyful Easter, even if we did have only a live oak tree for a home.

When we sheared the sheep and took the wool into San Angelo I went along, and when we reached the big divide and I looked afar over the vast expanse of the western country, I thought that indeed this must be paradise. We had to camp on the way, and the few who passed stopped and ate with us. On this trip we got six months' supplies and above all else a cook stove. No kind of stove can ever again look to me like that one did. Later when we had more hands, I have cooked hundreds of biscuits at a meal on that stove. When there would be prairie fires or mustang or antelope drives, they would all gather at our place for food and we never disappointed them.

The nearest I ever came to seeing a gunfight was between my husband and a man who came to our place asking for water for his stock. "I am very sorry," said my husband, "but we have only drinking water here, and that was bought and hauled five miles."

"I must have that, my stock are starving," said the man, and he made for our water barrel while Mr. West made for his gun, with me hanging onto his coattail. I wasn't much force in size, but I hung onto him with all my might until the man saw what he was in for and fled.

There was plenty of trouble over the water and grass between the sheepmen and cattlemen, and fight after fight ensued, but I never knew of any dangerous gunfights that we sometimes hear of. Fistfights were common, such as occurred between (I'd better not call names though, they are still living), but Mr. Cowman found Mr. Sheepman on his grass. "Don't you know those d--n things will ruin my grass?" he said.

"Get off, yourself," answered the sheepman, "This is as

much my land as yours and it will take more than you to put me off." The fist-a-cuffy was on, and the sheepman won, proving further his equal rights to the wide-open spaces.

For some time the only post office in the county was a large wooden box nailed on a big live oak tree on the Vermont ranch. All the mail for every resident of the county was placed in this box by the stage drivers, and going to this unique post office amounted to an event with the few settlers.

Mr. West established the first post office in the first store building in what is now Eldorado. He was also the first justice of the peace after the county was organized, and I believe the joke still goes around that my two children came in and said, "Ma, are we justices of the peace too, cause Pa is?"

"No, children, no," I replied, "Just me and your pa—me and your pa."

Speaking of stage drivers, I have seen them put hot bricks to their feet and veils over their faces and then come in with their faces frozen. I believe it used to get colder here than it does now.

I was called to sick relatives once and took the earliest stage out. On down the line when the mules seemed about run down, bang went a revolver right out over their heads. Without thought of announcing his intention, the driver had fired away, and the team lurched forward into a new pace. "Excuse me, madam," says he, "I only fire like that to hasten them on a bit."

"You can't go too fast for me," I replied, "I'm answering a sick call and can ride as fast as you can drive." With that, he used his six-shooter freely the rest of the way, and our arrival must have been hastened considerably by this means.

People comment on my living in such luxury now. I am grateful for every comfort, but I know exactly how it all came. I've done most every kind of work known to man or woman. When we were molding the concrete blocks out there in the back yard for this nine-room house, I helped just like a man. I scarified the walls of all nine of these rooms and that big hall by myself before they were calcimined. We have our own light and gas plants and enjoy many comforts from them, but I always tell people that with any showing at all a person can have nearly anything they set out for if they work to that end long enough and hard enough. When I was living under a tree, herding sheep with my babe in my arms and using one big skillet for a whole kitchen outfit, I was a long way from the big steam-heated home I am enjoying now. Our present basement would have been paradise then.

My greatest regret is that Mr. West couldn't have lived and enjoyed these comforts with us.

Elizabeth Doyle

Mrs. Jack Miles

FEW women in the entire history of the cow country ever threw their suggins [bedding] in the wagon and rode the range with their husband like a man as I did. My love for horses has always amounted to a passion, and I have owned some of the finest ones in the country.

We had few diversions in the early days, and when my favorite uncle, a ranchman of the Concho country, came to visit us at Uvalde, Texas, we were thrilled to death. On one of these visits he brought me a picture of his buddy, who had become famous for his expert riding and roping all over the wild and woolly West. One glance at the handsome pictured face of this dashing young Lochinvar changed my heart toward all my cowboy suitors and set me wondering if I had fallen in love with a picture.

My family decided to move to Tom Green County. We settled on the North Concho River, and I was at last in my own element. I could stay in my saddle from morning until night, eat out of the chuck wagon, and attend all the square dances for miles around. I hunted and fished and ran races with the dashing vaqueros, and at last the day of days came. I shall never forget the day I met the young Lochinvar of my picture. He was in his proper setting, at the head of a big drove of horses. Jack was of one of the oldest families in the state. Their landholdings consisted of fifty sections which stretched across Tom Green and Runnels counties and another ranch of fifty-nine sections in the Fort McKavett country. The town of Miles and also Rowena, as well as Harriett, were all named for members of the Miles family. They were in this country when San Angelo was a mere village of picket houses and adobe huts, when gambling tables stood on the sidewalks and the first theatre company performed in a livery stable.

Jack and I attended many frontier socials, picnics, fish fries,

A family group sitting in the shade of a tree behind their covered wagon, which has a chuck box and working table at the rear, 1905–15.

races, and glorious old-time square dances, where the fiddle, banjo, and guitar made "Sally Gooden," "Turkey in the Straw," and "Pop Goes the Weasel" famous. Thirty or forty miles was not considered a long distance to go on horseback to a dance. After a night of hilarious breakdowns we were served black coffee and cake to stimulate our flagging muscles, for the old-time dance was a test of endurance as well as skill.

I rode like an Indian and at the age of sixteen did not lack for suitors. I led them all a wild race from one end of the Concho country to the other.

The most treasured gift that love could buy for me was a horse, so one of my suitors presented me with a fine steed, which I called Ball Stockings. My young heart swayed mightily toward the donor. Then another suitor presented me with a still finer steed to add to my mount and asked me to return Ball Stockings to his former owner, which I refused to do. One night as a bunch of us were riding out to a dance at the Doak ranch, I was proudly mounted upon Ball Stockings, riding beside my latest suitor, when crack went a whip across my horse's hips. The jealous donor of Ball Stockings had only meant to interrupt our conversation, but he succeeded beyond his intentions, for my adorable Ball Stockings broke into a startled and furious run and I had a race as wildly exciting as my heart could crave while my anxious comrades flew after me. This settled my interest in the jealous suitor.

Jack's lariat had already ensnared my heart, anyway, so we were soon engaged, and we married at the old Bailey home on the T&F Ranch. A big dinner followed the ceremony, and the festivities ended in a big square dance that night. Each friend took a piece of my wedding veil as a souvenir, and my husband and I came to San Angelo next day in grand style, riding in a big barouche behind a Negro driver. Again the wide-open spaces claimed me; I lived in the saddle from then on. My honeymoon was spent on horseback, and Jack liked nothing better than to have me at every roundup and often said he wondered how he had ever made the long drives without me. Of course I knew he said these things only to please me, but I liked it just the same.

One of his first presents to me was a fine thoroughbred dun

horse. He was imported from England by Lord Durand and was the darling of my heart. He could pace his mile in three minutes. I called him Baby Dun, and the magnificent creature became the apple of my eye. I spent months in gently training him, the result of which would have given him entry into a circus. Jack taught him to kneel for me to mount him, bow to the judge, tell his age by pawing with his left foot, and we would have to teach him to paw one more time each year. When I would go out to bridle him, he would stand on his hind feet, shake his head at me, then come meekly up and take the bits in his mouth. His tricks always delighted his many admirers. Jack gave two choice lots in the business section of San Angelo for Baby Dun.

For years the greatest events of our Concho country was our fair. It was a gala week of riding, roping, branding, contests, racing, and cowboy tournaments of every description. In the many races I won at the fair, I rode sidesaddle with big black hair saddle pockets. These were always filled with candy, won in racing with the cowboys. For my racing I used a little brown pony called Pumpkin.

My saddle, bridle, blanket, spurs, quirt, and rope cost one hundred dollars. My bridle bit was silver-mounted. My riding habit was made of waterproof flannel trimmed in big brass buttons. My hat was a John B. Stetson. I wore buckskin gauntlet gloves. My boots were calfskin and laced to the knees. I still have a pair of them. I was a good shot but never wore a pistol.

The hardest ride I ever made was after a big mustang horse. He was a beautiful creature with long silken mane and tail. Jack and I captured several of them. This one got with an old outlaw horse that had on a big bell. We knew we would have to run him down to catch him, so we started toward the ranch. We ran them about fifteen miles, and the clang of that bell got louder and louder. I can hear it yet when I think of that ride. We captured the old rascal about sundown. I didn't have a dry thread on me. I made this ride on my big Baby Dun horse.

Stray horses bothered us so much by getting into the pasture that one day we roped a bunch of them and tied an old dry cowhide to each one of their tails. The last we saw of them, they were going over the hill with the cowhides standing straight out in the air. We had a good laugh and never saw the horses again.

On one occasion we gathered eleven hundred cattle out of the Fort McKavett pasture to be moved to Tom Green County. We threw them together on the side of a rocky hill. Jack cut out all the strays, and it fell my lot to be placed between the cut and the herd, which is a very hard place. One old wild cow was thrown with the cut-backs. She tried to run over me and get back into the herd. I was riding a little grey pacing pony named Grand Pap. He was as quick as lightning. I ran that old heifer for thirty minutes. All at once she made a break, simply sniffing the air. I slapped my spurs into Grand Pap and wheeled around to head her off when my saddle turned under his belly and I fell to the ground among the rocks and mesquite bushes. My horse planted his foot on the skirt of my riding habit and stopped dead still. Bless his heart! Jack and the boys came running to me, but I only had a few bruises and scratches. They fixed my saddle back on and I went on duty again. This time I took after that old cow and ran her so far she never came back. That ended the excitement until that night.

At sundown the cook struck camp and pitched my tent (I always had my individual tent). Then he prepared supper, which consisted of chili beans flavored with garlic, fried calf meat, or broiled calf ribs, biscuit bread baked in a big iron skillet (now called a Dutch oven), black coffee, stewed dried apples, and molasses. Sometimes we had a dish called "son-of-a-gun." All the cowboys considered that a treat, and I must say it was good. When a meal was ready, the cook would holler, "Come and get it, or I am going to throw it out." A part of the boys held the herd while the others came in and ate, then they went back on duty and the other boys came in and ate.

After supper Jack and I went on first guard. We were riding around and around, singing to keep the cattle quiet, when all of a sudden a big black cloud came up and in a few minutes the lightning was playing around on the cows' horns. The thunder was terrific; big drops of rain began to fall. I was riding a white horse, but it was so dark I could see him only when the lightning flashed. The cattle were milling and stirring. All the boys were called out, and we were doing pretty well holding them, but the storm was growing worse and worse and the cattle getting more and more restless. There had been some wire fences built near where we camped, and none of us knew how they ran, so as the cattle began to break away, the boss hollered, "Let 'em go." We all went to the wagon, got in, and sat there the rest of the night. We ate breakfast before daylight next morning and overtook the lead cattle about seven miles from camp. We only missed about fifty head, and we got them back in the spring roundup.

Jack's father owned three of the largest ranches in West Texas, and Jack bossed them all. I have worked for months at a time with my husband, rounding up and branding cattle. I went on the drive and helped to throw the cattle on the roundup grounds. When all the drives were in, we held the herd while the boss rode in and cut out all stray cattle. The cut is hard to hold. The cattle cut out to try to get back into the herd, and as we keep them out, they get very unruly and it takes a lot of riding to hold them.

I had seven dandy saddle horses in my mount, and they were all number-one cow horses. Jack was a natural cowboy and became the champion roper of the world, still holding this title. He roped six- and seven-year-old steers weighing eight and nine hundred pounds, not calves like the champions of today rope. I would not waste my time looking at a calf or goat roping now.

Jack and I rode the range together, in all kinds of weather. When we had a tenderfoot with the outfit, the boys played jokes on him all the time. Some of them were pretty rough, too. If he made a mistake, which he did in most everything he tried to do, not knowing anything about the cow business, the boys would bend him over the wagon tongue and hit him six or eight licks with a pair of leather leggings. They called that putting the leggings on him. If there was a creek nearby they would throw him in, clothes and all, and tell him to swim or drown.

Rattlesnakes are the worst enemies the cowboys have. They seem to want to share the boys' warm beds and often crawled in among their blankets.

One night two of the boys made their beds together. One of the boys could make a hissing sound exactly like a rattlesnake.

After they went to bed and got warm, Frank began to hiss through his teeth. The other old boy came out of that bed like a wildcat and could not be persuaded to go back to bed that night; what sleep he got was leaning against a tree by the fire with a big stick in his hand.

On another occasion we moved a herd to the Colorado Ranch on the Colorado River. We had been branding, and I was keeping tally. After we had finished, we were so tired and dirty Jack said, "Let's go to the river and take a bath." He saddled old Dun, I mounted, and he rode behind me. When we got to the river, we saw that it was rising. The water looked dirty and red. I did not go in, but Jack took his bath and we started back to camp. Old Dun was single footing and Jack slapped him on the hips; he got faster, and pretty soon down he went, and I went on over his head about five feet and landed right on my head. Jack, old Dun, and I were all piled up together. My horse scrambled to his feet, and Jack jumped up and picked me up. I was only stunned and came out of it in a minute with no bad effects except a big knot on my head. Jack was not hurt, but my darling horse was standing there shaking all over and covered with dirt. His mouth was bleeding, as the bit had broken and cut it. The sight of him in that condition hurt me worse than the fall I got. Baby Dun had stepped into an old ant bed and that caused him to fall. Ordinarily he was as light-footed as an elk.

When we got back to the ranch, we were rested and someone suggested that we go hunting. We kept a pack of hounds in the barn loft, so we saddled fresh mounts and turned the dogs out. They were frisky and eager to run, barking and yelping, ready to go. It was fun to run and keep up with them. When we came to a wire fence the boys would jump down and kick the staples out and stand on the wire until we all rode over. When the dogs would catch the coyotes, they had great fun killing them.

I certainly enjoyed ranch life and wish I could live it all over again, but time has brought such changes that ranching is not what it used to be. I want to say that the old-fashioned cowboys were the finest fellows I ever knew, loyal and true in every respect and had the greatest respect for women. They would lay down their lives if necessary for a woman. They were congenial among themselves and would give their boss the best they had in them. I will always say luck to the cowboys wherever they may be found, and sing to myself, "I'm a jolly cowgirl, I hunt cows all the time. I always catch the Son-of-a-Gun who steals a cow of mine. I can ride a bronco and ride him with all ease. I can rope a streak of lightning and ride it where I please."

Elizabeth Doyle

Samuel Thomas ("Booger Red") and Mollie Privett. (*Courtesy, Mrs. A. Futch*)

Mrs. (Mollie) Samuel Thomas ("Booger Red") Privett

WHILE we were running the wagon yard in San Angelo, people from all over the Southwest would bring wild horses to Mr. Privett to ride. He had never been thrown, and of course there were those who were envious and wanted to see his laurels hauled down. One man even brought along a camera with his outlaw horse, so sure was he that no one could ride him; he was going to take a picture of Booger Red as he was thrown. The picture was not taken, and during the ride the man himself became so excited that he threw away his camera and joined in the applause. Booger Red had the utmost confidence in his ability to ride, and he wasn't afraid to back it up with cash.

One year during a San Angelo Fair a man imported a famous young horse from Montana and bet his whole bankroll that Booger Red could not ride him. Other bets were piled up, and excitement ran high. The horse was a dun color with a black stripe right down his back, and the same black stripes encircled his legs. He was sixteen hands high and altogether a magnificent-looking creature. As Booger Red mounted him, he was very cautious not to excite him, and the horse actually stood dead still for

---

Throughout our research, our curiosity was whetted by repeated references to "Booger Red" Privett made in many of the narratives, including some that were not selected for this book. Each mention reflected great admiration for Privett. We were happily surprised to discover that Elizabeth Doyle, an FWP worker, had interviewed Mrs. Mollie Privett and recorded her story, which was primarily a recollection of her husband's life. Privett's contribution to the West has been virtually forgotten, based in part on his aversion to photography, including movies of his performances at Wild West shows and rodeos. He died in 1924, long before the hyperbole of mass communications produced national folk heroes. Nevertheless, at a time when literally thousands of cowboys earned their living on a horse, Booger Red's skill and reputation were a standard or model for all other bronco busters.

The memory of Booger Red Privett continues in San Angelo. One of his daughters presently makes her home in the area where her father married, had his first wagon yard, and produced his first Wild West show. She proudly relates that her father was inducted into the National Rodeo Hall of Fame, Oklahoma City, Oklahoma, in November, 1975.

"Booger Red" Privett on a bucking bronco, a rare photograph. (*Courtesy, Mrs. A. Futch*)

a moment, then Booger Red yelled to the crowd, "Folks, he's come all the way down here from Montana to get a booger on his back and here we go." With that he thumbed him in the neck, and the battle was on. So was Booger at the end of the ride, but I'll have to admit that there were times when even I wondered if he would make it, and I believe that I had as much confidence in his ability to ride as he did himself, but this was the toughest number I had ever seen him tackle. The money won was used to buy the horse, and we called him Montana Gyp.

This was the only one of the many battles between Booger Red and Montana Gyp, as each ride was only a temporary conquering, and the spirit of Montana Gyp was never conquered. For twenty-three years almost daily, sometimes ten or fifteen times daily, this battle was renewed. Old Montana never threw Booger Red, but he tried just as hard the last time as he did the first. I often think of when he rode him here once at a San Angelo Fair. He bucked all over the grounds, then broke through the fence and out through a bunch of horses which were tied on the outside. One horse became so frightened that he reared up and fell on his head and broke his neck. Booger was with Montana Gyp when he stopped, though, and rode him back on the tracks. As he rode by the grandstand, he said, "Ladies and gentlemen, I knew I was ugly, but I never knew before that I was ugly enough to scare a horse to death." They tried to pay the man for his horse, but he wanted an exorbitant price and refused any reasonable offer, saying that he had rather have nothing at all than less than he asked.

Another time at the fair here Booger Red rode a big old white steer that was said to be rideproof. Many bronc busters had tried him but had been thrown. He was so wild that the rider had to climb up on the gate and drop on him as he came through. Booger Red hit on him backwards, so he grabbed him by the tail and pulled it up over his shoulder with one hand and used the other to fan himself with his big white hat as he came by the grandstand. He really got a hand on that ride.

I used to have to exercise the show horses around the tracks when we were not showing. Ella and Roy were little shavers then, and I usually left Roy at the grandstand with Ella but not without a squall. He would cry to ride in the little two-wheeled carriage I drove. "Stick him down in the foot of that thing and let the horses out," his daddy said to me one morning, "One time will do him." I stuck his feet through the slats in the bottom of the thing and put the horses out at their best. When we got back to the grandstand, you wouldn't tell what that kid was. His eyes, nose, and mouth were filled with dirt, and as his daddy predicted, he was cured of wanting to ride.

The children were already as fond of horses as their father was. We got them a little paint horse when he was two years old and kept him until he was twenty-five. All six of the children learned to ride on Little Prince. He was the smartest horse I ever saw. One of his many intelligent acts was to stop at a railroad crossing if he heard a train blow, and no amount of whipping could force him to cross until he saw the train go by. The children could ride just as long as one could stick on anywhere. We kept him twenty-three years, and when he died at Miami, Oklahoma, we buried him with much grief and ceremony.

After we bought old Gyp and he and Mr. Privett became the attraction at every show, the idea of a Wild West show of our own was born in our minds, so we got our small possessions together and started out with two bucking horses, a covered wagon, and two buggies. The teams and Little Prince were just family equipment.

Mr. Privett originated the act of riding with his thumbs in his suspenders and looking back at the crowd. It had always been the custom up to then for the bronc rider to keep his eyes directly on the mount in an effort to anticipate his next movement, but Booger Red would tuck his thumbs in his suspenders and look all about, talking to his audience as he rode.

We started off showing in ball parks with a twenty-five-cent admission charge and did well from the beginning. Our success always out-balanced the usual knocks and bumps encountered.

Booger was a proud, clean fellow, always so jovial and witty that he made everyone, including himself, either forget his misfortune or regard it only as an asset to his business. His announcements were always wound up with, "Come and see him ride, the ugliest man dead or alive, Booger Red."

We had lots of fun and many good times. We put on a show once at a church in Midlothian, Texas. The "old man" (Booger Red) was always donating our exhibitions to some charitable cause, and on this particular occasion a woman rider was needed and I could not fill the place, so Booger put on my skirt and hat and a good wig and would have fooled everyone, I believe, if he had not failed to fasten them on right; but when the horse had made two or three rounds, off come his entire disguise. The crowd went wild when they saw that it was Booger Red himself.

Our camp life was our most fun while we traveled in wagons, camping on streams and in the most beautiful places we could find. We always had a general cleanup, even to washing the harness at such times.

Each Saturday night we would have kangaroo court. There were regular rules to be obeyed, and when they were broken, the victim was put on trial in regular cowboy style. On one occasion the old man was the offender. He had gotten about half sore one morning when the boys were late to breakfast and had rung a third bell after the first for rising and the second for breakfast had been rung. He was tried, found guilty, and sentenced to ten licks with the chaps as he was bent over a wagon tongue. He was a good sport and started off taking his medicine like a man, when Jack Lewis, who loved him like a daddy, ran into the guy, caught his arm, and stopped the punishment. This created great excitement, and Jack was then tried for contempt of court and sentenced to double punishment. The usual punishment was to have to buy candy for the ladies or cigars for the men.

Many people try to say that show people are no good, and so on, but I've seen more honesty and true principle shown by show people than many so-called higher-ups. I was just talking the other day about a boy we had with us down in East Texas. We called him Texas Kid and loved him like one of the family. He took sick down there, and Mr. Privett sent him to the hospital in Little Rock, Arkansas. We continued with our shows, but one night when we had a nice crowd we all kept feeling so depressed that we couldn't seem to get going. Even the band couldn't play right, and just before we were to start everything, the old man received a telegram stating that Texas Kid was dead.

We all just went to pieces, and Mr. Privett went out and read the message to the crowd, offering them a free pass the next night if they would excuse us and come back. They removed their hats and filed out of the tent in respectful order. The next night the crowd was almost double, and not one would accept the free pass. "Use the extra money to defray funeral expenses," they would say, and that was what was done.

Many were the kind deeds I have seen the old man perform. He was a fun-loving, witty man and carried on a lot in a joking way, but when it came right down to principle and honesty, he couldn't be beat. I have seen him go out to a little bunch of ragged children and say, "Boys, aren't you coming in the show?"

"We'd sure love to, Mr. Red," they would reply, "but we ain't got no money."

"Come on in," he would say, "and bring me some money next year when I come back here." It was surprising how many little shavers would walk up to him at different towns and offer him money, long after he had forgotten all about them. He always gave the money back to them, but that was his lesson in honesty for them. The same was true of old or trampy people who could not pay their way into the show, and many times I have seen him call back the customers for change, which in their excitement they would leave at the ticket window.

Booger Red was not a drinking man, but he was broad-minded and lenient with his boys. On Christmas Eve one year he told all the boys that if they would perform good that night, they could have four days for celebration, with the lid off. That was the funniest four days I ever spent. The old man set a keg of beer on the Christmas table, and every fellow had his own cup. It seemed each one had an extra stunt all his own to pull off.

The boys all called me Mother, and they took a notion for hot biscuits one day. I cooked their biscuits in a Dutch oven over an open campfire. "Why, I can't cook biscuits today, boys," I said, "it is raining and will put out the fire."

"Make 'em, Mother, make 'em," they all shouted, "we will get out there and hold our slickers over you and the fire, while you cook them."

That was too much, and I made up the dough while they

built the fire under the canopy of slickers, and we cooked and ate biscuits like that until everyone was filled.

At one time we were at Mill Creek, Oklahoma, during a big picnic, and the crowd insisted that we put on a morning as well as an afternoon show. We tried it, but somehow the unusual time of day for the performances threw us all off balance and everything went wrong. Several riders were thrown, and the whole thing was a flop. We felt sure that we would have no audience that afternoon, but I guess our reputation was bigger than our blunders, for the crowd very soon outgrew the tent, and Mr. Privett raised the sidewalls and told them to stack up, all outsiders free. Pretty soon all the trees around the tent were filled, and I believe we put on one of the best shows we ever produced.

Booger Red always advertised ahead of his appearances for people to bring in anything they could lead, drive, drag, or ship, and he would ride it or pay the standing forfeit of one hundred dollars. He never had to pay off, and there were plenty of bad horses brought in. He won twenty-three first prizes in all and rode at the World's Fair at Saint Louis forty years ago when Will Rogers and Tom Mix made their first public appearance.

His bronc riding saddle was merely a frame or tree, certainly no fancy affair but almost as famous as the old man himself.

In a rodeo contest in Fort Worth once he won five hundred dollars and a fine saddle. When he went to the hotel with the rest of his crowd, he took both his old and new saddles with him and hastily checked the new saddle as his buddies were rushing him to come on and eat. He pitched the old one in as he rushed after the boys. "Come back," called the clerk, "You haven't checked your other saddle."

"That's all right," Booger shouted back, "If any one uglier than I am comes along, just give it to him."

Our show was growing all the time. We now had twenty-two broncos, twelve saddle horses, and thirty-two wagons and had become known as the best Wild West show on the road. It was then that the circus sought us out. We sold everything except our best bucking horses and went with the circus. We traveled by rail then, and our good old wagon days were over. At different times we were with Al G. Barnes, Hagenbeck-Wallace, Buffalo Bill, and others.

I have to laugh every time I think of an incident which took place while we were with the Barnes Circus. Booger had twenty-five or thirty bucking horses, all good performers, and with them and our crew we put on the Wild West part of the show. He wanted a strong line in the parade, so we dressed up everything available and put them on horses. Old Frog Horn Clancy was our announcer, and when he came out to tell them of the fame of Booger Red's wife, it was pitiful how he spread it on. In truth, I was not much of a rider, but the way Frog Horn Clancy told them of the loving cups and handsome prizes I had won would have convinced the most skeptical. His blarney extended into time, and my horse became very restless, so when he finally did close his spiel with, "Behold, the famous Mrs. Privett in action," my horse lurched forward with an impatient gesture which sent me right off on my head. Wonder of wonders that I was not killed, but I was hardly hurt. Tickled at my plight, but shamed to tears, I gathered myself up with all possible haste and ran from the tent as the applause died upon the lips of my spectators.

In show life there is sadness as well as gladness—lots of fun and some sorrow, like when we were to show in Wichita Falls once. We were approaching the town and were met out on the highway by Pat Flynn's brother, who knew we were coming in and who had come on out to meet his brother in an effort to persuade him to quit the bronc riding business. Booger Red had taught little Pat to ride, and he was good—also crazy about riding, much to the objection of his family. We were all crazy about Pat and hated to see him leave us, but he had already promised his brother that he would go home with him the next day. A few hours before the show, we all began to feel some of our old signs of depressed feelings returning. We couldn't account for this, but it was so noticeable that we all commented on it. Pat's brother begged him not to ride that night. "Ah, just this last time," begged Pat, "You know we are going home tomorrow, and I want to ride for the last time."

"O. K.," said his brother, "If you will let me hold the horse."

Mr. Privett knew he didn't know how to snub a horse, and he insisted that he keep out of it. Nothing else would do him, however, and in getting off to an awkward start, the horse became excited and broke away in a wild run, tangling himself in the rope and falling. This slung little Pat's head against a tent pole and crushed his skull. Feeling the sense of depression that I had before the show began, I had remained at the wagon. When I noticed the awful stillness, the hushed exclamations, and the agonized groans of the audience, I knew the thing had happened, but who the victim was I was not to know until Thomas, my son, came running out to the wagon and said, "Oh! Mama, little Pat is killed." He was not really dead right then, but he never regained consciousness and died about two hours later. Mr. Privett rushed to him and held his bleeding head on his lap until the inquest was held. No means of cleaning ever removed that dying blood from the old man's chaps and jacket. The body was sent to the boy's home town in Oklahoma, and we all felt that we had lost one of our best boys.

While we were with the Barnes Circus, Mr. Privett had Alexander here in San Angelo make him a fine silver-mounted saddle and ship it to him. Of course it had "Booger Red" and our address all over the big wooden box. When it arrived at the station and was being unloaded, the children all gathered around and began saying to each other, "Booger Red has arrived; he's in that box." Excitement grew until I really believe some of the grownups believed it, too. Booger Red enjoyed the joke so much that he would walk around the box and tell the children that they should have Booger Red something there to eat when he came out—that he would be hungry. By the time the box was opened, the kids had enough peanuts, candy, milk, and sandwiches there to feed several people. When the box was opened and the saddle was taken out, the look of disappointment on the poor little kiddies' faces was pitiful. The old man enjoyed the joke so much that he repeated it in several towns where we showed.

Booger had many wonderful horses and riders in his different shows, but it always took Montana Gyp and Booger Red to produce the star act in any show. We kept the old horse over twenty years, and when he died we had another funeral and the family grief was not far different from our experience when Little Prince died.

Some of our famous horses were Flaxy, Moon, Texas Boy, Rocky Mountain Steve, Black Diamond, Grey Wolf, Hell Set, and old Pay Day. Texas Boy was the one that never pitched twice the same way, and Booger Red maintained a standing offer of fifty dollars per minute to anyone who stayed on him, but he was the only one ever to win the money. They were all bad horses, but none ever equaled old Montana Gyp with the old man. He held one grudge against the horse, though, until his dying day. In 1915 he won the world's championship at the San Francisco World's Fair and received a $750.00 silver-mounted saddle, and one day after he had ridden his old horse down and thought he was conquered for that once, he made an extra lunge just as the old man was dismounting, causing the rowel of his spur to make an ugly scratch across the seat of his beautiful saddle. He often remarked that he would never forgive the horse for this one deed.

Booger Red's last performance was at the Fat Stock Show at Fort Worth in 1924 just a short time before he died. He had retired and went to Fort Worth just to see the show. To keep from being recognized, he wore a cap instead of his big white hat and low-quarters instead of boots and slipped in on the top seat of the grandstand. He was enjoying the performances when trouble arose in the arena with an outlaw horse. The rider was thrown, and the crowd yelled, "Give us Booger Red." He sat as still as a mouse until an old lady at his elbow recognized him and shrieked, "Here he is!" The crowd went wild and would not be put off. He made his way calmly down through the audience until he reached the bottom step, where he was hoisted on the shoulders of the cheering throng and carried to the arena. He rode the old horse to a finish, and many said it was the prettiest riding they ever saw. He was at that time probably the oldest man on record to make such a ride.

He had lots of trouble during the last years of his performances, with movie companies trying to steal pictures of him. Many were the times he would start into the arena and see a machine set up in some obscure place, but they never tricked him. If he had lived until the picture business became more prominent, he would have been as famous in the movie world as he was in the show life of his day.

He always thought of his family first and was a kind husband and father, doing all the good he could wherever he was.

He died in March, 1924, at Miami, Oklahoma, with these

words on his lips: "Boys, I'm leaving it with you. Take good care of Mama and little Bill. Always be honest, for it pays in the long run. Have all the fun you can while you live, for when you are dead you are a long time dead."

After his death the children and I went back to the Buchannon Shows and tried to carry on, but it was never the same any more. Ella, the eldest girl, who had done a beautiful riding and roping act with her father for some time, rushed from the arena in tears the first time she attempted to put on the act without her father.

All the children were taught the riding and roping acts and were called famous by many.

We are all pretty well scattered now though. Ella married one of her father's performers by the name of Linton, and they are with the Tom Mix Circus in California. Roy never went back to the show after the World War. He has a nice family and is in the oil business in Electra, Texas. Thomas is with the Ringling Circus in New York. Luther is in California. Alta, who suffered a broken leg in the Hagenbeck-Wallace Circus, married a Mr. Futch and lives in San Angelo. And Little Bill, as we all call the baby boy who weighs only 115 pounds, trains race stock on the Santa Anita tracks at Arcadia, California.

Thomas and a bunch of boys went to Belgium in 1937 and put on a Wild West show in answer to a request from there, and when they were through showing, they wouldn't pay them. They had to sell all their fine saddles and equipment to live until relatives could send for them. It cost us over one hundred dollars to get Thomas back across the "pond." They then attempted to pull the same stunt with Tom Mix, but before he started he asked them to put up a forfeit. When they refused, he broke up the plans and never went.

I've never learned to drive an automobile. I didn't take my hat off to any man when it came to handling a team, but I tell them when they start making cars without fenders so I can see where my wheels are going, I will learn to drive then.

Elizabeth Doyle

Bibliography

Adams, Andy. *The Log of a Cowboy: A Narrative of the Old Trail Days.* Lincoln: University of Nebraska Press, 1964.

Banks, Ann, ed. *First Person America.* New York: Knopf, 1980.

Brown, Lorin W; Charles L. Briggs; and Marta Weigle. *Hispano Folklife of New Mexico: The Lorin W. Brown Federal Writers' Project Manuscript.* Albuquerque: University of New Mexico Press, 1978.

Clarke, Mary W. *The Slaughter Ranches and Their Makers.* Austin: Jenkins Publishing Company, 1979.

Collins, Ellsworth. *The 101 Ranch.* Norman: University of Oklahoma Press, 1971.

Couch, William T., ed. *These Are Our Lives.* Chapel Hill: University of North Carolina Press, 1939.

Crawford, Leta. *A History of Irion County, Texas.* Waco: Texian Press, 1966.

Dary, David. *Cowboy Culture: A Saga of Five Centuries.* New York: Alfred A. Knopf, 1981.

Davis, J. Frank. *The Road to San Jacinto.* Indianapolis and New York: Bobbs-Merrill Company, 1936.

Douglas, Claude L. *Cattle Kings of Texas.* Fort Worth: Branch-Smith, 1968.

Durham, Philip, and Everett L. Jones. *The Negro Cowboys.* New York: Dodd, Mead, 1965.

Ford, Gus L., ed. *Texas Cattle Brands: A Catalogue of the Texas Centennial Exposition Exhibit.* Dallas: Clyde C. Cockrell Company, 1936.

Frantz, Joe. *The American Cowboy: Myth and Reality.* Norman: University of Oklahoma Press, 1955.

Gard, Wayne. *The Chisholm Trail.* Norman: University of Oklahoma Press, 1954.

Garrett, Patrick F. *The Authentic Life of Billy, the Kid.* Norman: University of Oklahoma Press, 1954.

Grisham, Noel. *Tame the Restless Wind: The Life and Legends of Sam Bass.* Austin: San Felipe Press, 1968.

Haley, J. Evetts. *George W. Littlefield, Texan.* Norman: University of Oklahoma Press, 1943.

————. *Life on the Texas Range: Photographs by Erwin E. Smith*. Austin: University of Texas Press, 1952.

————. *The XIT Ranch of Texas and the Early Days of the Llano Estacado*. Norman: University of Oklahoma Press, 1953.

Hendrix, John. *If I Can Do It Horseback: A Cow Country Sketchbook*. Austin: University of Texas Press, 1964.

Holden, William C. *Rollie Burns; or, An Account of the Ranching Industry on the South Plains*. Dallas: Southwest Press, 1932.

Holt, R. D., ed. *Schleicher County*. Eldorado, Texas: The Eldorado Success, 1930.

Hoopes, James. *Oral History: An Introduction for Students*. Chapel Hill: University of North Carolina Press, 1979.

Hunter, J. Marvin. *The Trail Drivers of Texas*. New York: Argosy-Antiquarian, Ltd., 1963.

Jackson, Clyde L., and Grace Jackson. *Quanah Parker, Last Chief of the Comanches*. New York: Exposition Press, 1963.

Jordan, Teresa. *Cowgirls of the American West*. Garden City, N.Y.: Anchor Press, 1982.

Katz, William L. *The Black West*. Garden City, N.Y.: Doubleday, 1971.

Kielman, Chester V., ed. *The University of Texas Archives: A Guide to the Historical Manuscripts Collections in the University of Texas Library*. Austin: University of Texas Press, 1967.

Loftin, Jack. *Trails through Archer*. Burnet, Texas: Nortex Press, 1979.

McDowell, Bart. *The American Cowboy in Life and Legend*. Washington, D.C.: National Geographic Society, 1972.

Mangione, Jerre G. *The Dream and the Deal: The Federal Writers' Project, 1935–1943*. Boston: Little, Brown and Company, 1972.

Murrah, David J. *C.C. Slaughter, Rancher, Banker, Baptist*. Austin: University of Texas Press, 1981.

————. *The Pitchfork Land and Cattle Company: The First Century*. Lubbock: Texas Tech University Press, 1983.

Nordyke, Louis. *Cattle Empire: The Fabulous Story of the 3,000,000 Acre XIT*. New York: Arno Press, 1977.

Pearce, William M. *The Matador Land and Cattle Company*. Norman: University of Oklahoma Press, 1964.

Porter, Kenneth Wiggins. *The Negro on the American Frontier*. New York: Arno Press and the New York Times Company, 1971.

Rawick, George P., ed. *The American Slave: A Composite Autobiography*, Vols. 4–5, *Texas Narratives*. Westport, Conn.: Greenwood Publishing Company, 1972–73.

————. *The American Slave: A Composite Autobiography*, Vols. 2–10,

Texas Narratives, Supplement, Series 2. Westport, Conn.: Green-wood Press, 1979.

Rogers, Mondel. *Old Ranches of the Texas Plains*. College Station: Texas A&M University Press, 1976.

Skaggs, Jimmy M. *The Cattle-Trailing Industry between Supply and Demand, 1866–1890*. Lawrence: University Press of Kansas, 1973.

Terrill, Tom, and Jerrold Hirsch, eds. *Such as Us: Southern Voices of the Thirties*. Chapel Hill: University of North Carolina Press, 1978.

Thompson, Albert W. *They Were Open Range Days: Annals of the Western Frontier*. Denver: World Press, 1946.

U.S., Work Projects Administration, Federal Writers' Project. *Slave Narratives: A Folk History of Slavery in the United States from Interviews with Former Slaves*, Vols. 3–4, *Texas Narratives*. St. Clair Shores, Mich.: Scholarly Press, 1976.

————. *Texas: A Guide to the Lone Star State*. New York: Hastings House, 1940; St. Clair Shores, Mich.: Somerset Pubs., 1974.

Worchester, Don. *The Chisholm Trail: High Road of the Cattle Kingdom*. Lincoln: University of Nebraska Press, 1980.

CPSIA information can be obtained
at www.ICGtesting.com
Printed in the USA
LVOW04s1029021116

511236LV00008B/24/P